Guide to Netscape Navigator 2.0

Guide to Netscape Navigator 2.0

James Barnett
Edited by Karen Wickre

Ziff-Davis Press
Emeryville, California

Development Editor	Karen Wickre
Copy Editors	Nicole Clausing and Stephanie Raney
Technical Reviewer	Clay Shirky
Project Coordinator	Barbara Dahl
Proofreader	Jim Stanley
Cover Design and Illustration	Regan Honda
Book Design	Paper Crane Graphics, Berkeley
Screen Graphics Editor	P. Diamond
Word Processing	Howard Blechman
Page Layout	Janet Piercy and M.D. Barrera
Indexer	Valerie Robbins

Ziff-Davis Press, ZD Press, and the Ziff-Davis Press logo are licensed to Macmillan Computer Publishing USA by Ziff-Davis Publishing Company, New York, New York.

Ziff-Davis Press imprint books are produced on a Macintosh computer system with the following applications: FrameMaker®, Microsoft® Word, QuarkXPress®, Adobe Illustrator®, Adobe Photoshop®, Adobe Streamline™, MacLink®Plus, Aldus® FreeHand™, Collage Plus™.

If you have comments or questions or would like to receive a free catalog, call or write:
Macmillan Computer Publishing USA
Ziff-Davis Press Line of Books
5903 Christie Avenue
Emeryville, CA 94608
800-688-0448

■ Contents at a Glance

■ Table of Contents

1

Netscape Unveiled

- *Two Handy Acronyms: HTML and URL*
- *Give Me Just One Good Example*
- *The Web and Netscape*
- *Caution: The Web May Cause Cranial Damage*

1

What Is the Web and Where Did It Come From?

THE WORLD WIDE WEB IS A SYSTEM OF LINKING AND ACCESSING pieces of information over the globe-spanning Internet. The Internet is the system of wires and computers and networks that the information travels over. While the Web is certainly an important part of the Internet, the two systems are far from interchangeable. The relationship between the Internet and the Web is similar to the one between the worldwide phone system and various things you actually can *do* over the phone—make a person-to-person call, participate in conferencing calls with several others, leave voice mail or a message on an answering machine. The Web's strength lies in its ability to link together various pieces of information, allowing you to easily jump from one piece to the next by simply clicking your mouse button.

The Web is a *hypermedia* environment. This means various types of information on the Web can be linked to each other. Text linked to other text is called *hypertext,* and is typically highlighted with a color or underlined to differentiate it from "normal" text. Throw pictures, sound, and movies into the mix and you have hypermedia. For instance, a Web page may contain a picture that when clicked plays a sound. Have you ever used a touch screen at your local bank's ATM machine, or at a kiosk in a museum or record store? Ever played a CD-ROM game or even used a Windows help file? If the answer is "yes" to either or both of these questions, you've used hypermedia.

Basically, in a hypermedia environment some stuff appears on your screen. You may see highlighted text and graphics that look like buttons. Click on one of the on-screen buttons by using the mouse or your fingertip, and another screen with more stuff on it appears. Voilà—hypermedia. The links between the pieces of information are called *hyperlinks.*

■ Two Handy Acronyms: HTML and URL

HTML (Hypertext Markup Language) is an easy-to-learn language that was developed for writing hypermedia documents (*Web pages*) to be published on the Web. Web pages may be part of a group of pages called a Web *site.* For instance, if my sister decided to make her resume available on the Web, that'd be one Web page. If she linked that page to several other pages, each containing related information, that'd be a (tiny) Web site. There might be a page with further information about her education and professional interests, one with pictures of her and our family, and one containing a portfolio of multimedia work she'd done, with downloadable samples. All of the pages together would form a coherent unit of Web pages related in their subject: in this case, Rachelle Barnett. Web pages are the bricks of the Web and hyperlinks are its mortar.

To view documents written in HTML, you use a program called a Web browser over an Internet connection. Web browsers allow you to view information on the Web as well as information available on many of the various Internet information systems. Netscape Navigator is one such browser. With Netscape, you can look at HTML documents, send e-mail to pals (maybe pointing them to a great new Web site you've come across), download files or software from various sites, and lots more. Netscape can't do everything, but it can do an awful lot. And it'll do it relatively quickly and make it look nice, too. HTML is covered more closely later in the book, where I'll even show you how to write your own.

Each piece of information or Internet service you access with Netscape has its own address, called a URL (Uniform Resource Locator). URLs are like an e-mail address for a document. Armed with a URL, you can access most kinds of information on the Internet with Netscape. URLs look like this:

URL	Type
http://www.echonyc.com/~spingo/Spingo/	Web page
gopher://echonyc.com	Gopher site
telnet://echonyc.com	Telnet address
ftp://ftp.netscape.com	FTP site
news:alt.culture.www	Usenet newsgroup
mailto:spingo@echonyc.com	E-mail address

By the way, those were all real URLs that'll work if you try 'em. Fan mail and invitations for free beer are encouraged.

■ Give Me Just One Good Example

To further explain what the Web is like, let me set up a little fictional scenario. You're at work, connected to your office network. Let's say there's a company report for the previous year on your office's common drive, containing a page of text with a headline or two and a picture of your beloved boss. Now, from your computer on the network, you can bring the file up on the computer at your desk, look at it on screen, print it out, make a copy and save it to your local hard drive. Pretty standard, though handy.

You with me? Okay, now imagine that there's a caption with your boss's name under his picture, and the text of his name is highlighted. You click on his name and another document comes up on your screen: a page about your boss, including his home address. That'd be a hypertext link from the first document to the bio page.

Now, imagine you want to send him a nice birthday present, because you love him so much (I told you it was fictional). You look through a list of his hobbies and one is, say…collecting cuckoo clocks. And there's a picture of a particularly nice clock. Thinking you can score some extra points at bonus time by getting him a swell clock for his birthday, you click on the picture of the clock, and it takes you to a page of cuckoo clock info. That'd be a hypermedia link. And though it was as easy to access as the pages that sat on your common drive, the cuckoo page happens to be sitting on the hard drive of a computer in Switzerland. And you didn't have to do anything different to get there, didn't have to know anything about where on the Internet the cuckoo page resided, didn't have to know any complex commands to get to it. That's kind of how the Web works. Pretty nifty, eh?

■ The Web and Netscape

So where did the World Wide Web come from, and where does Netscape figure into the picture? In 1989, the father of the Web, Tim Berners-Lee, (see Figure 1.1) was working at CERN (the European Laboratory for Particle Physics, located near Geneva, Switzerland). He saw a need for collaborating physicists to readily share information across the Internet. He'd come up with a hypertext notebook program called Enquire that he'd been using for his personal notes, and figured it would serve him well to do what he needed at CERN. He proposed that CERN adapt Enquire to serve the uses of the laboratory. CERN decided to officially support development of his hypertext system made it available to the public, and the Web was born.

Figure 1.1

Tim Berners-Lee's home
page

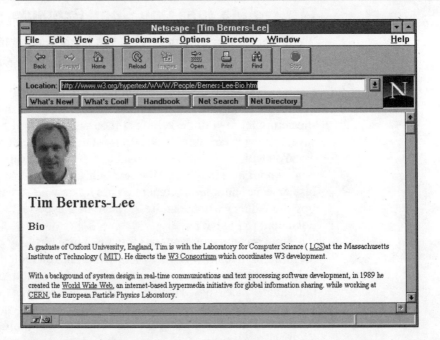

By Christmas 1990, CERN released demo versions of a text-only Web browser and a graphical browser for the NeXT computer. In 1991, these were released to the public, and the world had a new Internet service, along with browsers, server programs and protocols. See Figure 1.2 for a look at how Lynx, a current text-only browser, displays a Web page. Lynx was written by Lou Montulli, currently a member of Netscape's programming team.

Figure 1.2

Web page viewed through Lynx

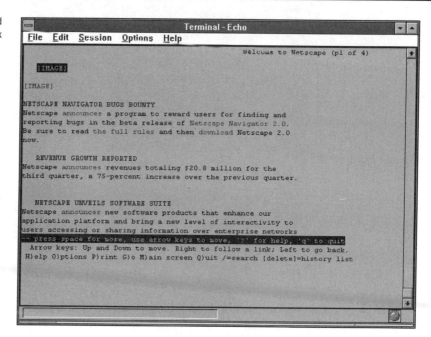

Marc Andreesen (see Figure 1.3) and a team of programmers at the National Center for Supercomputing Applications (NCSA) (see Figure 1.4) at the University of Illinois at Urbana-Champaign took the development of the Web to the next level. Basing their efforts on the publicly available code of CERN's browsers, in February 1993 they released a version of the Mosaic Web browser for UNIX-based computers. PC and Mac versions were available shortly after, and that's when things really took off. To many Internet users, including myself, Mosaic was an eye-popping, completely new way of looking at information on the Internet, and over a million people soon downloaded Mosaic browsers from NCSA. The popularity of the Web boomed, making Mosaic the most popular Internet service.

Jim Clark thought Mosaic was cool, too. Cool enough to leave Silicon Graphics, a computer company he'd helped found, and start Mosaic Communications Corporation (which later became Netscape Communications Corporation) with Andreesen in April, 1994. Netscape Communications hired away a good chunk of the original NCSA Mosaic programming team and got to work creating the next generation of Web browsers and servers. The first

Figure 1.3

Marc Andreesen

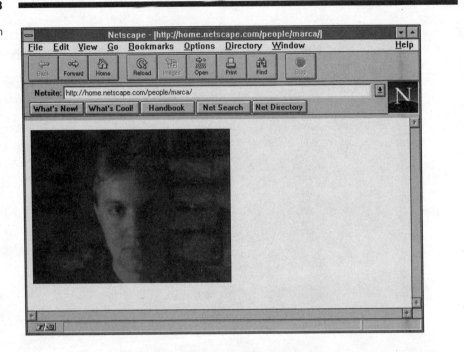

Figure 1.4

NCSA home page

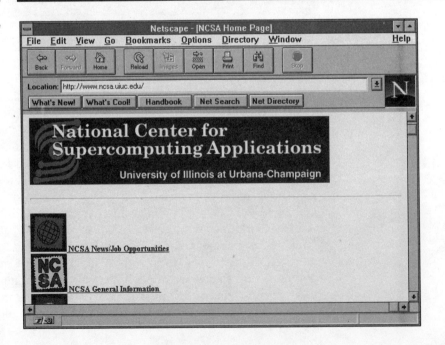

version of Netscape Navigator was released in early 1995. It quickly became the browser of choice for Web fans on PCs, Macs, and UNIX computers. Evaluation copies of the program, available at ftp.netscape.com, flew out the door at an even faster rate than Mosaic. Check out Clark's home page, shown in Figure 1.5.

Figure 1.5

Jim Clark's home page

As I write this, an estimated 75 percent of people who browse the Web do so via some version of Netscape; among those who use only graphical Web browsers, the percentage is even higher. Andreesen even made it into *Newsweek*'s "Technomania" issue as one of "50 for the Future." Not bad for a recent college grad, huh?

The Web is growing in size and popularity at an incredible rate. In mid-1993, there were around 100 Web servers in the world. As I write this, there are about 30,000 servers, serving up 3.6 million Web pages at the rate of 3 million megabytes a month, and millions upon millions of people with access to the Net and a Web browser of some kind. By the time you read this book, your mom will probably have her own home page and will be filling your e-mailbox with URLs of cool Web sites. Send some good ones back to her with the help of Part 3 of this book, "Spingo's Web Guide."

The Web is growing at an astronomical rate, and it's spilling over into real life. *The New York Times* regularly quotes URLs in stories about the Web. *Entertainment Weekly* magazine, on sale at your local grocery or 7-Eleven, reviews Web sites the same way they review a CD, movie or TV show. Trade magazines for professionals creating Web sites are even beginning to appear. URLs for Web sites are making debuts in corporate press releases, in magazine and newspaper ads, on street posters and on business cards. Look for URLs scrawled in spray-paint on an abandoned building near you soon.

How the Web Changed My Life—No, Really

I first saw the Web in January of 1994 at the office of Echo. Echo, my Internet homebase, is a New York City-based computer conferencing system where I cohost the Web conference. While I was there, famed computer expert Phiber Optik gave me my first tour of the Web via NCSA's Mosaic. When Phiber brought up that first Web page, my jaw dropped. Here were pages that looked like simpler versions of the Quark Xpress and Pagemaker documents I worked with at my day job, but with the hypermedia capabilities of some of the HyperCard stacks I'd seen. My first thought was, "You can't *do* that on the Internet!" I just couldn't grasp how this was possible.

Very soon after that fateful evening, I got myself a PPP account (these are discussed further in Appendix A), and began to look at Web pages at home. A completely new world opened up for me and I soon ended up monkeying around with HTML and setting up a home page for myself (see Figure 1.6).

Now I set up Web sites for a living and write about Netscape and the Web on the side. It's not a bad life. Can't say it'd be the same if I didn't stop by Echo that time.

■ Caution: The Web May Cause Cranial Damage

The Web will change everything you thought to be true about the Internet and make your head hurt trying to comprehend the possibilities. For starters, anything you can get into your computer, you can put on the Web. Digitized sounds, movies, pictures, text, homebrew programs—you name it. Anyone with access to a computer, an Internet account, and a little knowledge can add to the Web.

As a matter of fact, I'm working a Web site called the Internet Soul Archive (ISA). When I have enough of it done to go public, it'll hopefully be an encyclopedia site packed chock-full of information about the people and artists behind some of my favorite music. Other like-minded music fans will

Figure 1.6

My home page

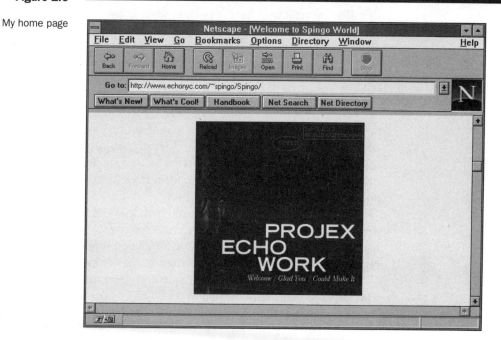

be able to contribute information about their favorite artists. I could gather all the information and write a book, shopping it around to publishers in hopes one of them will believe my idea to be profitable enough to sink the money required to produce a book. But if I put the same information on the Web, I can distribute information I think is important to a potential audience of millions with much less hassle and cost. I don't need a publisher for that type of work—I *am* the publisher, with no printing or distribution costs, promotional tour, or publishing groupies to worry about. Look for a link to the ISA on my home page, http://www.echonyc.com/~spingo/Spingo.

The audience for a Web page truly *is* worldwide. I've received fan e-mail about my home page from a nice woman in the Netherlands. I've never been to the Netherlands and I've never met her. People are at the other end of Web pages, and the community of Web users is only getting bigger. It's an exciting time for geeks like me.

NOTE. *While the term Web page, as used in this book, refers to any HTML document on the Web, I use the term home page to refer to the main Web page of an individual or organization, which may or may not be the entry point to an entire Web site.*

Every day there are new sites to check out as a variety of information is added to the Web. Later in this book I'll list some Web sites that regularly publish "What's New" pages. People are putting up all kinds of stuff. You can virtually dissect a frog, have a peek at what the surf is like across the country, look at family pictures of people you've never met. You can even get the day's news from the other side of the world—mere hours after any major news event, you can bet there'll be a Web page up with the latest details and photos.

And your audience can get to what you publish on the Web much more easily than ever before. The major online services all offer access to the Web or plan to shortly. Major computer manufacturers are building Internet connectivity into their system software. Already, thanks to the efforts of many skilled part-time programmers and the shareware and freeware they produce, the Web is accessible in some form from pretty much any kind of computer or terminal you care to mention.

The Web's open-ended ability to encompass all manner of new developments and information, will ensure that it only gets bigger and more amazing. Technical advances such as VRML (Virtual Reality Markup Language) and the ever-evolving HTML will offer increasing capability to Web pages.

Organizations like the World Wide Web Consortium, led by Web Daddy Tim Berners-Lee, are dedicated to coordinating the evolution of the Web. These groups want to make sure the Web doesn't splinter off into technically incompatible factions. They also want to ensure that the Web remains open to everyone with a browser, any browser.

As much as I hate the term, the Web is a leading candidate for the computer industry's next "killer app." While the existence of the Web may not cause people to buy machines just to access it, its arrival will undoubtedly up the sales figures of modem manufacturers. The Web is big, and it's only gonna get bigger.

The Web is a beneficent latter-day Blob (of B-movie fame), gurgling and oozing across counts boundaries, across oceans and continents, engulfing Internet resources (see Figure 1.7). It's growing, becoming stronger, gathering more and more of the world's information and computers in its pervasively easy-to-use grasp. Only this time around, the old guy at the beginning of the movie'd poke the Blob with his walking stick. And instead of becoming a tasty snack he'd run home and put up a home page featuring pictures of his grandkids. Instead of cornering the thing in a diner, armed with a fire extinguisher, the Steve McQueen character'd be staring dry-eyed into a monitor, with an itchy mouse finger and a 1 a.m. pot of java bubbling over on the stove.

Figure 1.7

From the Internet Movies
Database at Mississippi
State University—http://
www.msstate.edu/
Movies/

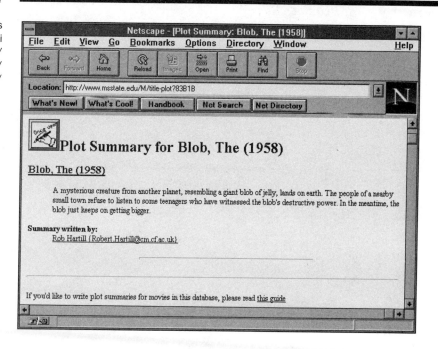

- *Get Clicking: Image Maps, What's Cool, and More*
- *One Site Forward, Two Sites Back*
- *The Visible Netscape: What Everything Does*

2

Netscape Quick Start

OKAY, NOW THAT YOU'VE GOT THE BASICS UNDER YOUR BELT, HITCH up those pants and get ready to dig into the main course. We're going to fire up Netscape and have a look around Netscape's Web site. First, I'll walk you through a quick Web-browsing session, then I'll go down the line and explain what all of Netscape's different buttons and menu options do.

Go ahead and get your Internet/Web connection up. See Appendix A if you some need help with this.

Now, let's launch Netscape. The first page that'll come up when you launch Netscape will be the entryway to the Netscape Communications Web site. The main menu or front door to any Web site is commonly known as a home page. What you're looking at is known as the Netscape home page.

The phrase "home page," as people use it when talking about the Web, tends to be a little confusing at first. As I mentioned, the front door to a Web site is called a "home page." The URL for Netscape's home page is http://home.netscape.com/. The URL for mine is http://www.echonyc.com/~spingo/Spingo/. The Home button on your Netscape screen refers to the page your browser loads when you launch Netscape. If you click the Home button in the middle of a session of Web browsing, it'll take you to the first Web page that loaded when you started the session. In your Netscape preferences, you can change the URL that Netscape goes to when it starts up; I'll show you how to do that in the next chapter.

While we're discussing terms, let me quickly add that Web pages are made accessible to Web browsers such as Netscape by programs called *Web servers*. A Web server is a program that runs on a machine connected to the Internet, waiting for requests for the Web pages that reside on its hard drive. The server program runs and waits for an incoming request for a Web page. When it gets a request, the server sends the page out to the browser asking for it. The Web page then downloads to the Web browser which in turn displays the page for the user.

The Netscape Web site is hardly skimpy on information, as we'll soon see. However, things on the Web change quickly. In the time between my writing these words and your reading them, the screen that appears should still look *something* like Figure 2.1.

The status message area at the bottom of the window will tell you something like "Document: Received 231 of 19580 bytes," and the red portion of the progress bar will give you an idea of how much longer you have to wait. Web pages don't come up immediately because the file that contains the HTML of the Web page is actually in the process of downloading to your computer. It also takes awhile for any inline graphics files—that is, pictures integrated into the page's layout—to find their way to your computer.

The downloaded image and HTML files are kept in your Netscape directory under the cache subdirectory. The cache subdirectory, one of several that Netscape creates for itself when you install it, holds recently downloaded HTML and image files so Netscape can quickly display recently visited Web pages. If you're the curious sort and peek into the cache subdirectory, you'll see files with names like "m0nvf4g3.moz." These have been renamed from their original file names to a file name in a code that allows Netscape to keep

Figure 2.1

Netscape home page

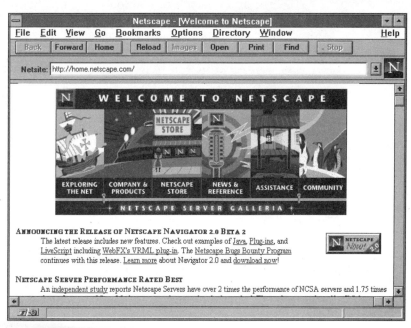

[handwritten note in left margin] .moz files stored in cache.

track of them. Why .MOZ? Because the Netscape Communications mascot is a fire-breathing lizard named Mozilla. Later in the book, I'll go into further detail about Mozilla, Netscape's cache directory, and the rest of the directories Netscape creates for itself. But by now, I'm sure, you're anxious to start exploring.

■ Get Clicking: Image Maps, What's Cool, and More

Netscape's home page is full of hypertext links, the colored, underlined text you'll notice here and there. Clicking these will take you to other Web pages on the Netscape Web site. Clicking on any of the different scenes or area names in the picture at the top of the page (Exploring the Net, Company & Products, and so on) of the graphic at the top of the page will also take you elsewhere. This kind of Web image is called an *image map*. Not only is the image map a festive page-enlivener, but it is also sprinkled with helpful, clickable hyperlinks, usually made evident by titling or appearance. For example, if you click on the phrase *Exploring the Net* in this image map, it takes you to the Exploring the Net page.

Other image maps you may come across in your Web travels may have a 3-D look, as if to say, "I'm a button. Click me." Image maps present a graphic on screen and different areas of the image map are hyperlinked to various URLs. Clicking on an image map may take you to another Web page, play a sound, or display an image, among other things. Some image maps you'll come across in your travels on the Web may also be outlined in the same blue of the hyperlinked text. I'll talk more about image maps and URLs in Chapter 9.

Now scroll down and have a look at the rest of the page. The latest news about Netscape is briefly discussed, with hyperlinks to Web pages containing more information. Further down, you'll find various areas of Netscape's Web site listed. Here you'll notice hyperlinks to most of the things you'll want to know about Netscape Navigator. This is also where you can scope out hyperlinks that'll take you from the Netscape Web site to all manner of things. That's where the fun stuff is.

Scroll back up to the top of the page and click on the phrase Exploring the Net in the image map there. That'll take you to the screen shown in Figure 2.2, Netscape's Exploring the Net page, where they list other sites on the Web that you may be interested in. Scroll down until you see the What's Cool hyperlink and click on it. That'll take you to Netscape's What's Cool page (Figure 2.3). You can also reach this page—you guessed it—by clicking on the What's Cool button in the row of Directory buttons just above the content area of your screen.

The thoughtful folks at Netscape provide this page so you don't have to search all over to find stuff that'll impress your non-geek pals. Some of the choices wouldn't exactly make my What's Cool page, but hey, that's the nice thing about the Web—diversity, right?

Scroll down until you see the link for The Amazing Fish Cam (Figure 2.4). If it's not on the list, chalk it up to the ever-advancing changes of progress—you'll then have to type in the URL of the Fish Cam page by hand. Look at the top of your Netscape screen and find the word *Netsite:* and a white text field that contains the URL of the page. Select the text in that field and hit Backspace. Now type in http://www2.netscape.com/fishcam/fishcam.html and hit Enter. (Anytime you want to go to a new Web site, you do the same thing.)

Now you're at the Fish Cam page where you can glimpse firsthand an occurrence of a great Web (and Internet) phenomena for which we are thankful: the preponderance of smart, creative people with perhaps too much time on their hands. Netscape programmer Lou Montulli keeps two video cameras focused on the saltwater aquariums in his office. These cameras are connected to a computer, which digitizes stills from the video and then serves them up to the Web. (Lou, you might remember, was the programmer of Lynx, the text-only Web browser mentioned in Chapter 1.)

Figure 2.2

Exploring the Net

Figure 2.3

What's Cool

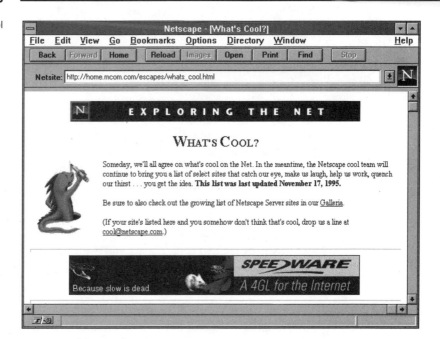

Figure 2.4

The Amazing Fish Cam!

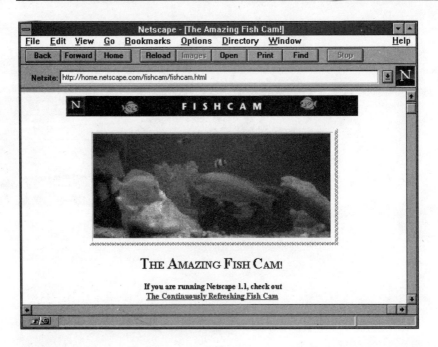

A nifty shortcut: *Netscape is smart enough to know that you generally want to look at a Web site—you can get away with leaving the "http://" off of any URL you type in the Netsite: text field.*

As part of your fish gazing, click on the "If you are running Netscape: Check This Out" link. As the picture loads you'll see a live image, more or less, of Lou's fish. This is one of the tricks that only Netscape browsers can do on the Web. The server is sending your browser a continuous feed of images, instead of just one. You're getting a video feed from somewhere that may be thousands of miles away, armed with nothing more than a modem, Netscape, and I may humbly add, this book. You can't do that! Or can you? (Note: unsubtle plug for Chapter 8, "Stretching the Web and the Future.")

Now, let's say you want to keep the live-feed Fish Cam address handy for the next time you use Netscape, to amaze friends and neighbors (and possibly, to feebly attempt to justify to your spouse all the time you spend in front of the computer). Netscape handily has a built-in way for you to keep track of noteworthy sites you come across and want to return to: the *bookmarks* file. In the menu bar click Bookmarks, and then select Add Bookmark (or just hit Ctrl+A on your keyboard). You've just added the continuously refreshing

Fish Cam image to your list of bookmarks. Select the Bookmarks menu again, and you should see The Amazing Fish Cam! in the pull-down menu underneath View Bookmarks (Figure 2.5).

Figure 2.5

Netscape's Bookmarks menu

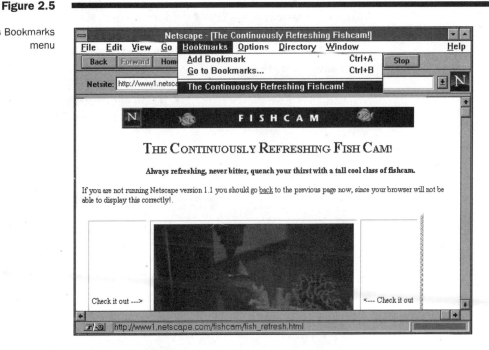

There you go. You've added the first of what's sure to be many URLs to your bookmarks list and lived to tell the tale. In the next chapter, I'll show you how to edit and organize your bookmarks list to perfection. For now, rejoice in the knowledge that you won't have to rifle through a stack of crumpled Post-It notes next to your computer every time you want to find the URL for that great site you had handy "just a few days ago."

Oh, and by the way, the word *Netsite* next to the field where you typed in the URL for the Fish Cam page appears when you're looking at a Web page that resides on a Netscape server. When the page is served up by a non-Netscape server, the title of the field will read Location instead. The text in this window is editable. As you type in a new URL or are in the process of editing the existing one, the title *Go to* will be displayed.

Lastly, here's a neat trick I learned from the About The Fish Cam page: Ctrl+Alt+F will bring you to the Fish Cam page, regardless of the Web page currently being displayed in your Netscape window. Those nutty Netscape guys crack me up.

■ One Site Forward, Two Sites Back

Having experienced a taste of one of the most revolutionary ideas in computing, you're probably hungry for more. Let's go back to the What's Cool page. To get there, you can click the Back button in the toolbar and cycle back through the trail of pages that got you here, or you can jump directly back. To do this, click the Go menu item. You can also select History from the Window menu (Figure 2.6). This option displays a list of all the sites you've visited during your current Netscape session. Double-clicking the titles of any of the Web pages listed or selecting the title from the list and clicking the Go to button will take you to that page. If you click the Create Bookmark button, Netscape adds the selected Web page to your bookmarks list.

Figure 2.6

Session history

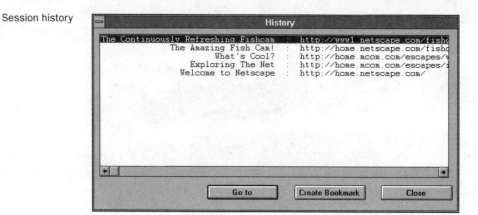

In your main Netscape window, the Back button goes back through the sites in your history list, one by one; the Forward button will take you forward through that same list. Now that you're back at the What's Cool page, the Forward button will no longer be grayed out; go ahead and click it, and then the Back button. The pages will load much quicker than when you first visited them. Netscape's caching system makes this possible; these pages are now available to Netscape as files in your cache directory. You're not actually downloading the pages this time, you're just reading them off your hard drive.

At this point, I'm gonna leave you to your own devices. I've left you back at the What's Cool page, and you'll find a good bit here to keep you occupied and maybe giggling for a while. Be sure to check out the Cool Site of the Day (http://www.infi.net/cool.html) and Random Light Bulb Joke (http://www.crc.ricoh.com/~marcush/lightbulb/random.cgi/).

When you're done, read on to see a quick explanation of all of Netscape's menu choices and buttons.

■ The Visible Netscape: What Everything Does

Netscape presents you with a myriad of buttons and menu choices, some of which provide multiple ways to perform the same function. In this section, I'll give you a quick rundown on the secrets behind each of Netscape's buttons, menu choices, and functions. You can always get a quick description of each menu choice by hitting the Alt key, moving the arrow key to the menu you're interested in, and arrowing down to a menu choice. The description appears in the status message area at the bottom of your main Netscape window. And now, on to a discussion of individual menu-bar choices.

The Famous Netscape Icon

Here's how it looks:

When you click this icon, it takes you to Netscape's home page. Its main feature, though, is that it animates to show you that Netscape's busy downloading something. (Those nifty meteors beat the pants off the Windows hourglass, no?) It's officially called the Status Indicator by Netscape in their online documentation (accessible via the Handbook menu choice under Netscape's Help menu). The meteor's animation is the idea of Christopher Skinner of Fairfax, Virginia. Skinner won $1,000 in a Netscape-sponsored contest for his troubles. The previous icon, a thick 3-D "N" that moved backward and forward in "space" was somewhat less than beloved by the Net population; Netscape said, "You don't like it? Fine, design a new one!"

Meandering through the Menus

Netscape's menus, while not as full-to-bursting as, say, Microsoft Word's, allow quick access to all manner of useful things. Some of these functions are duplicated by the onscreen buttons and/or zippy key commands. If there's a button that's an equivalent to a menu option, I'll show it.

Flipping through the File Menu

Netscape's File menu lets you do the following with Web documents:

- Load them from the Web or your hard drive
- Save ones you've found or send them to your pals
- Check their security status
- Print them, to provide coffee-break discussion fodder when you tack them up on the office bulletin board

You can also close Netscape windows or quit Netscape. But why would you wanna do that?

The Open Location Option

The Open Location button looks like this:

Selecting this option (or hitting Ctrl+O) brings up a dialog box with a blank URL field. Typing a URL into the Open Location field and hitting the Enter key (or clicking the OK button) does the same thing as typing a new URL into the Netsite field of the main Netscape window and hitting Enter. Doing any of these operations takes you to the URL you've entered.

The Open File Option

Making this selection brings up a standard Windows Open dialog box that lets you select a file from your hard drive. Netscape can open text files with the .HTM extension (.html shortened to the DOS three-letter standard), plain text files, and .GIF or .JPEG (.JPE or .JPG) picture files from your hard drive. Open File is most useful for browsing saved Web pages or your own pages in progress. You can also poke around the .MOZ files found in your Cache directory.

The Save As Option

Choosing this option saves the current document being displayed in Netscape's content area. If you're looking at a Web page, you can save it as either an HTML (.HTM) file or a text (.TXT) file. If Netscape is currently displaying an image in its content area, you can save the image.

The New Mail Message Option

Selecting this option brings up the Message Composition window shown in Figure 2.7, with the From: field showing your name and e-mail address.

Figure 2.7

The Message Composition window

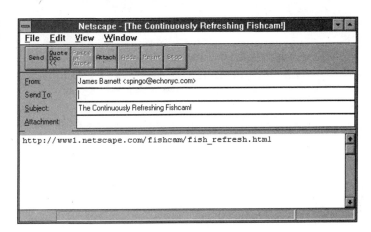

Before you can e-mail anything, you must properly set up your Mail and News preferences tab. See "Customizing Your Preferences" in the next chapter for more information.

The Mail Document Option

Selecting this option opens the same Message Composition window shown in Figure 2.7, with the title of the current document displayed in the Subject field and with the document's URL in the body of the message.

In your e-mail you can send the text or HTML source code of the current Web page being displayed, if you so desire. This is useful for sending yourself or a pal the contents of a cool Web page you've found without having to cut and paste the URL and text into a separate e-mail program. You can only quote Web pages or text files in the body of e-mail sent from Netscape; when you're viewing a picture independent of a Web page, the Quote Document button will appear grayed out. For instance, while preparing the Web guide in the back of this book, I sent myself e-mail containing URLs of good Web sites I found while poking around the Web using Netscape. I received the mail in the excellent freeware mail program Eudora (available at ftp://ftp.qualcom.com/pceudora/quest/windows/eudora/1.4/; a commercial version with more whizzy features is also available) and then filed them by category into separate Eudora mailboxes like Fun & Games, Art, and so forth.

In the Send To field, you would type the e-mail address of the person you'd like to send e-mail to. Clicking the Send button sends the e-mail off on its merry way, and the Cancel button lets you back out of the e-mail sending process gracefully, should you decide you'd rather not send e-mail right now.

The Attachment field in the Message Composition window is blank until you specify a file to be sent along with the e-mail. Most e-mail you send won't have attachments. Occasionally, though, you'll want to include a file from your hard drive or from the Web in a message to a friend or associate. To do this, click the Attach button, which will bring up the Mail/News Attachment dialog box shown in Figure 2.8.

Figure 2.8

Mail/News Attachments
dialog box

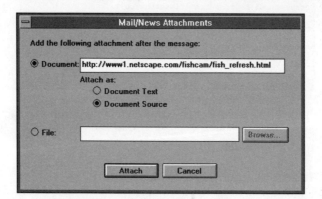

From this dialog box, you can specify files to be delivered along with your e-mail. The Mail/News Attachments window comes up with the Document radio button selected and the Document field automatically filled with the URL for the document currently being displayed.

The Document Source radio button is automatically selected in case you'd like to include the HTML of the document being displayed. For instance, if you're looking at a Web page and the author has included something particularly clever in his or her layout, you might want to send the Document Source to a friend who's conversant in HTML and is interested in writing better HTML documents. Generally, though, what you and your e-mail recipient will be interested in is the content of the Web page. In that case, click the Document Text radio button to send the text of the document currently displayed attached to your e-mail.

If you have a file on your hard drive that you want to attach to e-mail, click the File radio button. The Document information will gray out. To locate a file on your hard drive to attach, click the Browse button. The Enter File To Attach window comes up. Find the file you'd like to attach, and click OK.

Now you've selected a file to be attached to your e-mail, and you're back at the Mail/News Attachments window. Click the Attach button and you'll return to the Message Composition window. Type in a comment in the large field at the bottom of the window, click the Send button, and the e-mail and file go whizzing across the Internet, sure to enliven the existence of the lucky soul on the other end.

Before sending someone e-mail with a document attached, you might want to check with the recipient first to make sure he or she can receive e-mail with attachments; some e-mail systems don't know how to handle attached files and might not deliver the attachment *or* the e-mail to the recipient.

I'll go into further detail about using Netscape for e-mail in the next chapter.

The Page Setup, Print, and Print Preview Options

The Page Setup option allows you to specify how Netscape will print the current document. You can choose margin width, specify text color, and so on.

The Print button looks like this:

Selecting the Print menu option takes you to the standard Windows Print dialog box. Selecting Print Preview brings up the screen in Figure 2.9.

Netscape's Print Preview screen allows you to see what the printed Web page or pages will look like before you send the currently displayed document to your printer. You can choose a one- or two-page view, zoom in to see detail, zoom back out to get the big picture, and, if it's a long document, step through the pages that will be sent to your printer one by one. The Print button takes you to the Print dialog box, and the Close button closes the Print Preview screen and takes you back to the main Netscape screen, should you decide that the document you're viewing isn't actually something you want to print right now.

Be forewarned that pictures that look great in the relatively low resolution of a computer monitor may be somewhat disappointing when printed out on a high-resolution printer.

The Close and Quit Options

As you might have guessed, selecting Close from the File menu shuts the frontmost Netscape window. If you only have one window open, choosing this option causes you to exit Netscape.

Figure 2.9

Print Preview

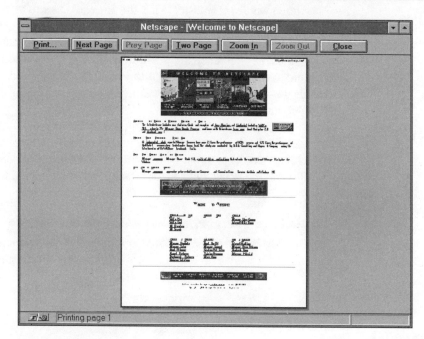

Selecting Quit closes the Netscape program and all of its windows. Make sure that after you quit Netscape you log off of your PPP connection through your Winsock stack; quitting Netscape leaves your line up and your Internet access meter running.

Exploring the Edit Menu

The Edit menu is our next stop on the menu bar tour, as we work our way down the line. Not much to see here, though you can avoid scrolling through a lengthy document and causing further eyestrain by using the Find command.

The Undo Option

Selecting this option or hitting Ctrl+Z undoes your last action when you're typing and/or editing information into any of Netscape's editable fields (such as a URL in the Location field) or on a Web page with a form.

The Cut, Copy, and Paste Options

As with other Windows applications, these options only work on text that's been selected with your mouse or Shift+Left or Right Arrow keys, either in the body of a Web document containing text or in an editable Netscape field. Paste won't work on a Web page unless you have the cursor in a form field, but it will paste text into an editable Netscape field, say, into the Message Composition window.

The Find Option

The Find button looks like this:

Selecting Find from the Edit menu or hitting Ctrl+F brings up the window in Figure 2.10. Typing a keyword or words into the Find What field and then clicking the Find Next button searches the current Web document for instances of the chosen keyword. If you've clicked so that the cursor appears in the text of a Web page, selecting either the Up or Down radio button under Direction tells Netscape to begin its search from there and work toward the beginning or end of the document. For instance, if you're looking for a specific word in a long document and have already scrolled down several screens before getting fed up, you can click and place the cursor in the Web page's text and use Find to begin your search where you left off, by selecting the Down radio button. You can also specify that Find match the case of the keyword you've entered in the Find What field.

Figure 2.10

The Find dialog box

Keep in mind that the Find button is only useful for searching the Web page you have on your screen. To search the Web for instances of a certain word or topic, click on the Net Search button in the bar of Directory buttons and use one of the Web searching tools you find there.

Peeking at the View Menu

Netscape's View menu will let you grab a fresh copy of a Web page hot off the server, bring up images that may not have loaded when you first came upon the current Web page, refresh your screen image if it's become untidy for some reason, and most importantly, view the HTML guts of the Web page you're looking at. Appearance is everything, you know.

The Reload and Reload Cell Options

The Reload button looks like this:

Selecting Reload from the View menu or hitting Ctrl+R redownloads the current Web page (the one currently displayed in Netscape's content area) from the server. This is useful for a couple of reasons. Say you go to a promising Web page and it just takes *forever* to load. Naturally, being the busy person you are, you get impatient and hit the Stop button. This stops the download of the document, and Netscape displays what's come through so far. You start looking at the portion of the page that's downloaded, and decide "Ah, what the heck. I may as well see the whole thing." You then would select Reload, hit Ctrl+R, or click on the Reload button to start the download of the page again. Unfortunately, there's no way to continue the downloading of a document that's been partially downloaded. You have to start again from scratch.

The Reload Cell option reloads only the selected frame of a document written to use Netscape Navigator 2.0's frames capability. This capability allows multiple Web pages to be displayed in their own panes within one main Netscape window.

Reloading Web pages is essential if you're writing your own Web pages from scratch. It allows you to change the HTML file, preview it in Netscape, make some more changes to the HTML file, and hit Reload to see the effect of those changes. This technique and much much more about slinging your own Web pages will be covered in Chapter 9.

The Load Images Option

The Load Images button looks like this:

Load Images is useful if you have turned off Auto Load Images under the Options menu, loaded just the text of a Web page, and subsequently decided you'd like to see the graphics. Click the Load Images button, and only the images come across. This differentiates Load Images from Reload, which goes and gets the whole Web page again. The Load Images option also comes in handy when the creators of Web pages forget to design them to be legible in text-only circumstances.

The By Document Source Option

Selecting this option will pop up a window showing the HTML code of the current document. This option is especially useful when you're writing a Web page of your own and want to swipe a nifty layout or see how a particular effect was achieved. The first page I wrote in HTML was spawned from someone else's HTML. There, I said it and I'm not ashamed.

You can copy HTML code from the View Source window, switch over to your favorite HTML editing program or text editor, and pop in your own information. You can do all this while still leaving the HTML tags intact. Don't be scared of all the greater-than and less-than signs; basic HTML is easy as pie to write (see Chapter 9).

The By Document Info Option

Selecting this option brings up a new Netscape browsing window that looks something like the one in Figure 2.11. This two-pane window tells you all kinds of things about the Web document in question. No, there won't be a quiz.

Figure 2.11

Document Info window

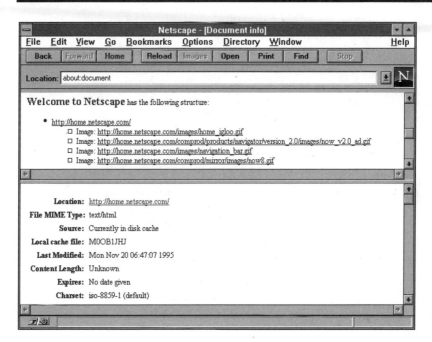

The upper pane displays the structure of the current document. If there are inline images, their URLs are given, as are those of supporting documents if the Web page contains frames.

The information on the Security line can be important if you're planning to do much shopping over the Web, or sending private information to an organization via a Web site using forms. *Forms* are Web pages with fields intended to be filled in by the user and submitted to the server. Typically, this is done by clicking on a button on the Web page itself (and not in the Web browser). More about forms in Chapter 9.

Why is security important on the Web? Because sensitive, unhackable information needs to be available on the Web. This applies both to the information published on a Web site as well as the information sent from a user. Commerce on the Web is a constantly growing concern of site publishers.

Visibly, Netscape uses a color bar and a key icon to indicate security status. The color bar is located between the Directory buttons at the top of your Netscape window and the content area. The color bar will turn from the insecure gray to secure blue when you're viewing secure Web pages. The key icon at the lower left of the Netscape screen appears broken on a gray background when viewing insecure documents. When viewing secure documents, the key icon will appear whole on a blue background, and will have two teeth for high-grade encryption, one for medium-grade. Note the difference between the color bars and key icons shown in Figure 2.12 (insecure page) and Figure 2.13 (secure page).

I'll go into further detail about security and Netscape in Chapter 8. To see what Netscape has to say about security on the Web, go on over to the On Security option under the Help menu, which will take you to the On Security Web page on Netscape's Web site.

The Go Menu

Think of the Go menu's choices as your own personal time-and-space travel machine. *Zip!* Back to the past! *Zip!* Back to the present! You can even see everywhere you've been in between.

The Back and Forward Options

The Back button looks like this:

Selecting this option or hitting Alt+Left Arrow takes you back to the most recent Web page in your session history; the Back menu option and the Back

Figure 2.12

Netscape displaying insecure document: color bar and key icon

Insecure gray color bar

Insecure key icon

Figure 2.13

Netscape displaying secure document: color bar and key icon

Secure blue color bar

Secure key icon

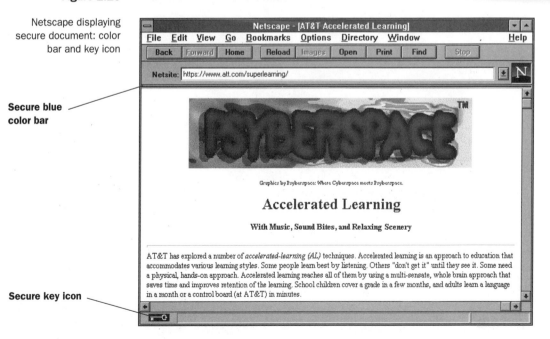

button will be grayed out if you're on the first Web page you've loaded in your current session.

The Forward button is shown below:

It works the same as the Back menu choice, but you use Alt+Right Arrow, and go forward through your session list. If you're still on the first page you've loaded and haven't gone anywhere from there, the Forward menu option and the Forward button will be grayed out.

The Home Option

Here's how the Home button looks:

Selecting the Home option or clicking the Home button takes you directly to the home page you specify in Netscape's Styles preferences tab. The section "Customizing Your Preferences" in the next chapter will show you how to do this.

The Stop Loading Option

The Stop Loading button looks like this:

Selecting this option or clicking on the Stop button stops the downloading in process on the Web page in the top-most Netscape window. If several Netscape windows are up at the same time, Stop Loading doesn't affect the downloading process of the others. Clicking Stop is a better way to halt downloading than just hitting Back; it gives Netscape the chance to halt things properly, and is less likely to cause problems.

The History List

A list of sites you've visited in your current Netscape session appears at the bottom of the Go menu. Selecting any Web site in this list will take you to that site.

The Bookmarks Menu

Netscape's bookmarks are the little black book of your Web travels. Unlike your session history, which starts from scratch every time you launch Netscape, your bookmarks list lets you keep URLs that you've deemed worthy to have on hand for easy access during future sessions. Plus, you don't have to mark up the wall next to your computer with scrawls of URLs you want to remember.

The Add Bookmark Option

Add Bookmark creates a bookmark in your bookmarks list for the current document. If no pointer is specified, the current site is tacked at the end of the list.

The Go to Bookmarks Option

Go to Bookmarks opens the Bookmarks window, a searchable, editable version of your bookmarks list. Editing your bookmarks is covered in the next chapter.

The Bookmarks List

This is a handy menu of your fave sites, as decreed by you, the ultimate judge of what's truly cool. Your bookmarks list will be empty until that first thrilling time when you select Add Bookmark. So get cracking!

The Options Menu

Here's where you fine-tune the appearance and engine of your Web-cruising mean machine. You still have to supply your own radio and drive-thru food, though.

The Preferences Option

Your Netscape Preferences allow you to customize Netscape to your heart's desire. (Chapter 3 details how.)

The General, Mail and News, Network, and Security Options

These options allow you to customize Netscape to your heart's desire. See Chapter 3 for more information.

The Show Toolbar Option

Show Toolbar toggles the visibility of the toolbar (the row of Back, Forward, Home buttons et al) on and off. If you like using the menus for the choices that are displayed in the toolbar, you can hide the toolbar and gain valuable on-screen area for Netscape's content area. I'd recommend you leave it on.

It's nice having the buttons for Netscape's most used functions available at a glance, without having to remember key commands or which menu they're under. Later, after you memorize all of Netscape's key commands, you might want to toggle Show Toolbar off.

The Show Location Option

Show Location toggles the Location field (where the URL for the current Web document is displayed) on or off. Ahh, leave it on. That way you always have the Location field available to type in a URL, which is one step easier than using the Open button or the file menu's Open location.

The Show Directory Buttons Option

Clicking this option toggles the row of Directory buttons (What's New!, What's Cool!, Handbook, and so on) on and off. You can get by pretty easily without them, unless you're a compulsive What's New checker, like I am. If that's your MO, you should probably change your start-up home page to a What's New page, like I do.

The Autoload Images Option

Autoload Images toggles between automatically loading images when you come to a new page or loading just the text of new pages. For faster browsing, turn it off. For prettier browsing or to impress your friends with snazzy graphics, leave it on. Courteous Web page authors will supply text descriptions of the images, if you're lucky, to give you (and those browsing the Web with a text-only browser) some idea of the content of unloaded images.

The Show FTP File Information Option

This option toggles between showing or not showing descriptive information when connecting to an FTP site. An FTP (file transfer protocol) site is a collection of directories and files usually available to the Internet public, though some sites have restricted access.

Figures 2.14 and 2.15 illustrate the the differences in appearance with this option turned on and off. Leave it on. That little extra bit of text can be helpful and isn't gonna slow you down much.

You'll find more about using FTP with Netscape in Chapter 5.

The Save Options Option

While Preference changes are saved automatically, settings in the Options menu aren't. Select Save Options to preserve them. One of these options is your default Netscape window size. You may find the default size of your Netscape window intolerable (some Web sites you visit might have graphics wider than the default screen). If this is the case, you can resize the window

Figure 2.14

Browsing FTP site with
File Information turned on

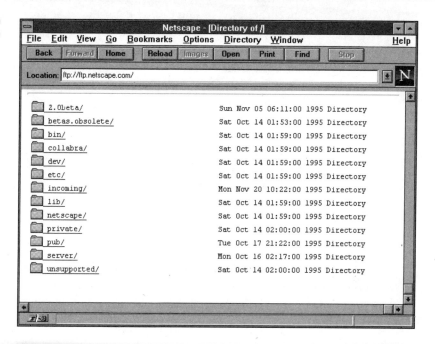

Figure 2.15

Browsing FTP site with
File Information turned off

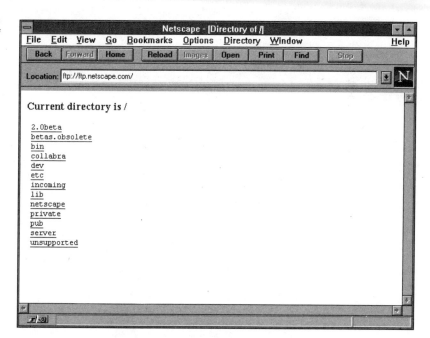

to perfection with the standard Windows window-sizing tool in the lower-right corner of your main Netscape window. Select Save Options and it'll be that size when you next start Netscape.

The Directory Menu

The Directory Menu (and its cousin, the Help menu) provide expeditious access to the most used areas of Netscape's Web site. Using the menu options is much quicker than going to Netscape's home page and poking around until you find what you're looking for.

Netscape's Home Option

Selecting this option takes you to the Netscape Communications home page. It's handy when you change your start-up home page to a different Web site because Netscape's Home is still only a menu choice away. Clicking on the "N" logo in the upper-right corner of the screen will also take you there.

The What's New and What's Cool Options

Here's how the What's New button looks:

It takes you to Netscape's What's New page, where you can look for new Web sites you may not have seen before. More about this Web page and others in Chapter 7.

The What's Cool button looks like this:

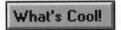

It takes you to Netscape's What's Cool page. Pressing this button provides quick access to Web sites that may cause your productivity to plummet from sixty to zero in four seconds flat.

The Netscape Galleria Option

The Netscape Galleria is a directory of sites that use Netscape servers. Guess they're kinda proud of 'em, huh?

The Internet Directory and Internet Search Options

The Internet Directory button looks like this:

Clicking here takes you to the Net Directory Web page on Netscape's Web site. The site contains hyperlinks to several Web directories that more or less serve as the Yellow Pages of the Web. The one I use constantly is Yahoo (http://www.yahoo.com/). If Yahoo doesn't have what you're looking for, try one of the sites listed in the page that comes up when you select Internet Search.

The Internet Search button is shown here:

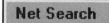

Selecting this option takes you to a page linked to several Web-searching sites; the one I use constantly is Lycos (http://lycos.cs.cmu.edu/), just because of the huge number of Web sites in its database. Lycos doesn't exactly greet the user with open, user-friendly arms, however. You might want to try the Web Crawler search engine (http://webcrawler.com/), TradeWave's Galaxy (http://galaxy.einet.net/) or one of the many sites discussed in Chapter 6.

The Internet White Pages Option

There's no one directory of everyone on the Net. The Internet White Pages option takes you to a page of sites that may be of use in locating someone's e-mail address on the Internet.

The About The Internet Option

Choosing this option takes you to a page that lists sites offering more information about the Internet than you can shake a stick at.

The Window Menu

The Window menu allows you to pop back and forth between the Netscape windows you have open on the screen at any given time, as well as providing quick access to Netscape's Address Book, Mail and News readers, and Bookmarks and History windows.

The Address Book and Netscape Mail Options

The Address Book option gives you access to your Netscape Address Book, in which you can keep handy the e-mail addresses of your closest friends, worst enemies, and others who fall in between. The Netscape Mail option takes you into Netscape's internal e-mail reader. More about e-mail and Netscape in the next chapter.

The New Netscape Browser Option

Selecting this option opens a new main Netscape window for browsing. New windows open to the first page visited in the current Netscape session. Attention-challenged? Open a new Netscape window to go to a second Web site while waiting for the first one to load!

The Netscape News Option

This option brings up Netscape's newsreader window, from which you can delve into the vast world of Usenet news, via Netscape's built-in Newsreader. Usenet news is really a whole world unto itself; entire books have been written about it. Luckily, you have this book, which will at least give you an introduction. Read more about Usenet newsgroups and learn how to use Netscape's newsreader in Chapter 5.

The Bookmarks Option

This option performs the same function as the Go to Bookmarks menu option under the Bookmarks menu, bringing up Netscape's Bookmark window. From there you can edit and reorganize your bookmarks list.

The History Option

History shows the trail of all the pages you've seen in your current session. Your session history resides in your computer's memory. This means when you quit Netscape that history is lost (unless you add bookmarks), and when you next run Netscape you'll be starting from scratch.

A list of sites you've been to in your current Netscape session also appear at the bottom of the Go menu. It's the same as the list brought up in History window, but it's handily located right there in the menu itself.

The Open Windows List

At the bottom of the Windows menu appears a list of all of the windows Netscape currently has open. Selecting any of the windows listed will bring that window to the front. Also, Ctrl+Tab cycles through all of Netscape's open windows.

The Help Menu

You're curious and want to know more about Netscape and the Web, I know you are. Otherwise you wouldn't have bought this book, right? The choices in Netscape's Help menu will answer a lot of your questions.

The About Netscape Option

This option brings up information about the version of Netscape you're using.

The Registration Information Option

Registration Information takes you to a Web page that'll let you register your copy of Netscape Navigator the company and sign up for paid tech support.

The Handbook Option

Handbook takes you to Netscape's online handbook, which is actually quite good. A printed version of the handbook is available if you spring for the full version of Netscape and the included tech support by registering your copy of Netscape via the Web page mentioned above.

The Release Notes Option

Release Notes takes you to a page with a somewhat extensive listing of features and known bugs of the version of Netscape Navigator you're using.

The Frequently Asked Questions Option

This is a guide to questions you might have about any and all the aspects of Netscape. The Frequently Asked Questions area of Netscape's Web site offers more extensive information about Netscape than is found in the Release Notes.

The On Security Option

On Security brings up a Web page with more information about Netscape's Web security measures than you'll probably ever need to know, unless you're thinking of opening a Web mall or store. A lot of the information found on the On Security Web page is fairly technical and intended for those interested in purchasing or knowing more about the workings of Netscape's secure server software. Nice to know it's there if you need it, though.

The How to Give Feedback Option

Here's where you can tell the nice folks at Netscape how much you love their program, or what you'd like to see changed in future versions.

You can order Netscape products and send bug reports from the Web page this menu choice takes you. Be sure to check all of the available online Netscape information as well as the list of known bugs on the Release Notes page before submitting your report.

The How to Get Support Option

You can sign up for tech support for Netscape's Navigator or server software from here.

The How to Create Web Services Option

Clicking here takes you to a Web page that lists good information sources for publishing your own pages on the Web.

The Versatile Status Message Area and Progress Bar

And now, we come to probably the most informative of Netscape's features. Talk about multipurpose—the status message area at the bottom of the screen dispenses all kinds of information like nobody's business. If you hit the Alt key and use your keyboard's arrow keys to poke around the menus, the status message area will display a brief description of each menu option. If you move the mouse so that the pointer hovers over a hyperlink, the URL of the link is displayed. Click on that hyperlink, and the connecting information is displayed with messages like "Looking up server," "Contacting host," "Host contacted," "Waiting for reply," and "Document: Done."

Once Netscape finds the server that the document resides on and begins downloading the document, the percentage of the document downloaded and the speed of the connection (in kilobytes per second) are displayed. At the same time the progress bar on the right fills with red, inching towards full until the document is fully downloaded, at which point it turns back to gray.

See the Status Message Area and progress bar in action in Figure 2.16, and observe them at rest in Figure 2.17.

Figure 2.16

Netscape's status message area and progress bar during loading of Web page

Figure 2.17

Netscape's status message area and progress bar after loading Web page

The Location Field Menu Button

This unassuming little button, when clicked, pops up a menu of URLs you've entered by hand into the Location field during the current Netscape session. Very handy.

Milking the Right Button Popup Menu

You may have noticed already that when you click the right button on your mouse, you get a small popup menu. The active choices of the menu vary according to the type of information or hyperlink your mouse pointer is over when you click the right button. Regardless of what your mouse pointer is over, these choices don't change: the Back and Forward choices, which do the same thing as the Back and Forward buttons and menu options.

When you place the pointer over a hyperlink (Figure 2.18), the popup menu's link choices are active. Open This Link does the same thing as just clicking on the hot link that the pointer is over. Add Bookmark For This Link adds to your Bookmark list the site you would go to on clicking the hyperlink, but doesn't take you there.

Figure 2.18

Right mouse popup menu
with pointer over a
hyperlink

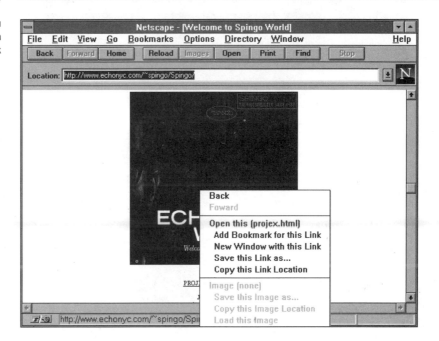

New Window With This Link opens a new window to display the URL the hyperlink points to, and leaves untouched the Netscape window in which the hyperlink appears. Save this Link As saves the contents of the document pointed to by the hyperlink directly to disk, without displaying it. This is useful when the hyperlink points to, say, a file that you want to save directly to your hard drive without displaying it.

Copy This Link Location copies the URL of the hyperlink to the clipboard. This is useful if you happen to be writing a book with a lot of URLs in the text and you don't want to have to select, copy, and paste them all from the Location field.

When you place the mouse pointer over an image (Figure 2.19), various selections in the image part of the popup menu become active. View this Image (with the file name of the image in parentheses) displays just that image alone in the Netscape browser. Save This Image as brings up the standard Windows save dialog box which that lets you specify where on your hard drive to save the file. Copy This Image Location copies the URL of the image to your Clipboard. Load This Image becomes active when you've loaded a Web page with Autoload Image turned off and you want to load just that image. Clicking on the generic image icon that Netscape uses for unloaded images will also load individual images on a Web page. Clicking the Images button would load all the images that may be on the page.

Figure 2.19

Right mouse popup menu
with pointer over an image

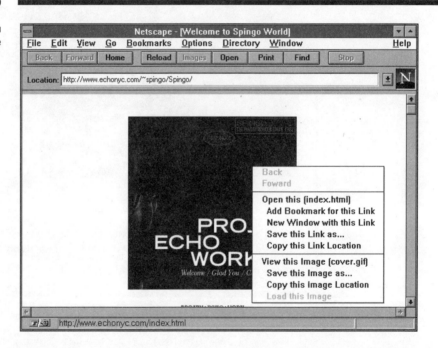

- *Customizing Your Preferences*
- *Customizing Your Bookmarks List*
- *Advanced Netscape: Tips, Tricks, and Silliness*
- *On to the Fun Stuff!*
- *Take Five, But Don't Get Too Comfortable*

CHAPTER

3

Intermediate
and Advanced Netscape

Y OU'VE BEEN USING NETSCAPE FOR AT LEAST A LITTLE WHILE NOW, but maybe you'd be a little happier if you could change a few things about it. Maybe you want to use larger or different fonts to ease the wear and tear on your bloodshot eyes. Maybe you want to change the color of the fonts or background. Maybe you want to organize your bookmarks to make it quicker to find that great site you were at a few days ago. Netscape provides a great deal of flexibility for these kinds of adjustments. In this chapter I'll show you how to tweak Netscape until it's just right for you. I'll give you some general tips on using Netscape, and then point you to some fun stuff you can do with Netscape. Are you just tingling with anticipation? I know I am.

■ Customizing Your Preferences

Are you ready to fine-tune Netscape so that it purrs like a kitten? I believe that was a "yes," so get your PPP connection in place, launch Netscape (if it's not still up), and pull down the Options menu to General. Let's get busy.

The General Options Window

Netscape's Options menu offers you several categories of preferences: General, Mail and News, Network, and Security. When you pull down to General, the window shown in Figure 3.1 appears. The different categories of preferences here are organized into tabs (as in the preference settings of other programs such as Microsoft Word 6.0), looking a bit like a file cabinet's drawer full of folders. I'll refer to the categories (Appearance, Fonts, and so on) as *preference tabs*.

Figure 3.1

The General
Options window

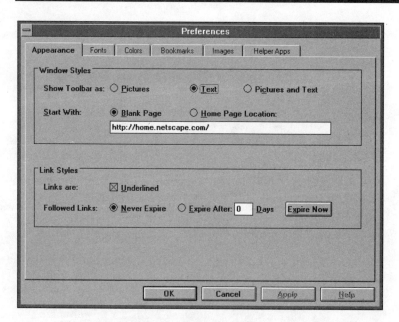

The Appearance Preference Tab

The choices you see before you are where you tell Netscape how to display its handy-dandy toolbar, what URL to load first when Netscape launches, and how to display hypertext links. Let's get to work.

The settings in the Show Toolbar As area of the Appearance preference tab set the look of buttons in the Toolbar at the top of your main Netscape screen (the row of buttons containing the Back, Forward, Home buttons, and so on). Try all the different variations for Show Toolbar As, and see what you like. "Try different variations until you find one that pleases you" may as well be the unofficial motto for this chapter—a lot of the decisions you'll make depend on your personal taste.

I usually set the Toolbar to Pictures and Text because selecting Text makes the toolbar buttons look kinda small to me, and because the Pictures setting gives you icon-only toolbar buttons. In general, I think icon buttons in any software tend to become useless, save for the few whose meaning you actually remember. For the rest of this book, however, I'll set Show Toolbar As to Text so that I can display more of the content of the Web pages I'll be showing you. While I'm at it, I'm going to turn off the Show Directory Buttons menu option in the Options menu to gain a little bit more screen area. Keep in mind that if you've previously unchecked the Show Toolbar choice under the Options menu, any changes you make in this section won't be visible until you recheck Show Toolbar.

The Start With setting allows you to specify a Web page to load every time Netscape starts up; as you see, the default is Netscape's home page. Selecting Blank Page tells Netscape to start with a blank page, which is handy in that you don't have to wait for Netscape to download a page every time you start the program. Later in this chapter, I'll show you a quick way to grab the URL from any Web page and make it your Start With page.

In the Link Styles area, I tend to uncheck the Underlined check box. With no underlining, the text of hyperlinks is easier to read and I can still identify hypertext links by their color. For this book, though, I leave underlining on to make hypertext links in the screen shots more visible.

Followed Links are hypertext links to sites you've already visited. For instance, let's say you're on Netscape's home page. You scroll down to where there's a hypertext link for What's Cool and click that hyperlink. You go to the What's Cool page, look around for a while, and decide you want to go back to Netscape's home page. Clicking on the Back button, you're returned to the page, and scrolling down again, you notice that the What's Cool hypertext link is now a different color than a hyperlink to an unvisited hyperlink. The What's Cool link, as it would appear in this example, is a Followed Link.

Your Followed Links setting determines the length of time until those links are displayed as unvisited again—that is, the length of time until the hypertext links of Web pages you've visited look the same as those of sites you've never been to.

Why is this setting useful? After you've been exploring the Web for a while, there's no way you'll remember all the sites you've been to. Your Followed Links settings give you a visual cue to remind you that you've already been to a Web page when you again see it listed as a hyperlink.

When you install Netscape, the setup program creates a file called netscape.hst in your Netscape directory. This file keeps track of all the URLs you've ever visited, and the dates and times you visited them. When you access a Web page that contains a hypertext link for a site you've visited previously, Netscape takes a look at the netscape.hst file to see when you last visited that site. Netscape then colors the hypertext link accordingly, depending on how you've set your Link Styles settings.

What you do in the Followed Links section is tell Netscape how long you want Followed Links to display differently from new, "fresh," hypertext links before once again making them appear the same as new links.

Clicking the Never Expire radio button tells Netscape to always display followed links differently than fresh ones. Expire After ___ Days allows you to set the length of time Netscape displays them as different from fresh ones. Expire Now tells Netscape to start over, in effect restarting the countdown until followed links are displayed as new ones once again.

I set Followed Links under Link Styles to Never Expire. I like coming across a hypertext link and being reminded I've been there at some point.

The Fonts Preference Tab

Here's where you tell Netscape what fonts to use for displaying text. If you're pretty happy with the way Netscape handles fonts so far, you don't need to change any of these default settings and can go ahead and skip to the next section.

In the For the Encoding area, Latin1 should come up as your choice. This setting tells Netscape which character set to use when rendering Web pages. If you click on this drop-down list box, you'll notice that Netscape can display sites written in Japanese, Korean, and other languages. Leave For the Encoding set to Latin1; setting this to Japanese or another language won't work unless you're running that language's version of Windows. You can find more information on using Netscape in different languages' character sets by selecting Release Notes in the Help menu of Netscape's main window.

Clicking on either Choose Font button next to Use the Proportional Font and Use the Fixed Font lets you select any of your installed fonts when displaying text in Netscape.

Proportional fonts are used for the majority of the text you'll see on Web pages (and in this book). Fixed fonts are used to display monospaced text, where each character in the font takes up the same amount of space.

This is an example
    of a proportional font.

```
This is an example
    of a fixed font.
```

Most of the text you'll see on Web pages will be in a proportional font. Text in a fixed font is commonly used for columns of words aligned with spaces. Play around with the fonts until you find something pleasing.

When browsing the Web, you can choose which font you view Web pages in; the designer of a Web page doesn't specify which font the page should use. They can't, actually. You have this choice because unlike a Microsoft Word document, where all the fonts are specified in advance so the same document uses the same font on different machines, HTML documents don't say anything about fonts except "This is a proportional font" or "This is a fixed font," and let your browser determine which fonts to use in each of those cases. This is because HTML is designed to be platform independent—that is, it doesn't care what kind of machine it is being read on—Unix, Windows, Mac, Amiga, or VAX. That way Web browsers can be made for specific kinds of computers, and any HTML document can be read by any of them.

The Colors Preference Tab

Authors of Web pages can specify colors for normal text, links, followed links, and background. Your settings in the Colors preference tab let you decide whether you want to accept the colors and background specified by the author of the Web page you're viewing, or always use colors and background that you specify (by clicking the Always Use My Colors, Overriding Document radio button).

If you're a stickler for consistency and hate to be surprised, you can find some combination of colors and background you like and set Colors to Always Use Mine, but hey—live a little! Be entertained by the good (and horrible) uses of colorful backgrounds and colors! Some Web authors have a real grasp on what makes for a great looking page and others, well, were probably the first on their block to use more than a dozen fonts on a printed page when desktop publishing first arrived. You wouldn't wanna forfeit your chance to be aesthetically impressed or horrified, would you?

Even if you select Always Use My Colors, you can still enjoy your own custom settings for a good portion of the Web pages you'll come across. Many Web pages don't have specified colors or backgrounds.

You may feel more comfortable reading sometimes-lengthy Web pages on screen using something other than the default colors. To test out colors for Links, Followed Links, or Text, click in the Custom check box and then on the corresponding Choose Color button. A standard Windows color palette window appears; you can then choose any of the Basic Colors or Define a Custom Color. Clicking OK returns you to the Preferences window with the new color displayed in the corresponding color box and the corresponding Custom check box is selected.

For Background, your choices are a bit different. Leaving the Default radio button selected will use the color you have specified in your Windows Color Control Panel as your background color.

NOTE. *Specifically, Netscape uses your Application Workspace color selection in the Color Control Panel as its default background color. Mine is set to a medium gray; if the color you've selected for Application Workspace is different, the screenshots in this book may appear slightly different from what you see on screen.*

Selecting a color to use as your Background works the same as selecting a color to use for Links, Followed Links, and Text. Click the Custom check box and then the Choose Color button and follow the directions above.

You can also specify a .GIF or .JPG file from your hard drive to use as a background for Web pages viewed in Netscape. A background image is a picture file that repeats to fill the background of the Web page displayed in your main Netscape window. Web pages can use background .GIF or .JPG images just like Windows can use .BMP files to wallpaper your desktop. To set your background to a file from your hard drive, click the Image File radio button, and then the Browse button. Locate a .GIF or .JPG file, and click OK. The text and pictures of the Web pages will then appear on top of your background. I'll talk more about image file formats in Chapter 9.

Not that my taste is necessarily any good, but I more or less leave the settings at the defaults, except for Followed Links, which I change from the default dull purple to a bright red. Makes 'em jump out a bit more.

The Bookmarks Preference Tab

This preference tab tells Netscape where to find your bookmarks file. When you first launch Netscape, it creates a file called bookmark.htm in which it saves any bookmarks you add. This file is saved in the same HTML language that Web pages are written in. You don't need to touch this setting unless you keep several bookmark files and want to specify one of them as the one to use upon starting up Netscape (for instance, if several people use Netscape on the same machine). If you're using more than one bookmarks file, you can click the Browse button and find the bookmarks file you'd like to use on your hard drive. For now, though, go ahead and leave this preference tab untouched. Later in this chapter I'll show you how to customize your bookmarks file.

The Images and Security Preference Tab

This is where you tell Netscape what method to use when displaying images. Regardless of how many colors your PC's color card can support, Netscape uses a somewhat limited palette of colors when displaying images in its content area. That palette is called a color cube here, after a 3-D method of describing the spectrum that's a little too complicated to go into here. Some images you come across on the Web will contain more colors than Netscape's limited palette, especially photographic images that may contain millions of colors.

When Netscape comes across an image to be displayed, it looks at the color information of the image and compares that against its own color palette. Then, based on which option you choose here, Netscape tries its best to display the image faithfully.

If, for Choosing Colors, you have Dither to Color Cube selected, Netscape uses a method called dithering to display the image. Dithering takes the image and attempts to display a rendition faithful to the original by scrambling its available colors throughout an area of the image that contains colors it cannot display directly. This method of using a limited palette to simulate many more is similar to that used by Impressionist painters and four-color printing presses.

Selecting Use Closest Color in Color Cube tells Netscape to compare the colors in an image displayed in its own palette, and to use the color in the palette that's closest to a color match. Images displayed using this method will sometimes appear to have bands of color where a range of colors is displayed using the closest color Netscape has available. Go ahead and set Choosing Colors to Automatic. Netscape will then have a look at the image to be displayed and decide which method will give the best image appearance.

When loading a Web page containing both images and text, the text of the page loads first and is displayed before Netscape begins downloading images. Images that are part of a Web page are referred to as *inline* images. For Display Images, if you select While Loading (the default), Netscape displays inline images as they download. The Web page will come up in the browser with holes in the text where inline images will appear. As more of each image file downloads, the holes gradually fill up, either filling in from the top down or filling immediately with a blocky version of the final image that comes into focus as more of the image file downloads. This effect is seen while Netscape loads .GIF images created in what's known as *interlaced* format. The data in such an image is arranged differently from that of other image files, so that different segments of data load in a sort of latticework fashion instead of from start to finish. Netscape can also display Progressive JPEG images, which act in a display in a similar fashion. I'll go into more detail about image file formats in Chapter 9.

Clicking the After Loading radio button will leave the image's placeholding hole in the Web page layout empty until the entire image loads, and then pop it into place whole. I leave this setting at While Loading. I like getting an idea of what inline images will look like as they download. I don't like being held in suspense because an image is large or its Web server is slow or overcrowded.

If you come to a Web page whose images take an unacceptable time to load, you can click the Stop button in Netscape's toolbar or hit the Esc key. The images halt downloading, and the text of the Web page will be readable. Depending on how far along the image downloading has gone, the images in the page are represented either as a generic picture icon or as partially finished versions of the actual images. If you later desire to see the images on the page, you can click on a picture icon to download that particular image, or click the Images button in the toolbar to download all the inline images on the page.

The Helper Apps Preference Tab

These preferences are worthy of their own chapter. See Chapter 4.

The Mail & News Options Window

The next stop on our tour is the Mail and News Options window. Within Netscape, you can send and receive e-mail. You can also read Usenet newsgroups as well as post your own messages. I'll go into more detail on Usenet in Chapter 5 and more about using Netscape's built-in e-mail reader later in this chapter. First, though, you have to tell Netscape a few things.

The Appearance, Composition, and Organization Preference Tabs

Go ahead and leave these preferences set to their defaults. Later, if you use Mail and News quite a bit, you can come back and tweak the settings here. For the most part, though, the defaults will serve you well.

The Directories Preference Tab

Ask your Internet provider's friendly support staff for the addresses of your Mail (SMTP and POP) Servers and your News (NNTP) Server. These settings tell Netscape how to get e-mail and Usenet News from and to the rest of the Net. Go ahead and leave the Mail Directory and News RC Directory settings as they are. If for some reason you later want to specify a different place to store your mail and news files, you can change these settings. Also leave the Messages are Copied... radio button set to Left on the server for now.

The Identity Preference Tab

Tell us about yourself! "Well, Alex, I'm an Internet consultant from New York City, and my hobbies include..." No, wait, that's Jeopardy. Sorry. What I meant to say was: in this preference tab, Your Name: is your name; Your

Email: is your e-mail address (if you don't know this, ask your Internet provider); Reply-to Address is the e-mail address you want e-mail replies to come to (probably the same address as Your Email); and Your Organization is your company or affiliation (my pal Andy uses "Tip-Top Hair Fashion Center," after a sign he found on the side of the road).

The Signature File setting will let you point to a brief text file to be affixed at the end of all outgoing mail and newsgroup postings. This file is commonly known as a .sig file—the original e-mail programs that used automatically included signatures put them in files labeled ".signature." Usually a .sig file will consist of contact information, such as your name, e-mail address, company name, and maybe a fun quote or saying. It's a good idea to make .sig files less than four lines long. Trust me on this one. If you have a .sig that's longer than your e-mail or posting, people will get mad at you. It costs money and time to send each bit of information to and from the many intermediate Internet sites that are likely to lie between you and your reader, and long .sigs are considered needlessly wasteful. I don't use a .sig file in Netscape. Your name and e-mail address are contained in every e-mail you send; I figure that's enough contact information, and if I have anything clever to say I'll say it in the body of the e-mail. I'll talk more about how to use Netscape's e-mail reader in the "Advanced Netscape" section later in this chapter.

The Network Options Window

The settings in these preference tabs tell Netscape how to use your RAM and hard drive memory; how to check for new versions of Web pages, where to put cache files, how much activity to send over your Internet connection, and what addresses to use to reach the outside world if you're behind a network firewall. You can get by just fine by not touching these settings and skipping to the next section of this chapter; if you'd like to know a bit more, read on.

The Cache Preference Tab

Your Memory and Disk Cache settings are what Netscape uses to know how much of your RAM and hard drive to commandeer. The settings are defaulted to 600K and 5,000K, respectively.

If you have lots of RAM, go ahead and bump up the Memory Cache—I have 8MB on my PC and don't usually run many other programs while I'm using Netscape—and set the Memory Cache to 1,000K. If you have more RAM than that, you might want to fiddle with that number and see if it speeds things up.

If you have plenty of hard drive space, Web pages and image files you download will remain on your hard drive longer, depending on how high you set your disk cache. As you visit more sites, the contents of the disk cache roll over and the older cache files are deleted automatically. I leave the Disk Cache set at 5,000K, as my hard drive is as yet uncramped. Later, I may bump this down to 2,000K or so.

The Clear Disk Cache Now and Clear Memory Cache Now buttons prove useful when writing your own Web pages. They ensure that you load only the latest version of your page and not the version in either of your caches. The Verify Documents settings are also useful in this situation; selecting Every Time ensures that every time you view one of your Web pages in progress, you get the most current version, and not one from your cache directory.

When downloading a page, Netscape actually checks first to see if the files are in its cache. If they are, Netscape checks the expiration information of the page. If the page hasn't changed, the cache files will be displayed. Otherwise, Netscape fetches the page from the server it resides on.

Which setting should you use? If you're working with Web pages that you're editing, displaying in Netscape, and re-editing, you'll want to change the Verify Documents setting to Every Time, to make sure you're getting the latest version of the document you're editing, and not a version from the disk cache. I honestly can't even think of a good reason to set Verify Documents to Never. For almost everything you do with Netscape, the Once Per Session setting will be fine.

Your Disk Cache Directory setting tells Netscape where to store its temporary files, which have the .MOZ extension. When Netscape is installed, it creates its own directory within the Netscape directory called "cache." You can go ahead and leave this setting at the default, and lose no sleep whatsoever.

The Network Connections Preference Tab

This section tells Netscape how to handle its traffic over your Internet connection. The Number of Connections setting tells Netscape how many simultaneous connections to use when connecting with servers over the Internet. For instance, when loading a Web page with several graphics, Netscape will load several of the graphics at the same time, allowing you to see them fill in at the same time. Remember, if you're using PPP over a modem, you're working from a relatively slow connection to the Internet. Each concurrent file you download causes the others you're downloading to slow down. Unless you're a hard-core Attention-Deficit-Disordered MTV junkie, a setting of four should sufficiently tax both your Internet connection and your attention span.

The Network Buffer Size is set at 6 kilobytes by default. It'll accept values from 1 to 31, but you can leave this at the default setting. I've never seen any difference in performance by changing these settings. Go ahead and leave this set to 6K.

The Proxies Preference Tab

Net users whose Internet access comes via a provider that uses a security measure called a firewall will need to take advantage of proxies. Firewalls are widely used at large corporate or educational Internet sites that prefer to take extra precautions in order to protect their internal networks. For this book, we're assuming you'll be using a Winsock-based dial-up PPP account, so don't sweat it. If for some reason you're going to use Netscape from behind a firewall, ask your provider or network administrator how you should fill out this screen. Most commercial Internet providers, such as the ones included in Appendix A, don't use proxies.

The Security Options Window

The check boxes here in the Alerts preference tab refer to various alerts Netscape uses to warn you about the security status of a Web page you're loading, a Web site you're entering or leaving, and of a filled-out form on a Web page you're about to submit information to. Unless you're browsing a Web store and plan to send them a credit card number or are sending extra-super-double-secret information via a form on a Web page, you can turn all of these off. I leave all of them off—I generally don't purchase items via the Web, and if I have confidential information that I want to keep relatively safe from prying eyes, I use e-mail, or heck, even the U.S. Postal Service.

■ Advanced Netscape: Tips, Tricks, and Silliness

We've gone through and set up most of your preferences and organized your bookmarks list to perfection. Now what? I'll give you a few tips on how to use Netscape to its fullest. Here are some helpful little tidbits that'll make your Netscape experience that much more fulfilling. After the actually help-ful stuff, I'll get to some less-than-serious uses of Netscape.

■ Customizing Your Bookmarks List

I know why you've come here. By this point you've been zipping around the Web adding bookmarks with a frenzied slapping of Ctrl+A and adding sites to your bookmarks list with reckless abandon. And now your bookmarks list's been turned into a painful aberration of a useful tool. Trust me, I've been there. Now, what you want to do is streamline your bookmarks list to reflect more accurately what a Conqueror of the Web you truly are.

On the other hand, maybe you're just starting to add bookmarks to your bookmarks list, and want to start things off on the right foot, laying the groundwork for a well-organized bookmarks list. If so, I commend you for your foresight! Either way, when you turn to the Web to manage information, Netscape's bookmarks list is your Rolodex, and a well-organized one is a terrific tool. I'll show you how to organize your bookmark list, using my own bookmarks list for the examples here.

In this discussion, I'll only use Web pages as bookmark items. While bookmarks are primarily used for Web pages, they can, however, be used for any Internet service that is accessible via URL. For instance, you can set up a bookmark for an ftp site, a gopher directory, or frequently downloaded individual files on ftp or gopher, among other things. For now, though, we'll only worry about Web pages.

The Netscape Bookmarks Window

Rip your Bookmarks menu on down to View Bookmarks (or hit Ctrl+B) and let's get started. The Netscape Bookmarks window (see Figure 3.2) appears.

Figure 3.2

Netscape Bookmarks window

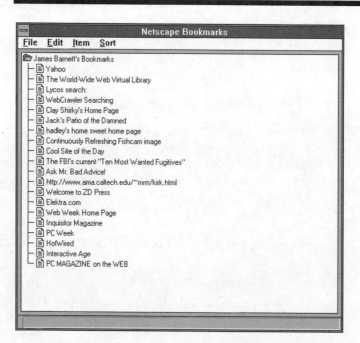

From here you can do all manner of things to fully customize your bookmarks list. All of your bookmarks appear as file icons in one large folder called Your Name's Bookmarks. This screen will probably look familiar if you've used Windows' File Manager.

Clicking on a bookmark or folder selects it and the arrow keys on your keyboard allow you to move the selection bar through the bookmarks list line by line. Left Arrow and Up Arrow will move your selection bar up and Right Arrow and Down Arrow move down. Bookmarks and folders in this window can be dragged up and down the list and into and out of other folders. Before we move anything, though, I'll give a quick overview of the different menu choices here.

The Netscape Bookmarks File Menu

Now, you're ready to get down to business. Let's start at the File menu. Selecting View in Browser displays your bookmarks list as a Web page in your topmost Netscape screen, as in Figure 3.3.

Figure 3.3

Bookmark list,
viewed in Browser

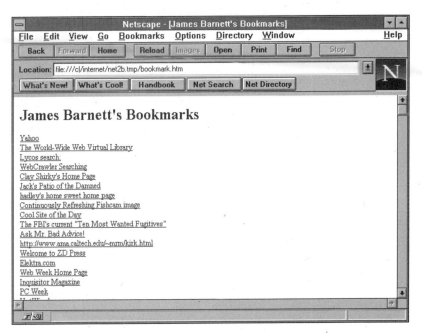

By the way, you can also view your bookmarks file as a Web page from Netscape's main screen. To try this, close out of the Netscape Bookmarks window, go to the File menu, pull down to Open File, and select the bookmark.htm file in your Netscape directory. Hit OK and the bookmark file will be viewed in Netscape's main window.

The next selection in the File menu is Preferences. I'm going to skip over Bookmark Preferences for now, and come back to this in a bit when the settings will make more sense.

The Import option will let you bring in other Netscape bookmark files. This is useful if you upgrade to a newer version of Netscape and want to bring your bookmarks list over to the new version, or if a friend gives you a copy of his or her bookmarks file.

Save As allows you to save your current bookmarks list as an HTML document. This is helpful if you keep separate bookmark lists for different users who use the same machine, or if, say, you like to keep your work and play bookmark lists separate.

Selecting Close will close the Netscape Bookmarks window. Alt+F4 also closes the Netscape Bookmarks window.

The Netscape Bookmarks Edit Menu

The selections in this menu affect the folders or bookmarks currently selected in the bookmarks list. Cut, Copy, Paste, and Delete do exactly what they say to the highlighted item in the bookmarks list. Find will search from the top of the bookmarks list for a keyword you type into the Find Next field of the Find Bookmark window.

Find searches the names (usually the title of the Web page) and URLs of the bookmarks in your bookmarks list. Clicking the Find Next button searches for the next instance of the keyword.

Selecting Find Again from the Edit menu will search for the last keyword specified in Find during your current Netscape session; when you quit Netscape, the Find What field is erased. Find Again works much the same as the Find Next button, though you don't need to have the Find Bookmark window open to use Find Again.

The Netscape Bookmarks Item Menu

Here's the menu you'll be using the most when customizing your bookmarks. With the choices in this menu, you can jump to the URL of the selected bookmark, add new items to your bookmarks list, and change the information in pre-existing bookmarks listings.

Selecting Go to Bookmark will tell Netscape to go to the URL of the highlighted selection. Double-clicking on any bookmark in the list will also take you to that URL. (Double-clicking on a folder will open and close it, displaying or hiding its contents.)

Insert Bookmark will insert a new bookmark (for the Web page currently displayed in Netscape's main window) into your bookmarks list directly below the currently selected item. If no item is selected, a new bookmark is added at the end of the bookmarks list. When you select Insert Bookmark, the window in Figure 3.4 appears.

Figure 3.4

Bookmark Properties window

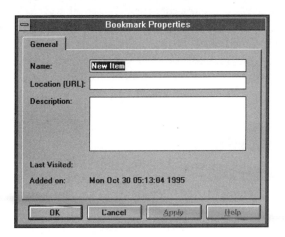

If you've selected this menu option with no page currently displayed in your main Netscape window, you can replace the default Name of New Item, typing in the Name of the bookmark as you want it to appear, as well as the actual URL of the Web page. This is useful for adding URLs from other sources to your bookmarks list without actually visiting them yet—for instance, you can go through the current issue of a magazine and add all of the interesting-looking URLs to your bookmarks list, to be further investigated later. You must fill in both the Name and Location fields for the bookmark to work properly. You can also add an optional Description of the bookmark item—for example, "from latest Wired, p. 37." Clicking the OK button then adds the new bookmark to your bookmarks list. For instance, if you came across a URL in a newspaper or magazine, you might type in the URL, a name to appear in your bookmarks list, and a note about where you came across the URL. You probably won't use this menu choice very much; most bookmarks you add will be from the Add Bookmark menu choice in Netscape's main screen.

Selecting Insert Header adds a new folder to your bookmarks list. Added headers will subsequently appear as hierarchical menus in the Bookmarks menu of your main Netscape window, and are the most important weapon in your fight to conquer an unruly bookmarks list; more about this in a moment.

Selecting Insert Header brings up a Bookmark Properties window similar to that of Insert Bookmark, with several differences. The default name is New Header. The field that was the URL field in the window that appears upon selecting the Insert Bookmark menu choice is present, but it is an uneditable placeholder. Clicking the OK button adds a new header folder in your bookmarks list directly below the currently selected item. If no item is selected, a new header folder is added at the end of the bookmarks list.

Selecting the Insert Separator menu choice places a horizontal line into your bookmarks list. Separators provide a nice visual cue when organizing your bookmarks list.

The Properties menu choice is operative only when you have an existing bookmark selected. The Bookmark Properties window appears with the Name field filled in, and the URL field filled in if a bookmark was selected. You'll use this menu choice when renaming bookmarks or headers or modifying URLs of bookmarks. Incidentally, if you click the right mouse button while the pointer is over a bookmark, you get a popup mini-menu of Go to Bookmark and Properties. Over a header folder, you get a mini-menu of Close Folder and Properties.

The Netscape Bookmarks Sort Menu

Selecting several bookmarks (by Shift-clicking on their listings in the Netscape Bookmarks window) and then pulling down to either the By Name or By Date options in this menu sorts the selected bookmarks, you guessed it, by the first letter of their titles or by the date they were added.

Now that you've completed your brief recon mission, I'll show you how to use that information for personal gain.

Managing Your Bookmarks List

Now, then. All of these bookmarks-list tools are fine and dandy, but when would you actually use them? Well, if you're both a Web junkie and a pack rat like I am, you'll find yourself with a long list of unorganized bookmarks along with pangs of guilt about deleting any of them. If you've ever tried to find an important letter on a desk full of papers, you have an idea what it's like to find a particular Web page in a long unsorted bookmarks list. You don't want that to happen in Netscape, right? Of course you don't. So let's go through a short bookmarks-list organizing session that'll give you a few strategies for organizing your own bookmarks list.

I've come up with a little bookmarks list for this chapter. From Netscape's main window, I pull down the Bookmarks menu and see the bookmarks list shown in Figure 3.5.

Figure 3.5

My bookmarks list in the Bookmarks menu

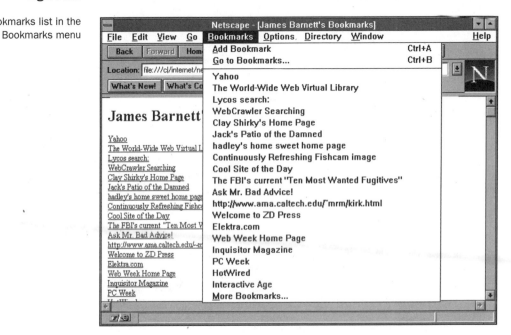

Pulling down to View Bookmarks in the Bookmarks menu, I'm greeted with the Netscape Bookmarks window shown in Figure 3.6.

The bookmarks here fall into several categories, handily enough. There are bookmarks for Web sites of Web searching, pals of mine, goofy stuff, work, and magazines. I'll set up header folders for each of these topics, and move the bookmarks for each topic into the appropriate folder.

To create a Searching header, I select the first item in the list, the header named James Barnett's Bookmarks. (No, Netscape isn't psychic; it gets the name for this header from the preferences you've previously given it.) With this header selected, I pull down the Item menu to Insert Header. Naming the Header "Searching," I click the OK button and now have a Searching header directly above the Yahoo bookmark, as shown in Figure 3.7.

Figure 3.6

My bookmarks list
in Netscape's
Bookmarks window

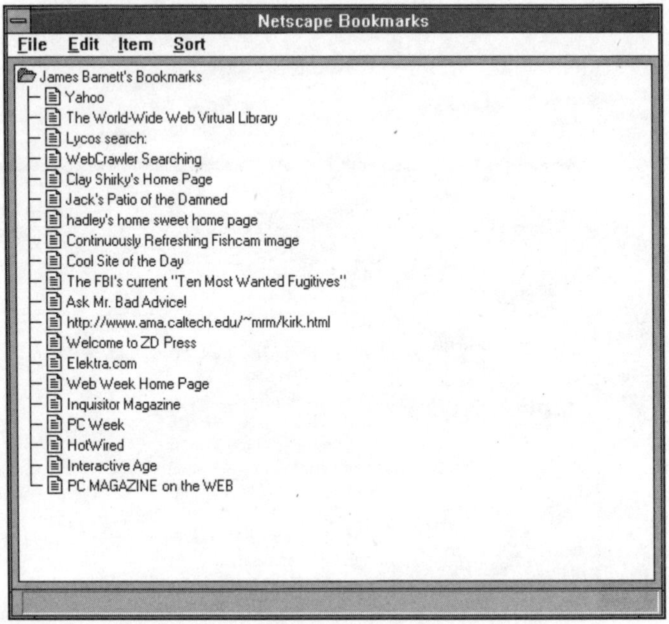

```
                    Netscape Bookmarks
File   Edit   Item   Sort

📂 James Barnett's Bookmarks
 ├─ 📄 Yahoo
 ├─ 📄 The World-Wide Web Virtual Library
 ├─ 📄 Lycos search:
 ├─ 📄 WebCrawler Searching
 ├─ 📄 Clay Shirky's Home Page
 ├─ 📄 Jack's Patio of the Damned
 ├─ 📄 hadley's home sweet home page
 ├─ 📄 Continuously Refreshing Fishcam image
 ├─ 📄 Cool Site of the Day
 ├─ 📄 The FBI's current "Ten Most Wanted Fugitives"
 ├─ 📄 Ask Mr. Bad Advice!
 ├─ 📄 http://www.ama.caltech.edu/~mrm/kirk.html
 ├─ 📄 Welcome to ZD Press
 ├─ 📄 Elektra.com
 ├─ 📄 Web Week Home Page
 ├─ 📄 Inquisitor Magazine
 ├─ 📄 PC Week
 ├─ 📄 HotWired
 ├─ 📄 Interactive Age
 └─ 📄 PC MAGAZINE on the WEB
```

Figure 3.7

My bookmarks list with
Searching header added

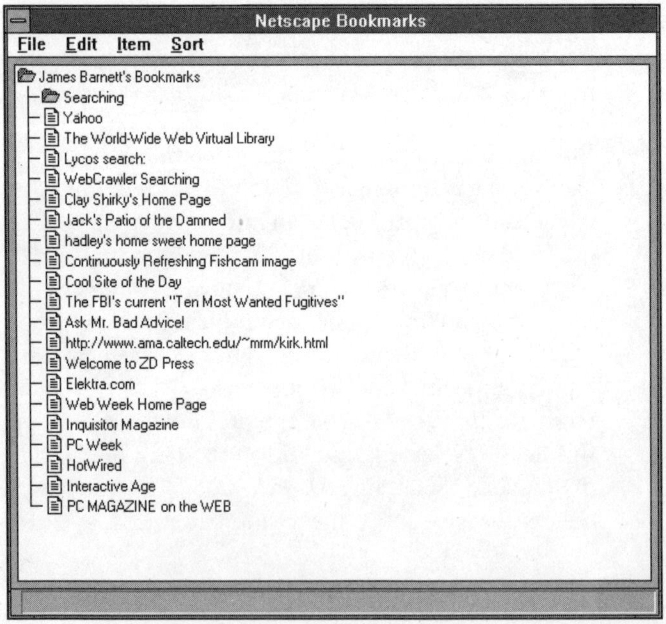

```
                    Netscape Bookmarks
File   Edit   Item   Sort

📂 James Barnett's Bookmarks
 ├─ 📂 Searching
 ├─ 📄 Yahoo
 ├─ 📄 The World-Wide Web Virtual Library
 ├─ 📄 Lycos search:
 ├─ 📄 WebCrawler Searching
 ├─ 📄 Clay Shirky's Home Page
 ├─ 📄 Jack's Patio of the Damned
 ├─ 📄 hadley's home sweet home page
 ├─ 📄 Continuously Refreshing Fishcam image
 ├─ 📄 Cool Site of the Day
 ├─ 📄 The FBI's current "Ten Most Wanted Fugitives"
 ├─ 📄 Ask Mr. Bad Advice!
 ├─ 📄 http://www.ama.caltech.edu/~mrm/kirk.html
 ├─ 📄 Welcome to ZD Press
 ├─ 📄 Elektra.com
 ├─ 📄 Web Week Home Page
 ├─ 📄 Inquisitor Magazine
 ├─ 📄 PC Week
 ├─ 📄 HotWired
 ├─ 📄 Interactive Age
 └─ 📄 PC MAGAZINE on the WEB
```

Going down the line, I add a header named Pals above the Clay Shirky's Home Page bookmark, a Goofy Stuff header above the Fishcam bookmark, a Work header above the Welcome to ZD Press bookmark, and a Magazines header above the bookmark for *Inquisitor* magazine. My bookmarks list now looks like Figure 3.8.

Figure 3.8

My bookmarks list with various headers added

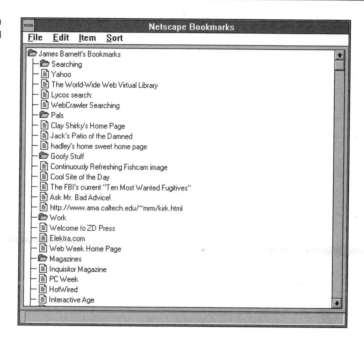

Okay, the header folders are in place. Now I need to move the book-marks into them. Shift-clicking allows you to select more than one bookmark at a time. I click once on the Yahoo bookmark, hold the Shift key down, and then click on the WebCrawler bookmark. Those two bookmarks and the two in between them are selected. (I could also have clicked the first, and then Shift-clicked the second, third, and fourth individually.) With these book-marks selected, I click once with the left mouse button, hold it, and drag up until the mouse pointer is over the Searching header folder. A thin black box appears around the Searching folder. I release the mouse button and the selected bookmarks are dropped into the destination folder. The searching bookmarks are now safely nestled in the Searching header folder, as shown in Figure 3.9.

I perform the same actions all the way down the line, until all of my header folders are full of bookmarks and the Netscape Bookmarks window looks like Figure 3.10.

Figure 3.9

Bookmarks placed within
Searching header

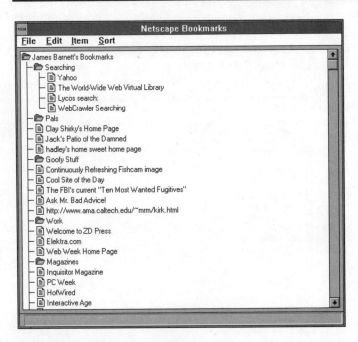

Figure 3.10

Header folders full of
bookmarks

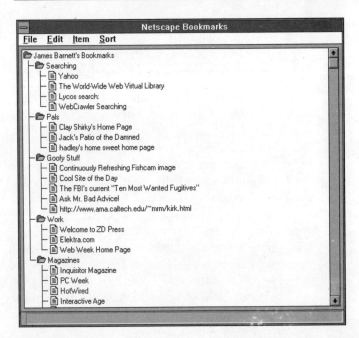

Hmmm. This looks pretty good. Let me give this layout a run in the main Netscape window to check. I close the Netscape Bookmarks window and select the Bookmarks menu in the main Netscape window. The Bookmarks menu then appears as shown in Figure 3.11.

Figure 3.11

New improved bookmarks list in Netscape's Bookmarks menu

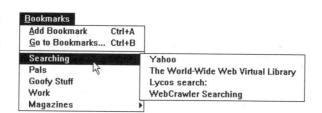

Not bad, not bad at all. The headers that appear as folders in the Netscape Bookmarks window appear here as hierarchical submenus. Had I wished, I could have created header folders within header folders in the Netscape Bookmarks window, which would appear here as multileveled hierarchical menus.

Ahh. That's so much better. Adding headers also makes it considerably easier to skim your bookmarks when viewed in Netscape's main window. One last time, I pull down the Bookmarks menu to View Bookmarks, and in the Netscape Bookmarks window's File menu, pull down to View in Browser. My bookmarks list appears in Netscape's main window's content area as shown in Figure 3.12, with handy indents for easier viewing.

When customizing your own bookmarks list, go ahead and add as many headers as you see fit. Add some headers that you think you'll use in the future. It's better to add empty headers (or headers that appear empty save for one or two bookmarks) now than to have to try and neaten up things later.

Another reason to make sure you use headers is that if Netscape's bookmark list gets too long (that is, with lots of sites and no headers), only part of your bookmarks list will appear in the Bookmarks pulldown menu, with a More Bookmarks choice at the end of the list. Selecting More Bookmarks there will bring you back to the Netscape Bookmarks window. Use headers. It'll make your life easier.

Netscape's Mail Reader

Pull down the Window menu to Netscape Mail and let's have a look at how Netscape handles e-mail. Netscape will ask you for the password for the e-mail account you've specified in the Identity preference tab in your Mail and News option window, accessible under the Options menu. The screen in Figure 3.13 appears.

Figure 3.12

New improved bookmarks list in Netscape's main window

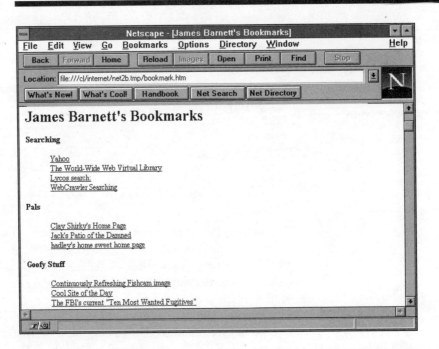

Figure 3.13

Netscape's Mail window

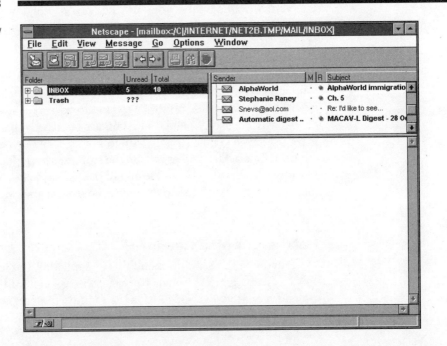

The first e-mail you'll have listed is from Mozilla himself. Well, from Netscape Communications Corporation, anyway. You'll see that it's possible to embed pictures into e-mail, as in Figure 3.14.

Figure 3.14

Mail from Mozilla

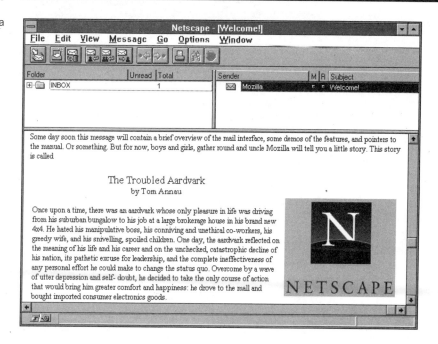

E-mail from normal folks looks a lot like Figure 3.15, depending on who your friends are.

The layout of the Netscape Mail window is customizable. Move your mouse pointer over the horizontal bar in the center of the screen and the cursor turns into a variation of Windows' standard window-resize cursor. Click your left mouse button and drag the center divider line up and down until you like the screen's appearance. Move the cursor over the vertical bar and you get the same cursor and capability. Additionally, the divider-move cursor appears over the bar between the Folder, Unread, Total, Sender, M(arked), R(ead), and Subject columns.

The full capabilities of Netscape's e-mail reader are somewhat beyond the scope of this book (there's a lotta stuff in those menus). The main thing you need to know is that to reply to the message you're currently reading, hit Ctrl+R (or pull the Message menu down to the Reply menu choice). You can read more about using Netscape to read your e-mail by pulling down the Help menu to Handbook and selecting the Mail News and Bookmarks hyperlink in the Reference section, or by going directly to the URL http://home.netscape.com/eng/mozilla/2.0/handbook/docs/mnb.html.

Figure 3.15

Mail from Andy

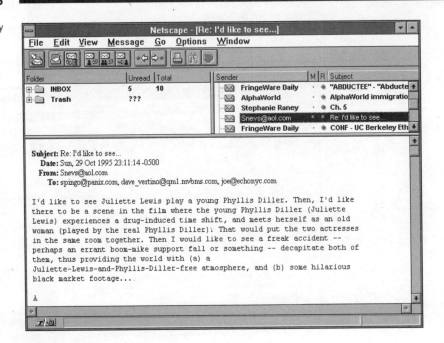

Netscape's Address Book

Pulling down the Window menu to Address Book brings up a window that you can use to keep your frequently used e-mail addresses handy, as in Figure 3.16.

New users can be added by pulling down the Item Menu to Add User, which brings up the window shown in Figure 3.17.

Browsing for Speed

The Web can present information in a much more aesthetically pleasing way than any other Internet service, but sometimes you're not concerned with the way things look. You may be hungry for quick information or not in the mood to wait for graphics files. You can use Netscape to browse Web pages without loading their inline images. Pages come up with background and text colors, but background and inline images are not downloaded. To load a Web page sans images, go to Netscape's Options menu and pull down to Auto Load Images. The check mark next to the menu choice disappears. The next Web page you access will load without pictures.

Figure 3.18 shows a Web page with Auto Load Images turned off and Figure 3.19 shows the same Web page with graphics loaded.

Figure 3.16

The Address Book window

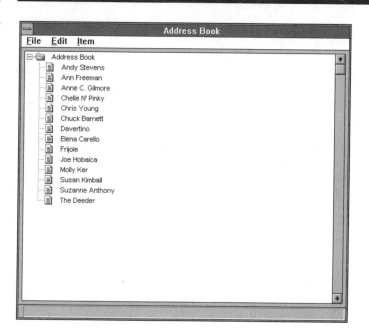

Figure 3.17

Adding a new user to
your Address Book

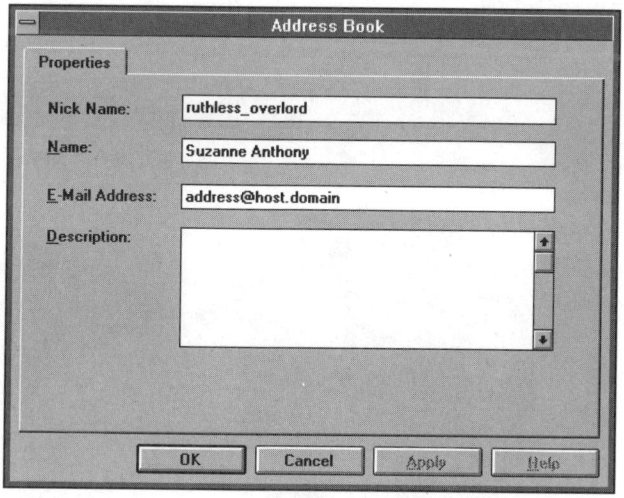

Figure 3.18

Web page with
Auto Load Images off

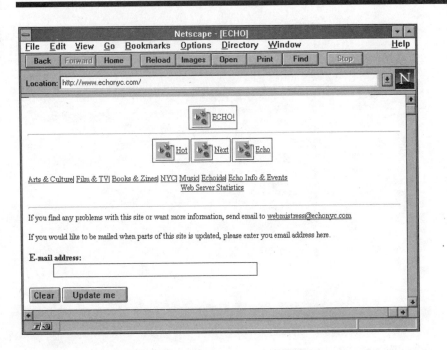

Figure 3.19

Web page with
images loaded

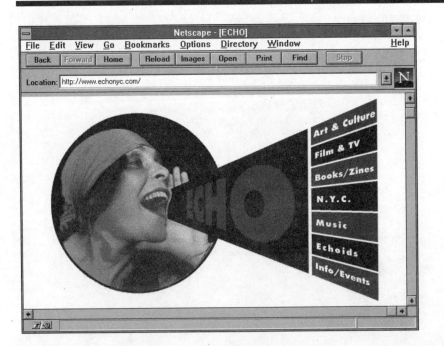

While turning Auto Load Images off does not allow you to see the pictures to grasp their content, a short text description of the image may appear. The HTML language supports the use of what's called the ALT tag, wherein Web authors can add an optional text description of inline images (more about HTML and the ALT tag in Chapter 9.)

Should you decide you'd like to see the images, clicking the Images button in the toolbar (or hitting Ctrl+I) will load all of the page's images. Clicking on any of the picture icons will download just that picture.

Doing a Little URL Detective Work

Let's say you come across a URL somewhere and are anxious to check it out. You type the URL into Netscape's location field, same as always, and hit Enter. Instead of being greeted with the page you desire, you get an error message saying the file you're looking for cannot be found. Now what do you do? First, check your spelling. This is an obvious solution, I know, but I can't tell you how many times (especially when I was just starting to use the Web) I typed an extra colon or slash when inputting a URL by hand. Spelling's okay? Try again. The Web page still doesn't come up. Hmm. Now what? Here's a little trick.

On the Web, authors sometimes move their pages around in an effort to fine-tune their Web sites. Sometimes they forget that an old URL for a Web page may still be in circulation, and leave no forwarding address. Occasionally, you can do a little snooping around and find the Web page you're looking for.

For instance, my home page is located at http://www.echonyc.com/~spingo/ Spingo/. A lot of people try to access it, but forget to type in the last part of the URL, the "/Spingo/" part. Those that do this are presented with the screen in Figure 3.20.

URLs usually point to files, but they can also point to directories, which is what's happening in this instance. Files in this directory are indicated by a file icon and the file name; subdirectories are indicated by folder icons. Clicking on the name of a file or directory loads that file or enters that directory. The directory we want here is the Spingo directory. Go ahead and click on the folder name "Spingo/" and you'll enter the Spingo directory, where my home page resides. My home page itself (as seen in Chapter 1) will load. When it does you won't be presented with another directory listing, even though you haven't explicitly typed the name of an HTML file to load. When Netscape accesses a directory on a Web server without explicitly asking for an HTML file, it automatically looks for a file called index.html. If an index.html file is present, Netscape loads that file instead of presenting a directory listing.

Figure 3.20

http://www.echonyc.
com/~spingo/

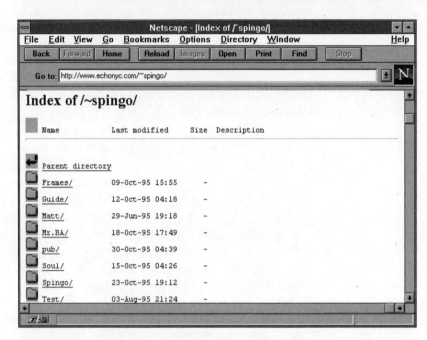

This process also works in the other direction: If you've gone looking for a specific HTML file and not found it, go into the Location field and click your mouse at the end of the URL there. Use your Backspace key to delete the characters back to the last slash, and hit Enter (or press the Reload button in Netscape's toolbar). This takes you up a directory level, to where maybe you can see why you missed the file you were looking for, or if the Web page author moved things around. This fiddling with the URL in the Location field also works quite handily when navigating ftp and gopher sites, which I'll get into further in Chapter 5.

Save Useful Pages to Your Hard Disk

You can save frequently accessed Web pages to disk, allowing you to save connect time and the uncertainty of connection with popular pages. If you frequently access a particular Web page and want to have it on hand whenever you need it, saving pages to disk may be the way to go.

Pages with often-accessed reference information or a lot of links are prime candidates to save to disk. For instance, you may want to save some of the Web pages at Yahoo (http://www.yahoo.com/), which are primarily lists of hyperlinks to other sites. Go to the Web page you'd like to save. Select Save As (or hit Ctrl+S) under the File menu, and name the file something memorable in the File Name field. Make sure to save as "Source (*.htm)". This'll save the page with HTML coding (including the link information) intact. Saving as a .TXT file will only save the text displayed in Netscape's content area; hypertext links will be saved as text and when reloaded will not be useful as hyperlinks. When you want to load the page into Netscape in the future, open the file with Open File under the File menu. The page will be displayed (sans graphics), the same as if you were at the site itself.

Some sites are also making available pages that can be saved to disk and then imported into your bookmarks list, adding a mini-directory of the site for little effort on your part. One site doing this is the Internet Underground Musical Archive, which calls it the "E-Z Bookmark Feature." Directions on how to save and import these pages are at http://www.iuma.com/IUMA-2.0/pages/ezbkmrk/.

Grabbing Any URL and Making It Your Startup Page

Getting tired of seeing Netscape's home page every time you launch Netscape? You can solve this, dear reader. Next time you're at a Web page that you figure would be just perfect to see every time you fire up Netscape, here's what you do:

1. Click in the Location field and highlight the entire URL you see there.

2. Hit Ctrl+C or pull the Edit menu down to Copy. The URL is now in your clipboard, securely biding its time until it reaches its final destination.

3. Pull down the Options menu to Preferences. In the Styles preference tab, have a peek at the Window Styles area, and in particular the Start With choices.

4. Click on the Home Page Location radio button and click in the field below.

5. Hit Ctrl+V, and the URL that will serve as your new entry to the Web will appear.

6. Click the OK button and confidently return to Netscape's main window, knowing that the next time you launch Netscape, you'll be immediately transported to the start-up Web page of your dreams.

Editing Your Netscape.ini File

While .INI files are somewhat beyond the scope of this book, you should know that Netscape saves all manner of operating and preferences settings in this file. It's created when you install Netscape and is located in your Netscape directory. See Figure 3.21 for a quick glimpse at your netscape.ini file. If you've never edited .INI files before, I'd recommend you leave it untouched. If you've been around the block a few times and are comfy doing such things, well, hey, be my guest!

Figure 3.21

Netscape.ini as viewed
in Windows Notepad

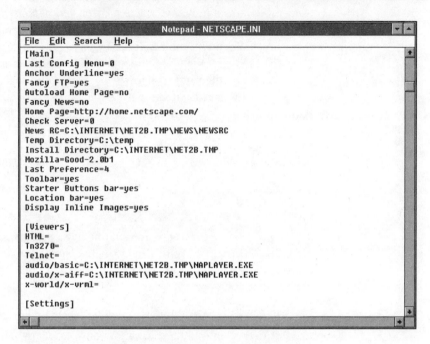

```
                          Notepad - NETSCAPE.INI
 File   Edit   Search   Help
 [Main]
 Last Config Menu=0
 Anchor Underline=yes
 Fancy FTP=yes
 Autoload Home Page=no
 Fancy News=no
 Home Page=http://home.netscape.com/
 Check Server=0
 News RC=C:\INTERNET\NET2B.TMP\NEWS\NEWSRC
 Temp Directory=C:\temp
 Install Directory=C:\INTERNET\NET2B.TMP
 Mozilla=Good-2.0b1
 Last Preference=4
 Toolbar=yes
 Starter Buttons bar=yes
 Location bar=yes
 Display Inline Images=yes

 [Viewers]
 HTML=
 Tn3270=
 Telnet=
 audio/basic=C:\INTERNET\NET2B.TMP\NAPLAYER.EXE
 audio/x-aiff=C:\INTERNET\NET2B.TMP\NAPLAYER.EXE
 x-world/x-vrml=

 [Settings]
```

TIP. *If you've opened more than one Netscape window using Ctrl+N or by selecting New Window from the File menu, hitting F6 or Ctrl+Tab will switch between the different open Netscape windows.*

Also, try a click on the N logo; when not being mercilessly pelted with meteors, it serves as a handy alternative to the Netscape's Home menu listing under the Directory menu.

■ On to the Fun Stuff!

I hope I've shown you some interesting ways to fully use Netscape. These tricks 'n' tips are all well and good, but as with anything, fun is where you find it. And who couldn't use a little more fun in their lives? Let's have a look at a few things you can do with Netscape that will do absolutely nothing to increase your productivity.

Prank E-mail

You can easily baffle your pals with prank e-mail sent from Netscape. Pull down Mail and News under the Options menu, and select the Identity preference tab. Change your name and e-mail address to something suitable, perhaps Sal Paradise for Your Name and jkerouac@the.road.net as your e-mail address? Click OK. Go to the File menu, select Mail Document (or hit Ctrl+M). Fill out the subject and body of the e-mail, send it on! The e-mail is sent along to your mark, with a spurious name and return address.

Oh, and don't tell anyone I told you this. And don't even *think* of doing any serious stuff with this. You'll be snagged; information that'll lead back to you is indeed placed in the headers of the e-mail you send this way. But if you just want to send dopey e-mail to a pal, well, why not?

Hunting for Netscape Easter Eggs

You don't think the clever programmers over at Netscape would be content with just putting out the most advanced Web browser to date, would you? Of course not. They threw in what are commonly called "Easter eggs." These are fun little undocumented treats hidden in the coding of a computer program. Easter eggs are only viewable via a certain key/mouse click sequence or, in this case, a URL typed into Netscape's Location field.

The first step to accessing Netscape's Easter eggs lies no further away than the Help menu. Go to the Help menu and select About Netscape. That takes you to a little page containing copyright information and links to the license and feedback pages. Look at the URL—"about:". This isn't exactly a standard URL; the sneaky devils made it up for themselves. Go ahead and change the URL in the Location field to read **about:mozilla**. You may have already had a sighting of Mozilla, Netscape's fire-breathing dragon mascot. Bet you didn't know he had his own book, did you? Oh, and by the way, I'm not showing screen shots here on purpose; I'd hate to kill the thrill of discovery, which is what Easter eggs are for. Go look for yourself!

I will, however, give you the Mozilla museum, as seen in Figure 3.22. If you can't get enough of Mozilla, check out Tilman Hausherr's Mozilla Museum at http://www.snafu.de/~tilman/mozilla. There you'll see pictures of Mozilla culled from previous versions of Netscape's Web site that show the many sides of Mozilla, certainly the most well-rounded reptile I know. There's also a Usenet newsgroup called alt.fan.mozilla; it's pretty quiet so far, and talk of said lizard is almost nonexistent, but hey, it's there. Mozilla, you see, is also the not-so-secret nickname of the Netscape Navigator program, too.

Next, try **about:authors**. You can even get specific about the authors. Try **about:jwz** to have a peek at Netscape Hacker Jamie Zawinski's home page. I'm told that on the Unix version of Netscape, accessing this page changes the meteor-showered N logo to a compass. With a bit more fiddling it goes back to the N, albeit one that has Mozilla looming over it and breathing fire. Try about: with the last names of the rest of the developers and see what you get.

Figure 3.22

The Mozilla Museum

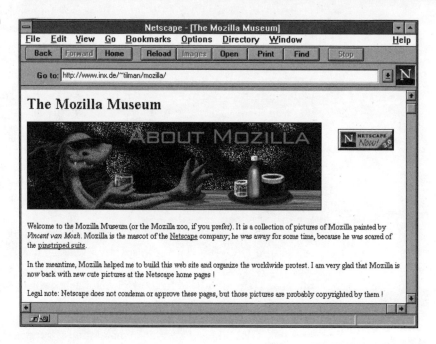

Netscape's Easter eggs are different on different platforms. For instance, typing about: and then something that Netscape doesn't recognize (that is, say, about:cheeseburgers) on a Windows machine will bring you an error unlike the others you're likely to come across. In Netscape's content area, you get the message "Yeah, whatever…." On the Mac, you'd get the somewhat more colorful "Whatchew talkin' about, Willis?"

For a fairly comprehensive list of Easter eggs contained in the different platform versions of Netscape, have a look at the Eric Perlman's Netscape Easter Eggs page at http://www.yikes.com/fun/netscape_eggs.html.

■ Take Five, but Don't Get *Too* Comfortable

You've come this far, making yourself at home within Netscape itself, arranging things so they're just right. Pat yourself on the back for a job well done. But there's still a bit more you'll need to get in place to be able handle the sundry images, sounds, video clips, and assorted files that the Web offers up. C'mon along to the next chapter and I'll show you how to set up the helper applications that will handle all those files.

C H A P T E R

Using Helper Applications

Y OU'VE GOT NETSCAPE FINE-TUNED AND HUMMING, AND NOW you're prepared to go out and browse the Web with the best of 'em. Netscape and the included Netscape Audio Player (naplayer.exe in your Netscape directory) will handle the bulk of multimedia files you come across. Keep in mind, though, that Web pages can contain hyperlinks to just about any kind of computer file you can think of: sounds, images, digitized video clips, and others. Eventually, you'll come across a multimedia file you want to watch or hear that either Netscape or its Audio Player can't handle. To take full advantage of the many different types of files that are available on the Web, you'll have to do a little work to set up Netscape to handle these files by downloading supplementary programs, called *helper applications* or *helper apps*, that will display or play multimedia files once you've downloaded them.

Really, this won't hurt a bit. I'll walk you through downloading, installing, and using several of the more popular helper apps, and I'll point you to where you can find some others. At the end of the chapter there's a chart showing the URLs where you can get some helper applications for the rest of the MIME types listed in your Helper Apps preference tab.

■ What Needs Helping?

Helper applications and the files they play or show take the Web into the realm of full-blown multimedia. Web pages with pictures and text can be visually attractive, but don't look that different from print pages displayed on a monitor. With sound, video, and other multimedia types thrown into the mix, you enter a whole new ball game. However, the constrictions of file size and speed inherent in accessing these files over the Internet instead of from your hard drive or CD-ROM drive is limiting, to be sure. You'll find few Web sites that immerse you in a full-blown multimedia environment like, say, the CD-ROM game Myst does, but hey—you're not shelling out fifty bucks for each Web site you access either.

As far as viewing files goes, Netscape's pretty versatile. It can show you several different kinds of image files, and it can play several kinds of audio files with the Netscape Audio Player included in the Netscape installation. You can look at text (.TXT) files and of course, HTML (.HTM or .html) files with Netscape. But files on the Internet come in all kinds of formats. For starters, there are sound files in various formats, MPEG and QuickTime movies, PostScript and .PDF (Portable Document Format) files that adopt the look of a printed document for onscreen use and cross-platform transportability. And though Netscape can view picture files internally, sometimes you'll want to view them in a more powerful dedicated image program.

When you use Netscape to download a multimedia file from the Web, it first looks to see whether it can display the file on its own, in its own window. If not, the next thing the browser does is look through your settings in the Helper Apps preference tab to see if you've specified a helper application that can handle it. When these settings are properly configured, Netscape will download files in formats that it can't show internally, and then automatically launch the proper helper app to deal with the information.

Let's take a look at Netscape's Helper Apps preferences by launching Netscape, pulling down General under the Option menu, and clicking on the Helper Apps preference tab. We'll come back and fiddle with these in a bit. First, though, I'll explain what the phrase *MIME type* means (it appears underneath the scrollable field). To set yourself up for managing the rest of the programs you'll download in this chapter, create a directory in your Netscape directory and call it *helpapps*. Using this directory for all of your helper applications will make them easy to find should you need to locate them later for playing saved files or when upgrading to newer versions. For greater organization, create separate directories within your helpapps directory for various types of files—image, sound, video, and so on. You can also read some more about Netscape and helper applications at http:// home.netscape.com/assist/helper_apps/.

MIME: Not an Excuse to Wear Tights and Whiteface

There's a standard for describing various kinds of multimedia files on the Internet, which Netscape and other programs use to define what kind of data goes with which helper app. This is akin to how Windows knows that a .doc file belongs to Microsoft Word, or a .txt file belongs to Notepad. This standard MIME (Multipurpose Internet Mail Extensions), was developed to attach multimedia files to Internet e-mail messages. You can read more about MIME at http://www.netscape.com/assist/helper_apps/mime.html.

WinZip, an Invaluable Tool on Your Utility Belt

We want to grab some of the most important helper applications. First, though, we need to get our hands on WinZip, which will be invaluable for downloading not only helper applications but many files on the Internet. Most Windows programs (and many files) on the Internet are distributed in compressed .ZIP format to save disk space and download time. Before you start downloading helper applications from the Net, you'll want a program such as WinZip that can unzip these compressed files. If you've already got a decompression program that handles .ZIP files, by all means use it. If not, I recommend WinZip, which you can download from the WinZip Web home page shown in Figure 4.1 (http://www.winzip.com/winzip/). WinZip is very easy to use, runs from within Windows, can install/uninstall programs, and has a handy "check out" option for you to try before permanently devoting valuable hard drive space to it.

Scroll down to the hyperlink that reads *Download WinZip*, and click on it. You're taken to a Web page listing the various permutations of WinZip available. As I write this, the most current version is WinZip 5.6; click the Download WinZip 5.6 for Windows hyperlink. The Unknown File Type window in Figure 4.2 appears.

Click the Save to Disk button, tell Netscape where on your hard drive to save WinZip (the helper applications directory you just created would be a fine place for it), and click OK. The Saving Location Window in Figure 4.3 appears, indicating the status of the download in progress.

Figure 4.1

WinZip home page

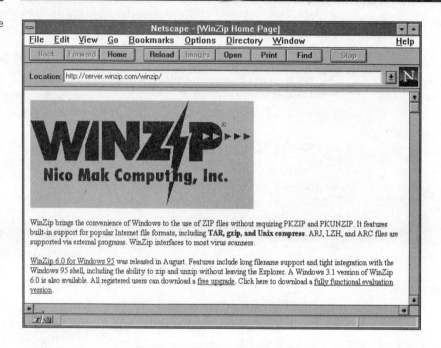

Figure 4.2

Unknown File Type window

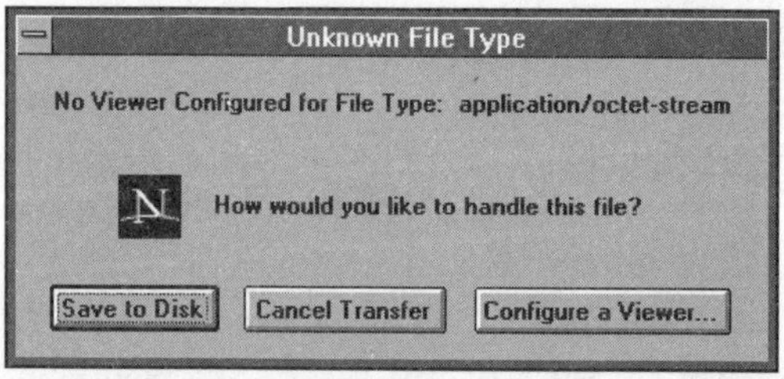

Figure 4.3

Saving Location window

While WinZip is downloading, you can bring Netscape's main window to the forefront. If you haven't already, click the Back button and read a bit about WinZip. Netscape allows you to continue browsing the Web while you're downloading files, which is handy especially for large files, and it allows you to continue poking around the Web while you are receiving the download.

You might want to have a look at the program and maybe take a quick spin through the help files. Once the download is finished, minimize Netscape and bring up Windows's File Manager. Locate and launch WinZip to see the screen in Figure 4.4.

Figure 4.4

WinZip program window

Now we want to make sure that any .ZIP files downloaded with Netscape are sent directly to WinZip for decompressing. In Netscape, pull the Options menu down to General and click the Helper Apps preference tab. Scroll down until you see the line beginning with *application/x-zip-compressed* in the scrollable File type list. Click once to select this listing so that we can modify it. In the Action area of the preferences tab, click the Launch Application radio button, and then click the Browse button. Locate WinZip on your hard drive and click the OK button. Your Helper Apps preference tab should now look something like mine, shown in Figure 4.5.

Click the OK button; now any .ZIP files you download—and there will be plenty, I bet—are shuttled right over to WinZip for decompression.

Figure 4.5

Helper Apps preference
tab: WinZip configured as
.ZIP helper app

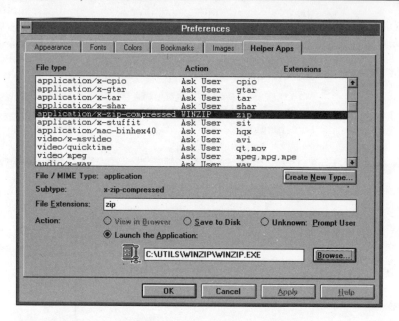

■ Harvesting Helper Applications

Though Netscape's sound player comes bundled with your Netscape Navigator package, you'll have to download the rest of the helper applications you'll need from the Internet. Don't worry, it's easy to do. Keep in mind that this book is a snapshot of the Web as it existed when we were producing this book; new versions of helper applications are constantly being released. Chapter 7 will point you to newsgroups and mailing lists where you can get the latest news about helper apps. Whenever possible, I refer you to the "official" Web home page of a helper app so you'll get the most up-to-date version.

Sounds? Good

Netscape comes prepared to play some of the sounds on the Web. As mentioned earlier, when you installed Netscape the Netscape Audio Player (naplayer.exe) went in your Netscape directory. If you'd like to read more about the Netscape Audio Player, have a look at http://home.netscape.com/info/winaudio.html.

For a lot of the sounds you'll find on the Web, Netscape's Audio Player will do you just fine; it can handle .AU and .AIFF sound file formats. .AU files are the sound standard on UNIX workstations, and .AIFF files were originally developed by Apple and are common on Macintosh computers as well as others. .AU sounds are the most prevalent kind of sound format on the Web, though various other sound file types are becoming more popular. Many Web authors, realizing this, are beginning to provide several different versions of the same sound in various formats, all of which come with their own pros and cons. I'll help you set up Netscape to handle the most popular of these.

In discussing sound helper applications, I'll assume you have a sound card. However, if your PC doesn't, the program spcak.exe will allow you to play sounds through the computer's speaker, of course with less quality than if you did have a sound card. Speak.exe and several sound players are available from VirtualRadio's Netscape Sound How-to Web page at http://burgoyne.com/vaudio/netsound.html, along with helpful tips on setting up Netscape to handle various sound helper applications. For an exhaustive technical reference to computer sound formats, have a look at the Audio File Format FAQ (Frequently Asked Questions) files at http://www.cis.ohio-state.edu/hypertext/faq/usenet/audio-fmts/top.html. Sound utilities are discussed in the Usenet newsgroup alt.binaries.sounds.utilities.

Netscape Audio Player

Netscape comes preconfigured with the Helper Apps preference tab set to use Netscape Audio Player for .AU and .AIFF sounds. Let's go to a Web site with lots of sounds and give it a test run. The Sounds Directory at Rob's Multimedia Lab (http://www.acm.uiuc.edu/rml/Sounds/) has oodles of .AU files organized into directories for your browsing ease and enjoyment, as you can see in Figure 4.6.

Scroll down and click on whatever directory strikes your fancy. I've used the Simpson-snds directory for this example. Clicking the hyperlink to any of the sound files brings up the Viewing Location window (which is essentially the Saving Location window from the earlier WinZip download, with a different title). Once the file is downloaded, Netscape Audio Player is automatically launched and appears as you see it in Figure 4.7.

The downloaded sound plays once automatically. To play it again, press the play button (the right arrow) in the Netscape Audio Player window. The simple controls in Netscape Audio Player mimic those of a cassette or CD player; for instance, to stop playing a sound file, click the stop button with the square icon. The double-arrow-forward and -reverse buttons search through the sound file, and the forward and reverse arrows with the bar at the point jump you to the end and beginning of a sound file, respectively. The open-folder button allows you to open a file from your hard drive, and the question mark button brings up a terse About Netscape Audio Player window. All of these commands are contained in Netscape Audio Player's menus as well.

Figure 4.6

Rob's Multimedia Lab
Sounds directory

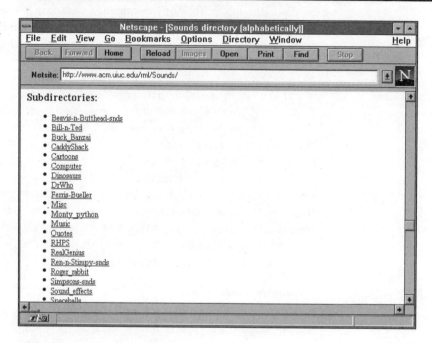

Figure 4.7

Netscape Audio Player

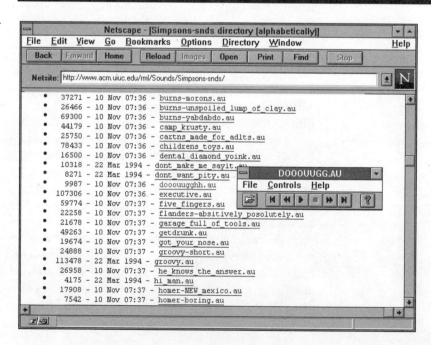

As you may have noted while perusing the Viewing Location window, files you download from the Web that are played or viewed in a helper app are stored in the Temporary Directory you've specified in your Applications and Directories preference tab. Unlike Netscape's cache files, which are deleted automatically as your disk cache (as specified in your Cache and Network preferences tab) fills up, downloaded helper-app-dependent files are saved in your Temporary Directory until you explicitly delete them with Windows's File Manager or another Windows utility. After your Netscape session, the files are still there to be played over and over again or moved to a handier directory, should you wish.

If you'd like a bit more power in your .AU/.AIFF player, you may want to try the WHAM (Waveform Hold and Modify) sound player; it's available from Netscape's Windows Helper Applications Web page at http://home.netscape.com/assist/helper_apps/windowhelper.html. WHAM is slightly more complicated and powerful than Netscape Audio Player, and it can handle more sound file formats, including .WAV format sounds.

WAV Sounds

.WAV files are the de facto standard for PC sound files. Your PC probably came with several .WAV sounds, as well as Windows's Media Player. We'll set up Media Player as your .WAV-playing helper app. To set up Netscape to play .WAV files through it, bring up the Helper Apps preference tab again. In Netscape, pull the Options menu down to General and click the Helper Apps preference tab. Scroll down until you see the line beginning with *audio/x-wav* in the scrollable File type list. Click once to select this listing so that we can modify it. In the Action area of the preferences tab, click the Launch Application radio button and then click the Browse button. Locate Media Player on your hard drive (probably c:\windows\mplayer.exe) and click the OK button. Your Helper Apps preference tab should now look something like mine in Figure 4.8.

Now we'll go to a Web site with a bevy of tantalizing .WAV files, Tiger's Sound Archive, at http://xx.acs.appstate.edu/~me9794/sound/tgr/snd/files.html, as shown in Figure 4.9.

Click on the hyperlink for Various Short Wavs, and then choose one of the sounds. Click on the hyperlink for the sound, and the Viewing Location window pops up to show you the status of the download. When the download is complete, Media Player launches, presenting something similar to the window in Figure 4.10.

The controls for Media Player are similar to those of Netscape Audio Player or almost any cassette or CD player you've used. The Contents menu choice in the Help menu provides a thorough discussion of Media Player's abilities.

Figure 4.8

Helper Apps preference
tab: Media Player
configured as .WAV
helper app

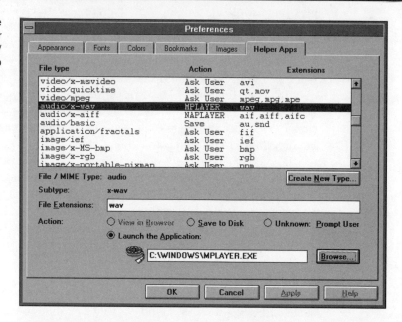

Figure 4.9

Tiger's Sound Archive

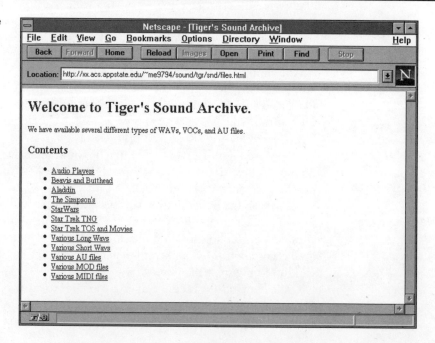

Figure 4.10

Sound in Media Player

Grabbing and Configuring .WAV System Event Sounds

.WAV files offer the added novelty of being usable as system event sounds on your PC. Say you're browsing through a directory of .WAV sounds and come across a particularly endearing clip you'd like to have. Clicking the hyperlink, you download the sound and play it in Media Player. To make it a Windows system event sound, open File Manager and move the .WAV sound file from Netscape's temporary directory to your c:\windows directory. In your Windows Control Panel, double-click the Sound icon. Select a System Event in the scrollable list on the left and your new favorite sound in the scrollable list on the right. Make sure the Enable System Sounds check box is checked and click the OK button. Stand back and watch the zaniness that ensues!

Using Your Other Existing Programs as Helper Apps

Before you download any new helper applications, you may want to look on your hard drive to see if any of the commercial programs you already own can handle any of the MIME types listed in the Helper Apps preference tab. Have a quick scan through the list of MIME types there, paying attention to the Extensions column. If there are file extensions that you already recognize from your day-to-day computer work, you may as well use the programs you have that handle them. For instance, in your Helper Apps preference tab is listed the MIME type application-rtf. Microsoft Word can handle .RTF quite nicely. And Adobe Photoshop, the amazing image-processing program, can handle many types of image file formats. If you're already comfortable with a program, why learn another program that does the same thing?

MPEG Audio

MPEG audio is possibly the best overall audio format in use on the Web, providing small sound files with good quality sound. Thanks to sites such as IUMA, the Internet Underground Music Archive (http://www.iuma.com/), MPEG audio is growing in popularity. IUMA houses music from scores of well-known and obscure musicians and bands. Be forewarned though: IUMA's site, though graphically well-developed, can be a image downloading time hog and may try your patience, especially if you're using a 14,400 baud modem. If you find that IUMA's graphics take forever to download, you might want to turn Auto Load Images off under your Options menu before accessing the site, or click your Stop button once the images have downloaded to the point where you get the general idea of each graphic.

To set up MPEG audio, go to http://www.iuma.com/IUMA-2.0/help/helpwindows.html (shown in Figure 4.11) and grab Xing SoundPlayer (mpgaudio.exe). A hyperlink to information about configuring SoundPlayer in Netscape is located just below the hyperlink to the program.

Figure 4.11

IUMA's Help for Windows

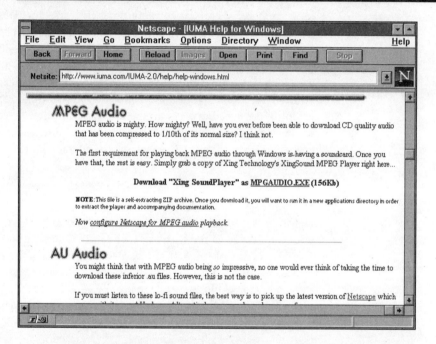

You'll have to define a new MIME type for MPEG audio. Under your Options menu, pull down to General. Click on the Helper Apps preference tab and click on the Create New Type button. In the MIME Type field, type *audio*, and in the MIME SubType field type *x-mpeg*. Click the OK button. In your File Extension field, type *mp2*. In the Action area, click the Launch the Application radio button. Click the Browse button and select the MPEG player, xing_ply.exe. Your Helper Apps preference tab should look like the one in Figure 4.12.

Now you can go to the IUMA site at http://www.iuma.com/ (see Figure 4.13) and hear weird and wonderful music from all manner of folks. Go to the IUMA home page and poke around until you find a promising artist and download a sound file.

Figure 4.12

Helper Apps preference
tab configured for MPEG
audio

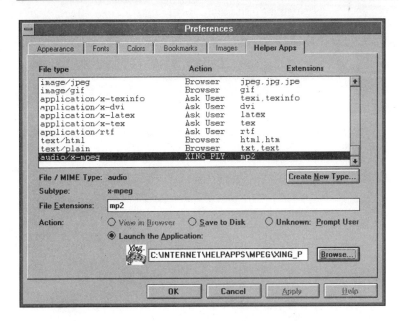

Figure 4.13

IUMA

The sound file will download and Xing Sound Player should launch, bringing up the window in Figure 4.14.

Figure 4.14

Sound in Xing Sound
Player

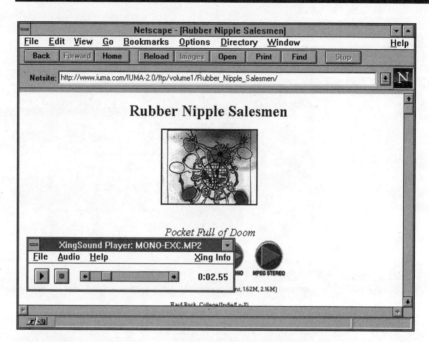

RealAudio

RealAudio is one of the latest and most impressive technologies to appear on the Internet, allowing almost instantaneous sound to play while downloading. Sounds on the Web are usually played by clicking a hyperlink to a sound, downloading the sound in its entirety, and then playing it back in a sound player. What RealAudio does is start the download, pause for a little bit, and then begin playing the sound, as it's downloaded from the server. Pretty cool. We'll go and grab the RealAudio Player from the RealAudio Web page (http://www.realaudio.com/), shown in Figure 4.15. Follow the Download FREE Player! hyperlink and download the RealAudio Player into your help-apps directory. (You'll have to fill out a brief registration form first.)

Download and install RealAudio, which will, as part of its installation, set itself up as a helper application—handy, huh? Go back to http://www. realaudio.com/ and scroll down to the Sights and Sounds area of the Web page. Click the hyperlink that takes you to the RealAudio Guide at http://www.realaudio.com/raguide.cgi (Figure 4.16) and select a site with RealAudio programming. Poke around until you see something you'd like to hear and click on its hyperlink.

Figure 4.15

RealAudio Web page

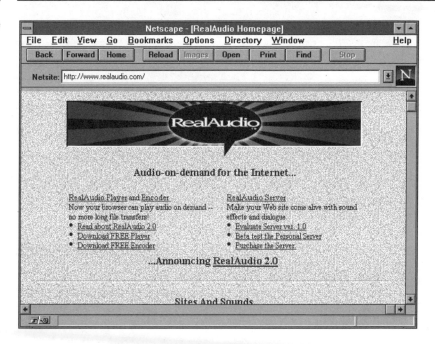

Figure 4.16

RealAudio Guide

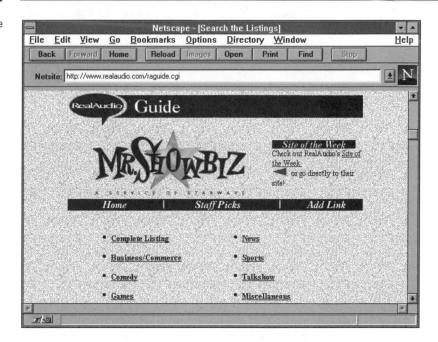

The sound begins downloading and then launches the RealAudio Player window seen in Figure 4.17.

Figure 4.17

Sound in RealAudio Player

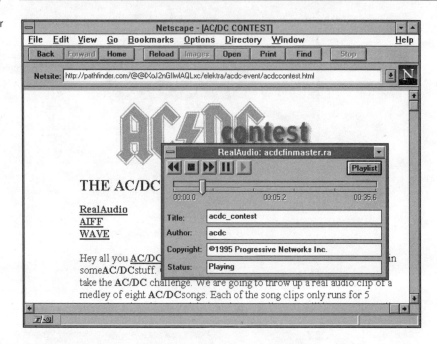

The current version of RealAudio sounds best when playing spoken-word files, but developers are working to improve the quality of music files.

Images

For all the impressive things that it does, Netscape doesn't make a particularly great image-viewing program. Can't fault them, really; heck, they were busy doing other stuff. But if you want to get the full aesthetic quality of the images on the Web, an image-viewer helper app is good to have around. Because Netscape can view .GIF and .JPG images by itself, you generally only need an image helper app for images that come in less popular file formats. Paint Shop Pro, an excellent shareware image-viewing and -processing program, is among the best. It can display almost all of the rest of the image MIME types listed in Netscape's Helper Apps preference tab, as a quick glance at the MIME Type chart at the end of the chapter will attest. Paint Shop Pro is also quite good at editing images and converting them from one image format to another. A Web page devoted to Paint Shop Pro and other fine software from JASC Inc. is located at http://www.winternet.com/~jasc/

and is shown in Figure 4.18. Go to this page to the hyperlink for the program and download it. You might want to take this opportunity to grab a magazine or get a cup of coffee—it's a big program.

Figure 4.18

Paint Shop Pro home
page

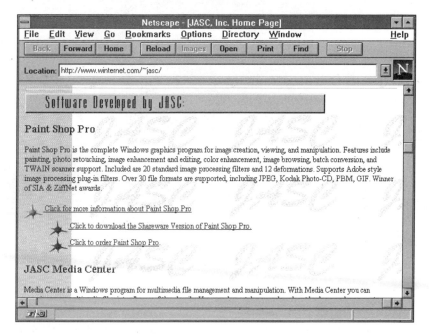

Launch WinZip, open the Paint Shop Pro archive, and unzip it into the image directory in your helpapps directory. Now that you've got Paint Shop Pro, let's go get something for it to chew on. Let's go to the Mona Lisa Web page in the Leonardo Da Vinci section of the Louvre's Web site (http://sunsite.unc.edu/wm/paint/auth/vinci/joconde/). Click once with the left mouse button on the small image of the Mona Lisa, and a full-page version appears. Click on the large picture with your mouse's right button and pull down to the Save This Image As option. Save the file to your hard drive, and then launch Paint Shop Pro from Program Manager. Now pull the File menu down to Open and locate the Mona Lisa image file. Opening it in Paint Shop Pro, you'll see the screen in Figure 4.19.

From here, you can transform (or deface) the image in any number of ways, without paying for a pricey flight to Paris or risking a possible roughing-up from Louvre museum guards. In addition, using Paint Shop Pro you can save images downloaded from the Web as .BMP files to be used as Windows wallpaper.

Figure 4.19

Mona Lisa In Paint Shop
Pro

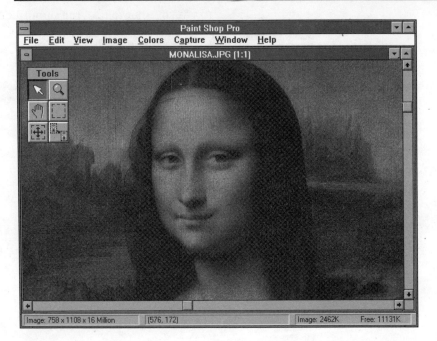

Video

If you've used many CD-ROMs containing video clips, you'll know that digital video is still pretty crude; memory-hungry digitized video files, as they appear on the Web, are postage-stamp sized, short in duration, jerky, compressed so that the image is blocky or noisy, or they take forever to download. More than likely, all of the above. Still, it is kind of fun to be able to download video from the Web, generally for free. You can watch somebody's home movies, the trailer for a new Hollywood blockbuster, or a 3-D rendering of molecules leaping around.

Most of the digital video you'll come across on the Web will be in either MPEG or QuickTime format. MPEG, more or less the Web video standard, tends to take up the least hard-drive acreage, in part because the MPEG standard used in movies you'll come across on the Web contain no capability for an accompanying soundtrack. (MPEG video shares compression routines with MPEG audio.) QuickTime, the digital video format developed by Apple, is gaining ground on MPEG video as the Web video standard as QuickTime movie players become more prevalent on other computer platforms.

MPEG Video

An MPEG video player, MPEG Play, is available from IUMA's Help for Windows Web page. Go to this Web page, at http://www.iuma.com/IUMA2.0/ help/help-windows.html, and scroll down to the MPEG Video section. Click on the hyperlink for MPEGW32H.ZIP and download MPEG Play.

Once the player's been downloaded, unzipped, and placed in your help-apps directory, go back into Netscape and go to the MPEG directory of Rob's Multimedia Lab at http://www.acm.uiuc.edu/rml/Mpeg/ (shown in Figure 4.20) to find plenty of MPEG movies to watch.

Figure 4.20

Rob's MPEG video
directory

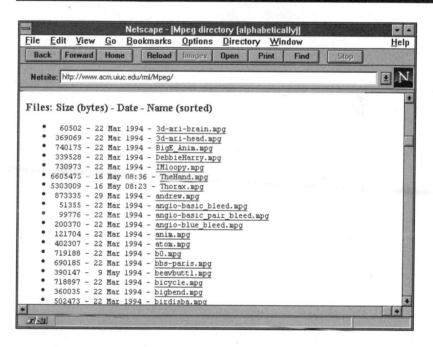

QuickTime Video

QuickTime is a digital video format created by Apple that has advantages over MPEG movies in that it includes sound where MPEG movies have none (though a new sound-capable version MPEG is starting to surface) and that it's somewhat more widespread among PC and Macintosh users.

QuickTime for Windows 1.1 is also available at IUMA, at http:// www.iuma.com/IUMA-2.0/help/help-windows.html, along with configuring information. Download and install QuickTime, and pop on over to Apple's directory of QuickTime archives at http://quicktime.apple.com/content.html (Figure 4.21).

Figure 4.21

Apple's "Cool Content!"
QuickTime archive

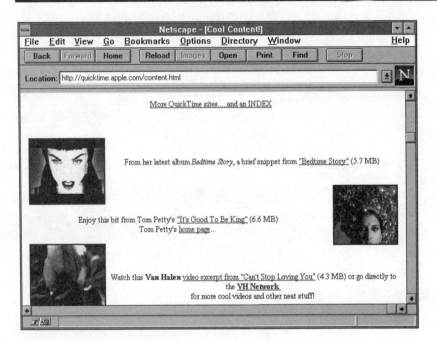

Webtop Publishing: .PDF and PostScript Helper Apps

.PDF (Portable Document Format) and PostScript files allow users to get the graphic formatting of a print document, something HTML was never intended to do. If a document's look is as important as the information within it, .PDF or PostScript renditions may be preferable to an HTML rendition. Either type of file can be viewed onscreen or printed out; manuals and newsletters are just a few of the uses.

The PostScript and .PDF formats were both developed by the software company Adobe. PostScript was originally released in 1985 as a page description language for use in developing documents for printout on PostScript-capable laser printers. Many popular graphic design applications use PostScript to describe the look of a Web page. These programs can output PostScript files directly from the program itself.

.PDF

.PDF files are PostScript files taken the next level; in addition to describing the layout of a PostScript document, a .PDF document can include hyperlinks, color, placed images, as well as approximations of a document's original fonts if the user doesn't have the fonts originally specified in the document. You can use full-blown computer design tools such as PageMaker, Xpress, or

Illustrator to design your documents, and then have them available electronically as .PDF files with little loss of aesthetics, and in some cases, increased functionality via hyperlinks. .PDF files require Adobe's Acrobat line of software to create and view them. Acrobat Reader, the .PDF viewer and helper app we'll download, is free and available at http://www.adobe.com/Software/Acrobat/ (Figure 4.22).

Figure 4.22

Adobe Acrobat Reader
download page

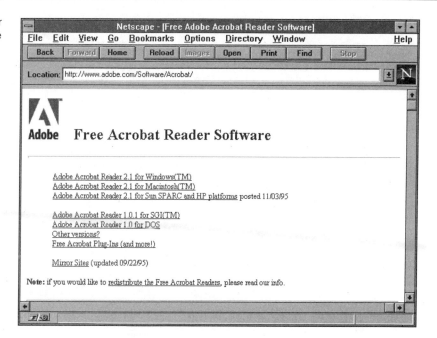

Click the hyperlink for the Windows Acrobat Reader and tell Netscape where to save the program. Once the program is downloaded and the program acroread.exe is placed wherever you keep your helper applications on your hard drive, go back to Netscape, and we'll set up the Helper Apps preference tab to handle .PDF files. Pull down Netscape's Options menu to General, and click the Helper Apps preference tab. Click on the Create New Type button, and the window in Figure 4.23 appears.

In the MIME Type field, type in *application*. In the MIME SubType field, type in *pdf*. Click on the OK button.

In the File Extensions field, Type in *pdf*. In the Action area, click the Launch the Application radio button, and then click on the Browse button. Find acroread.exe on your hard drive, and click OK. Your Helper Apps preference tab should now look something like Figure 4.24.

Figure 4.23

Configure new MIME
type: .PDF

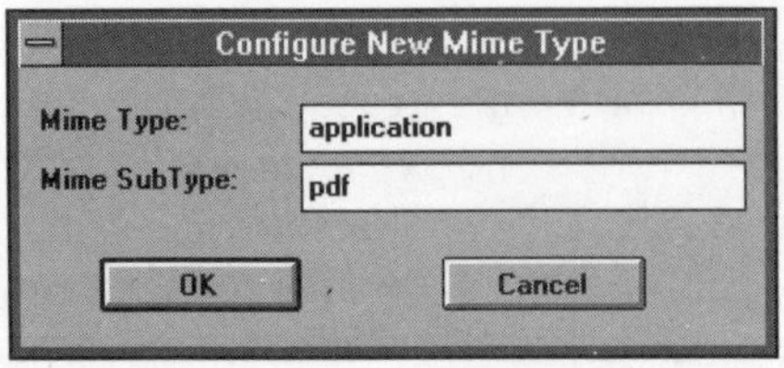

Figure 4.24

Helper Apps preference
tab setup for .PDF and
Acrobat

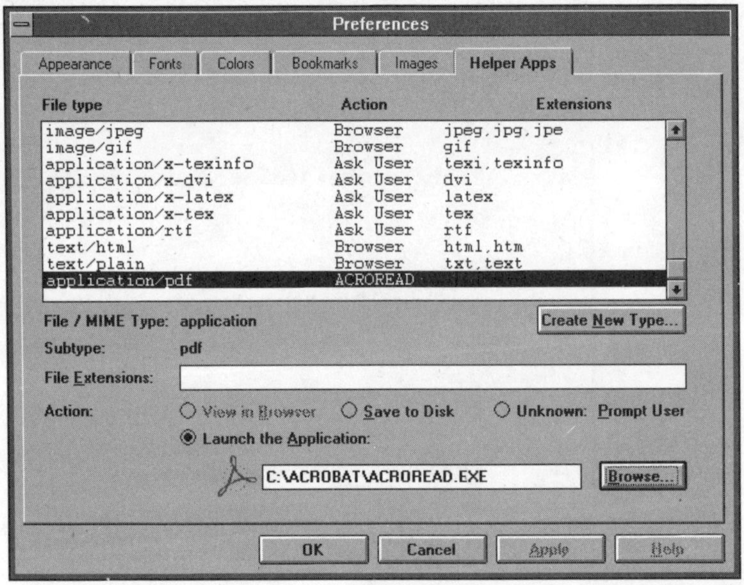

Now we'll check out The New York Times's TimesFax Internet Edition, a summary of the day's news in .PDF format. TimesFax is available at http://nytimesfax.com/ (see Figure 4.25).

Click the hyperlink for today's edition; the .PDF file downloads, which could take a while—neither .PDF nor PostScript files are small. Acrobat Reader should then launch, presenting you with the day's news as in Figure 4.26, served up piping hot, .PDF style.

You can view .PDF files onscreen and you can print them to your printer or fax them. It's a versatile little format, and it's becoming more and more popular all the time. Netscape has plans to include .PDF-viewing capability within the Netscape program itself, and the IRS's 1994 tax forms using .PDF (http://www.ustreas.gov/treasury/bureau/irs/taxforms.html), are available on

Figure 4.25

TimesFax Web page

Figure 4.26

TimesFax .PDF file viewed
in Acrobat Reader

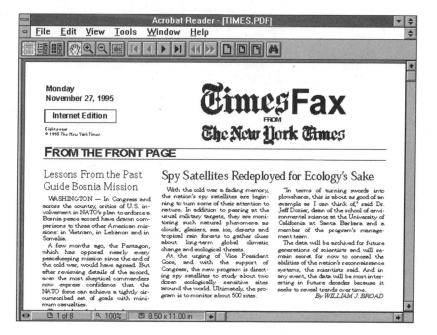

the Web. On Adobe's Web page, more information about Acrobat is available, as well as information on configuring Acrobat to work with Netscape. There's also a Usenet newsgroup, comp.text.pdf, where the creation, usage, and viewing of .PDF files are discussed.

PostScript

To view PostScript files (which typically have a .PS extension), you can use the Ghostscript interpreter programs. They're available from the Ghostscript home page shown in Figure 4.27 (http://www.cs.wisc.edu/~ghost/).

Figure 4.27

Ghostscript home page

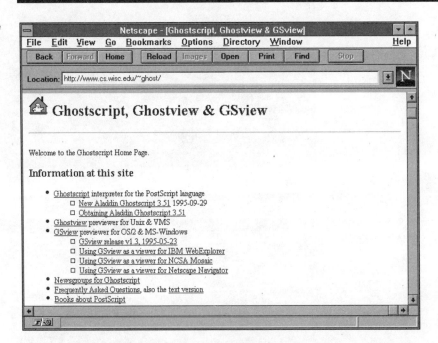

Installing Ghostscript is somewhat more complex than most helper applications, and beyond the scope of this book. However, a Ghostscript Web page containing information about Ghostscript and configuring Netscape to use Ghostscript as a helper app is worth checking out. It resides at http://www.cs.wisc.edu/~ghost/gsview/netscape.html. PostScript is also discussed at length in the Usenet newsgroup comp.lang.postscript.

■ The Never-Ending Parade of Helper Apps and MIME Types

The helper applications we've already covered are probably enough to keep you satisfied for a good long while. But as the short, action-packed history of the Web shows, more and more nifty MIME file types and helper applications will soon appear, stretching the limits or surpassing current capabilities possible for multimedia files on the Web. No doubt soon you'll come across a brand-new file format and corresponding helper app. Don't sweat it. The creators of the helper app will probably put up a Web page with help on configuring Netscape to use it. With the knowledge you've gained here, you'll be able to add any kind of MIME type or helper app to your toolkit, which is nice.

Associating New MIME File Types in Windows File Manager

You can make the new file types that you've downloaded from the Web double-clickable from Windows File Manager. For this example, I'll use .AU files and associate them with Netscape Audio Player.

Go into Netscape's temporary directory and locate any of the downloaded files with the extension .AU. Select the file and pull down the File menu to Associate, causing the window in Figure 4.28 to appear.

Figure 4.28

Windows File Manager
Associate window

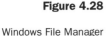

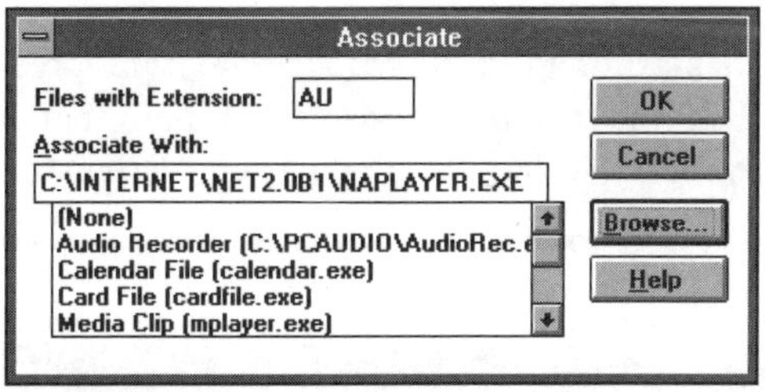

The Files with Extension field reads *AU*, and the Associate With field should be filled with the path name to naplayer.exe. If it isn't, click the Browse button, locate naplayer.exe in your Netscape directory, and click OK. You'll return to the Associate window. Click OK again and then double-click a file with an .AU extension. Netscape Audio Player will launch and play the sound. Maybe it's not a mind-shattering technique, but it will make downloaded files that much more accessible in the future.

MIME and Web Servers

Sometimes a Web creator will create a page with a hyperlink pointing to a file with a MIME file type that the server doesn't know how to handle. Even if you've installed the proper helper app for that particular kind of file, you won't be able to download it properly by the usual means because the Web server doesn't know how to serve it. Typically, this manifests itself as Netscape attempting to load a file of some sort and displaying it onscreen as gibberish text.

Should this happen to you, the thing to do is first hit the Escape key to halt further downloading. Hit the Back button to return to the Web page with the hyperlink to the file. Reclick on the hyperlink, this time with the right mouse button. Hold the button down and the right mouse button pop-up menu appears. Scroll down to Save this hyperlink as. The Save As browser window will pop up; tell Netscape where to save the file and release the right mouse button. The file will be saved to your hard drive; launch the helper app manually and open the document from the helper app's Open menu choice under its File menu.

Should this happen to you regularly with one Web site or page, you might want to find the e-mail address of the person who maintains the Web site or page (commonly known as the Webmaster), and inform him or her of your difficulties.

■ The Rest of the Supporting Cast

Table 4.1 is a chart of all of the MIME File types present in the default list in Netscape's Helper Apps preference tab. Where there's a popular or Windows-included program that handles the file type, I've listed it first, with no URL.

Table 4.1

Selected MIME File Types and Corresponding Helper Apps

FILE TYPE/ SUBTYPE	EXTENSIONS	HELPER APP	URL
video/x-ms-video	avi	Windows Media Player, AVIPro 2.0	http://home.netscape.com/assist/helper_apps/windowhelper.html
video/quick-time	qt, mov	QuickTime for Windows 1.1	http://www.iuma.com/IUMA-2.0/help/help-windows.html
video/mpeg	mpeg, mpg, mpe	MPEGPlay	hftp://gatekeeper.dec.com/pub/micro/msdos/win3/desktop/

**Table 4.1
(Continued)**

Selected MIME File Types
and Corresponding
Helper Apps

FILE TYPE/ SUBTYPE	EXTENSIONS	HELPER APP	URL
text/plain	txt	Netscape Navigator	
text/html	HTML, mdl, htm	Netscape Navigator	
image/x-bit-map	xbm	Netscape Navigator	
image/x-rgb	rgb	Paint Shop Pro	http://www.winternet.com/~jasc/
image/x-porta-ble-pixmap	ppm	Paint Shop Pro	http://www.winternet.com/~jasc/
image/x-porta-ble-graymap	pgm	Paint Shop Pro	http://www.winternet.com/~jasc/
image/x-porta-ble-bitmap	pbm	Paint Shop Pro	http://www.winternet.com/~jasc/
image/x-cmu-raster	ras	Paint Shop Pro	http://www.winternet.com/~jasc/
image/tiff	tiff, tif	Paint Shop Pro	http://www.winternet.com/~jasc/
image/jpeg	jpeg, jpg, jpe	Netscape, Paint Shop Pro	http://www.winternet.com/~jasc/
image/gif	gif	Netscape, Paint Shop Pro	http://www.winternet.com/~jasc/
audio/x-wav	wav	Windows MediaPlayer	
audio/x-aiff	aif, aiff, aifc	Netscape Audio Player	
audio/basic	au, snd	Netscape Audio Player	
application/x-tar	tar	WinZip	http://www.winzip.com/winzip/
application/rtf	rtf	Microsoft Word	

**Table 4.1
(Continued)**

Selected MIME File Types
and Corresponding
Helper Apps

FILE TYPE/ SUBTYPE	EXTENSIONS	HELPER APP	URL
application/ postscript	ai, eps, ps	Ghostscript	http://www.cs.wisc.edu/~ghost/
application/ octet-stream	exe, bin	No helper app; set Action to Save to Disk	
application/ xzip-com-pressed	zip	WinZip	http://www.winzip.com/winzip/
application/ xgzip	gz	WinZip	http://www.winzip.com/winzip/
application/ xcompress	Z	WinZip	http://www.winzip.com/winzip/

■ Other Helper App Resources

Several of the most important helper applications are available from Netscape's Windows Helper App Page (http://home.netscape.com/assist/ helper_apps/windowhelper.html), shown in Figure 4.29.

You may also want to swing by the Stroud's Consummate Winsock App list (http://cwsapps.texas.net/image.html). Its main menu is shown in Figure 4.30. Stroud's list covers not only helper applications for use with Netscape, but just about any program that interacts with the Internet over a Winsock-based connection. If you hear about a new helper app or a new version of an existing one, chances are the helpful Mr. Stroud will already have it waiting for you.

A Web site that will prove helpful in testing your helper applications and Netscape preferences tabs settings is the WWW Viewer Test Web page, located at http://www-dsed.llnl.gov/documents/WWWtest.html. Links to many MIME file types and their helper applications for all types of computers that access the Web are available here. Click the button on the right, and the indicated kind of file downloads; click on Comments on the left of the Web page, and you're presented with multiplatform helper app information.

Figure 4.29

Netscape's windows
helper app page

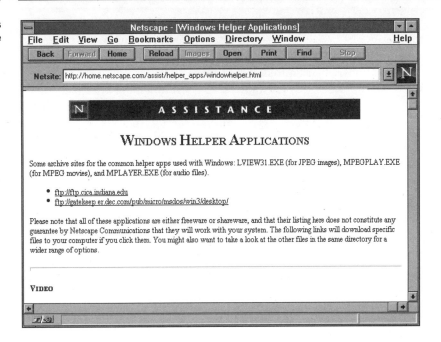

Figure 4.30

Stroud's Auxiliary Viewers
Web page

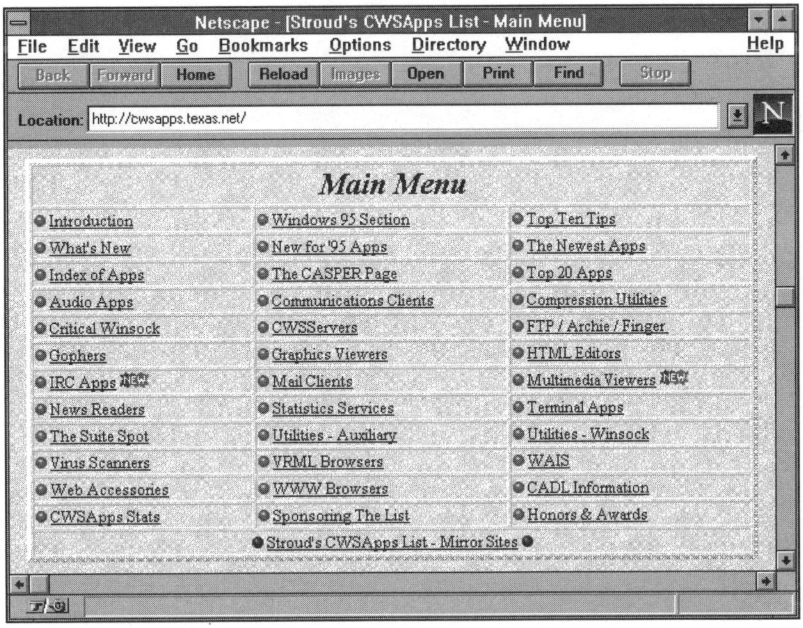

■ Armed and Dangerous and Hungry for Kicks

At this point, you've made yourself at home within Netscape, arranging preferences so they're just right for you. Now you should be fairly well prepared to handle pretty much any kind of data that the Web throws at you and know what to do when you come across unfamiliar files. Congratulations!

Now that we've got it humming along, our stay within the hallowed walls of Netscape itself is pretty much over. What's next, you ask? Well, there's all kinds of great stuff on the Internet that isn't delivered via Web pages, for starters. It's time now for me to set you loose on the Web and the Net. While the Web is pretty huge, it certainly isn't the whole enchilada. Since you've got a firm handle on Netscape, let's use it to check out all the other stuff on the Internet. No sense in resting on your laurels! Which takes us on to the next chapter, where you'll learn how to access a whole lot more of the Net's information.

2

Above and Beyond the Basics

- *Uniform Resource Locators (URLs)*
- *Usenet Newsgroups*
- *Gopher It*
- *FTP (File Transfer Protocol)*
- *Helper Application-Based Internet Services*
- *Gatewayed Internet Services*

- *Finding Various Internet Services on the Web*
- *Better Living through Distributed Networking*

5

Accessing Other Internet Services

T HE WEB, AS YOU'RE WELL AWARE BY NOW, IS NO SMALL POTATOES. And as vast as the Web is, there are all kinds of other Internet services you can access with Netscape. It accesses these using different types of URLs (Uniform Resource Locators), the address schemes that exist for many of the types of Internet services such as gopher or FTP. In this chapter I'll show you how to use these URLs to access other Internet services, and point you toward several worthwhile sites for each type of service.

■ Uniform Resource Locators (URLs)

URLs are a way of categorizing and accessing Internet files and documents. Each URL has a specific format and each piece of data or directory has a specific URL. I covered this briefly in Chapter 1; here I'll go into a bit more detail about the naming conventions they use.

All URLs have a standard syntax, pretty much: scheme://site.domain/path/file. *Scheme* is the type of service offered—http:// or gopher://, for instance. *Site.domain* is the name of the computer the information or directory resides on, for example, echonyc.com or compuserve.com. *Path/file* is the path through the Internet site's directories leading to where the file resides. In the URL http://www.echonyc.com/~spingo/Spingo/index.html, for instance, the */~spingo/Spingo/index.html* part is the path/file. URLs pointing to directories have no file name at their ends, as in http://www.echonyc.com/~spingo/Pix/. Web pages sometimes have no file name specified, yet point to a file in a directory without adding the file name into the URL. When you send a request for a URL without a specified file name, the Web server at the other end of the HTTP connection looks through the directory for a file with the server's default file name (such as index.html). If it finds that file, it displays the HTML document (such as in the URL http://www.echonyc.com/~spingo/). If it doesn't find the file, it gives you a listing of the files in that directory (such as in the URL http://www.echonyc.com/~spingo/Pix/).

A few types of URLs differ from this scheme. News and mail files use the scheme types, news:*newsgroup* and mailto:*user@site.domain*, respectively. That's because they don't refer to files or directories on a specific computer, but rather they depend on the addresses for NNTP (Network News Transfer Protocol) and SMTP (Simple Mail Transfer Protocol) servers at your Internet access provider, as specified in the information you enter into Netscape's Mail and News preferences tab. Several types of URLs are given in Table 5.1.

Table 5.1

URL Types

INTERNET SERVICE	URL ANATOMY	SAMPLE URL
World Wide Web Page	http://site/path/file	http://www.echonyc.com/~spingo/Spingo/index.html
Usenet Newsgroup	news:newsgroup	news:rec.arts.movies
Gopher	gopher://site/path/file	gopher://echonyc.com/
FTP	ftp://site/path/file	ftp://ftp.netscape.com/
Telnet	telnet://site/	telnet://echonyc.com
Mailto	mailto:user@site.domain	mailto:spingo@echonyc.com

Other types of URLs exist but are somewhat less common. For more information on URLs, check out *A Guide to URLs* at http://www.netspace.org/ users/dwb/url-guide.html and *Bruce Gingery's Guide to URLs* at http:// metro.turnpike.net/bagingry/URLs.html.

■ Usenet Newsgroups

Usenet newsgroups are Internet discussion areas available worldwide where readers discuss, via posted messages, topics ranging from science fiction to practical jokes to computer software. These thousands of newsgroups are collectively also known as *Usenet* or *Usenet news*, though most of the postings are those of laypeople, not official news sources. As Ronda Hauben (au329@cleveland.freenet.edu) puts it in Chapter 1 of her book *The Net: the Wonderful World of the Net* (http://www.columbia.edu/~hauben/ project_book.html):

> *Usenet was born in 1979. It has grown from a design conceived*
> *of by two graduate students at Duke University in North Carolina,*
> *to a logical network linking millions of people and computers to*
> *over 9,500 different newsgroups and millions of bytes of articles*
> *available at any given time to hundreds of thousands of sites*
> *around the world.*

Remember way back in Chapter 3, when you called or e-mailed your Internet provider and asked for the address of your NNTP (Network News Transport Protocol) server, and then typed this address in the Identity preferences tab in the Mail and News Options window? That's where Netscape looks to get Usenet news. See, you know more than you thought! If your Internet provider doesn't provide a Usenet newsfeed, have at look at the Public Access News Servers on the Net Web page at http://www.phoenix.net/ config/news.html. While some of the news servers will allow you to read and post articles to Usenet, some of the sites listed will only let you read Usenet news.

To help you appreciate Netscape's newsreading features, take a look at Figure 5.1. It shows you what a newsgroup looks like in the UNIX program nn, a newsreader that runs from an Internet dial-up shell account.

Nn is a program designed to be used from a UNIX dial-up account and over a slow Internet connection, while Netscape runs over your PPP connection and adds an interface that's somewhat more accessible, as we'll see in a minute.

Figure 5.1

Reading a Usenet
newsgroup in nn

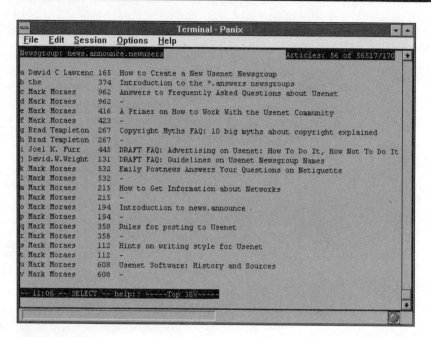

```
┌─────────────────────────────────────────────────────────────────────────┐
│ ─                        Terminal - Panix                       ▼ ▲       │
├─────────────────────────────────────────────────────────────────────────┤
│  File   Edit   Session   Options   Help                                   │
├─────────────────────────────────────────────────────────────────────────┤
│ Newsgroup: news.announce.newusers                  Articles: 56 of 56517/170 │ ▲
│                                                                           │
│ a David C Lawrenc 165  How to Create a New Usenet Newsgroup               │
│ b the           374  Introduction to the *.answers newsgroups             │
│ c Mark Moraes    962  Answers to Frequently Asked Questions about Usenet  │
│ d Mark Moraes    962  -                                                   │
│ e Mark Moraes    416  A Primer on How to Work With the Usenet Community   │
│ f Mark Moraes    423  -                                                   │
│ g Brad Templeton 267  Copyright Myths FAQ: 10 big myths about copyright explained │
│ h Brad Templeton 267  -                                                   │
│ i Joel K. Furr   445  DRAFT FAQ: Advertising on Usenet: How To Do It, How Not To Do It │
│ j David.W.Wright 131  DRAFT FAQ: Guidelines on Usenet Newsgroup Names     │
│ k Mark Moraes    532  Emily Postnews Answers Your Questions on Netiquette │
│ l Mark Moraes    532  -                                                   │
│ m Mark Moraes    215  How to Get Information about Networks               │
│ n Mark Moraes    215  -                                                   │
│ o Mark Moraes    194  Introduction to news.announce                       │
│ p Mark Moraes    194  -                                                   │
│ q Mark Moraes    358  Rules for posting to Usenet                         │
│ r Mark Moraes    358  -                                                   │
│ s Mark Moraes    112  Hints on writing style for Usenet                   │
│ t Mark Moraes    112  -                                                   │
│ u Mark Moraes    608  Usenet Software: History and Sources                │
│ v Mark Moraes    608  -                                                   │
│ -- 11:06 -- SELECT -- help:? -----Top 38%-----                            │
└─────────────────────────────────────────────────────────────────────────┘
```

Netscape's Usenet News Browsing Features

Netscape does a good job of managing Usenet newsgroups. Pull the Windows menu down to the Netscape News choice. Netscape's News Window (Figure 5.2) appears. Go ahead and click once on your news server in the upper-left pane. The first time you connect, Netscape downloads what's called your newsrc file, telling you that it must get the list of groups from the server, and asking your patience while it does so. Newsrc files can be pretty big—your Internet provider's newsfeed can include thousands of newsgroups. This file is a list of all of the Usenet newsgroups that your Internet provider offers, and it also contains information about which ones you've subscribed to, and which articles you've read.

Eventually, Netscape finishes downloading your newsrc file (which it then places in the news subdirectory in your Netscape directory). Since there are so many newsgroups, Netscape only automatically subscribes you to three: news.announce.newusers, news.newusers.questions, and news.answers. All of these are required "must-skim," at least for those new to Usenet. You should read these groups pretty thoroughly until you have the hang of Usenet news. To the right of the newsgroup name are three columns: Sub, Unread, and Total. Click the check box in the Sub directory to subscribe to the newsgroup, and click again to uncheck and unsubscribe. The number in

Figure 5.2

Netscape's
news window

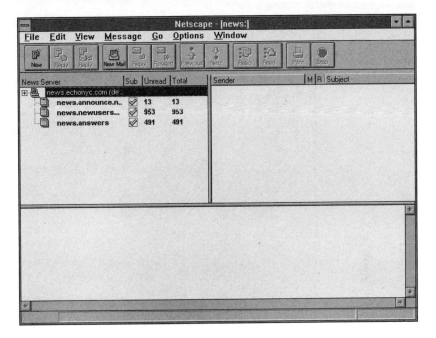

the Unread column is the number of articles in the group that you haven't
seen yet—your newsrc contains information about how much of a group
you've read. The number in the Total column is the total number of articles
available in that newsgroup.

Go ahead and double-click with your left mouse button on news.an-
nounce.newusers (which appears here as *news.announce.n..* due to the space
limitations in Netscape's newsreader). If this group doesn't appear at the top
of the listing, as it does here, scroll down and look in the "news.*" folder—
your newsgroup listings may look different, depending on what newsgroups
your Internet provider offers. Any group will do for this example. A listing of
the articles available appears in the upper-right pane, as shown in Figure 5.3.

You should have an article called "Welcome to Usenet!" somewhere in
the article list (though again, any article will do for this example). Double-
click on the article listing, and the contents of the article appear in the bottom pane, as in Figure 5.4.

Note that in this article, the names of other newsgroups appear as hyperlinks. Clicking those hyperlinks will take you to their respective newsgroups.
Hyperlinks can also appear in the body of a Usenet article, which is useful
when someone's talking about a new Web site, for example—you're one
click away from checking out the Web site (which will then be displayed in
Netscape's main window).

Figure 5.3

News.announce.newusers

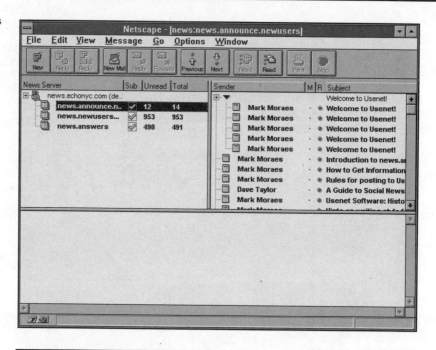

Figure 5.4

News.announce.newusers
Welcome to Usenet!

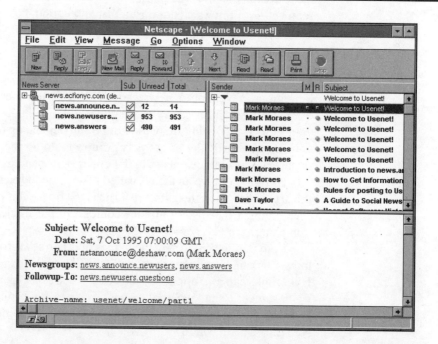

The scroll bar in the bottom pane allows you to scroll through the current article, or you can hit your space bar to jump forward one screen at a time. This is a handy feature for the lazy among us, including your humble author.

You've read your first Usenet article! Give yourself a small congratulation and scroll down through the list of newsgroups in the upper-left window pane to find newsgroups that appeal to you, or have a look at one of the newsgroups listed in Table 5.2.

Table 5.2

Useful Usenet
Newsgroups

USENET NEWSGROUP
news:alt.cult-movies
news:alt.culture.internet
news:alt.culture.usenet
news:alt.fan.cecil-adams
news:alt.humor.best-of-usenet
news:alt.internet.services
news:alt.national.enquirer
news:alt.winsock
news:alt.winsock.trumpet
news:comp.infosystems.www.announce
news:comp.infosystems.www.authoring.html
news:comp.infosystems.www.authoring.images
news:comp.infosystems.www.browsers.mswindows
news:comp.infosystems.www.users
news:comp.os.mswindows.apps
news:comp.sys.ibm.pc.games.marketplace
news:misc.forsale.computers.pc-specific.systems
news:rec.humor.funny

The layout of the Netscape News window is customizable, just like that of the E-mail window. Move your mouse pointer over the vertical bar in the center of the screen and the cursor turns into a variation of Windows's standard window-resize cursor. Click and drag the cursor and the center divider line moves left or right. Move the cursor over the horizontal bar and you get the same cursor and capability. Additionally, the divider-move cursor appears over the bar between the server/newsgroup subsection on the upper left and the article information subsection on the upper right, as well as Between the Sender, M, R, Subject, and Date columns.

This example has only been a *quick* spin through Usenet via Netscape. Read more about reading news with Netscape in the Mail, News, and Bookmarks section of Netscape's online handbook at http://home.mcom.com/eng/mozilla/2.0/handbook/docs/mnb.html.

Get the FAQs before You Post

Many newsgroups have their own FAQ files full of handy information about the subject of the newsgroup. You can access these at the Usenet FAQs Web page at http://www.cis.ohio-state.edu/hypertext/faq/usenet/FAQ-List.html. If you're new to this scene, you'll want to check the FAQ before asking any questions or posting to the group. Frequently Asked Questions files are exactly that: regular readers intensely dislike answering the same questions and having the same discussions over and over again. New users are also directed to the "Welcome to news.newusers.questions!" file, posted to news.newusers.questions weekly and archived at http://www.cis.ohio-state.edu/hypertext/faq/usenet/news-newusers-intro/faq.html. The newsgroup news.answers is full of all manner of information that should also be read by newcomers to Usenet.

Useful Usenet Newsgroups

Some Usenet newsgroups you might want to check out appear in Table 5.2. Remember, there are *tons* of the darn things. This is but a tiny sampling of what's available. Enter any of the URLs below into Netscape's Location field to see the following newsgroups.

Usenet Information Web Pages

For even more info about Usenet, check out the What Is Usenet? Web page at http://www.cis.ohio-state.edu/hypertext/faq/usenet/usenet/what-is/top.html.

The DejaNews search service at http://www.dejanews.com/ lets you quickly search for Usenet groups by keyword. The Find Newsgroups Web page at http://www.cen.uiuc.edu/cgi-bin/find-news offers a similar function; and a handy, skimmable listing of newsgroups (as well as information about Usenet itself) is available at the Usenet Info Center Launch Pad (http://sunsite.unc.edu/usenet-b/home.html).

Many Usenet newsgroups allow posting of binary multimedia files, typically converted into postable text files (*uuencoded,* from the UNIX program uuencode, whose files have the .UU or .UUE suffixes). The Usenet reader must convert these text files back into a binary file via a process called *uudecoding.* Many of these files are reconstituted and ready for download at the Usenet-Binary assemblage site (http://pmwww.cs.vu.nl/usenet/.news.html).

If your Internet provider doesn't offer Usenet news, check out the list of Public Access Usenet Sites at http://www.yahoo.com/News/Usenet/Public_Access_Usenet_Sites/ to find an NNTP server you can use.

■ Gopher It

Gopher, an Internet information system of hyperlinked directories containing files, first appeared at the University of Minnesota in April 1991 as a help system for campus computer users. Gopher files differ from Web files in that there is no linking from one file to the next, only from one directory to the next. And the name *gopher*? It honors the university's mascot. Gopher is a compact, efficient way of filing and finding information, and is an important evolutionary step in the development of the Web. Why use gopher when the Web is more advanced? Lots of useful information has made its way into gopher that hasn't yet or won't make it into Web pages. Gopher was developed to be quick and easy to use, and the advent of the Web hasn't changed that.

The main gopher, gopher.tc.umn.edu, is a good place to start your exploration of what's known as gopherspace (sort of the gopher equivalent of the Web). This is where it all started, and it's probably the best source for more information about gopher itself.

Again, to foster your appreciation about our progress, here's how we accessed gophers back when dinosaurs ruled the earth, as seen in Figure 5.5. This is the above gopher viewed in a UNIX-based gopher client. And now, the same gopher accessed via Netscape, in Figure 5.6.

All the gopher servers in the world, organized geographically, are listed at gopher://gopher.tc.umn.edu:70/11/Other Gopher and Information Servers. The most recent version of the Gopher FAQ file is at gopher://mudhoney.micro.umn.edu:70/00/Gopher.FAQ. You can also read about gopher in the newsgroup comp.infosystems.gopher.

Searching Gophers with Veronica

Veronica, or Very Easy Rodent-Oriented Net-wide Index Of Computerized Archives (yeah, yeah, I know), searches gopherspace to find documents or directories containing user-supplied keywords. The Veronica FAQ is located

Figure 5.5

Gopher via dialup
Internet account

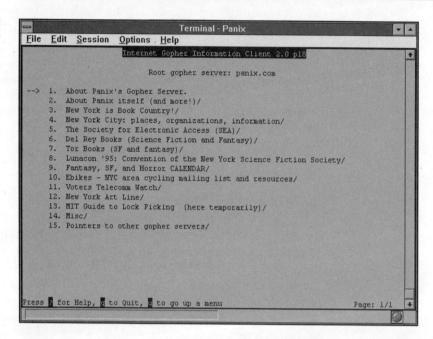

Figure 5.6

Gopher in Netscape

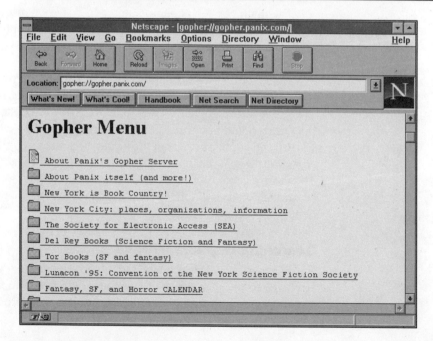

at gopher://gopher.scs.unr.edu/00/veronica/veronica-faq. The Index of Veronica Servers is at gopher://gopher.scs.unr.edu/11/veronica.

Great Gophers

Some of the most useful gophers (or gopher holes, as they're sometimes referred to by slangy geeks) appear in Table 5.3.

Table 5.3

Some Great Gophers

GOPHER NAME	DESCRIPTION	URL
Main Gopher	Gopher Central at the University of Minnesota, where it all started.	gopher:// gopher.tc.umn.edu
Gopher Jewels	Some of the best gopher sites, organized by subject.	gopher:/cwis.usc.edu:70/11/ Other_Gophers_and_Information_ Resources/Gopher-Jewels
ECHO (East Coast Hang Out)	Gopher of New York-based conferencing system that your humble author had a hand in developing—contains NYC info, e-zines, ECHO info, links to various sites.	gopher://echonyc.com/
Currency Exchange Rates	Exchange rates for global currencies against the U.S. dollar.	gopher://caticsuf.csufresno.edu:70/ 00/atinet/agtrade/rates
Small Business Administration	Useful info for small and new businesses.	gopher://www.sbaonline.sba.gov/
Webster's Dictionary and Thesaurus	Why spring for an expensive CD-ROM? Look up words with this handy online tool.	gopher://next2.msci.memst.edu: 70/11/webster
The Internet Wiretap	Government, e-text, and Internet info.	gopher://wiretap.spies.com/

You can read about current developments in gophers, gopher tools, and so on in the newsgroup comp.infosystems.gopher. To see a list of recently announced gophers, check out Washington & Lee University's New Gopher Sites at gopher://liberty.uc.wlu.edu:70/11/internet/new_internet/new_gophers.

■ FTP (File Transfer Protocol)

FTP (file transfer protocol) lets you log in to other machines on the Net and download files from them, kind of like grabbing a file from your office network's common drive. FTP sites can be public sites that are open to all or systems that require an account in order to be accessible.

In the olden times, an FTP session would look like the listing below. You'd log in to the remote computer, have a look around and download what you'd like, and then log back out. (The commands typed in by the user appear after the ftp> prompt.)

Listing 5.1

Pre-Netscape
FTP session via dialup
Internet account

```
$ ftp ftp7.netscape.com
    Connected to ftp7.netscape.com.
    220 ftp7 FTP server (Version wu-2.4(3) Tue Dec 27 17:53:56 PST 1994) ready.
    Name (ftp7.netscape.com:spingo): anonymous
    331 Guest login ok, send your complete e-mail address as password.
    Password:
    230-Welcome to the Netscape Communications Corporation FTP server.
    230-
    230-If you have any odd problems, try logging in with a minus sign (-)
    230-as the first character of your password.  This will turn off a feature
    230-that may be confusing your ftp client program.
    230-
    230-Please send any questions, comments, or problem reports about
    230-this server to ftp@netscape.com.
    230-
    230 Guest login ok, access restrictions apply.
    ftp> ls
    200 PORT command successful.
    150 Opening ASCII mode data connection for file list.
    betas.obsolete
    bin
    collabra
    dev
    etc
    incoming
    2.0beta
    lib
    netscape
    private
    pub
    unsupported
    226 Transfer complete.
    102 bytes received in 0.0043 seconds (23 Kbytes/s)
    ftp> cd 2.0beta
```

**Listing 5.1
(Continued)**

Pre-Netscape
FTP session via dialup
Internet account

```
250 CWD command successful.
ftp> ls
200 PORT command successful.
150 Opening ASCII mode data connection for file list.
mac
unix
windows
226 Transfer complete.
20 bytes received in 0.002 seconds (9.7 Kbytes/s)
ftp> cd windows
250-This software is subject to a license agreement.  Be sure to read and
250-agree to the license BEFORE you use the software.
250-
250-EXPORT
250-You may not download or otherwise export or re-export Netscape
250-Software or any underlying information or technology except
250-in full compliance with all United States and other applicable laws
250-and regulations.  In particular, but without limitation, none of the
250-Software or underlying information or technology may be downloaded or
250- otherwise exported or re-exported (i) into (or to a national or
250-resident of) Cuba, Haiti, Iraq, Libya, Yugoslavia, North Korea, Iran,
250-or Syria or (ii) to anyone on the US Treasury Department's list of
250-Specially Designated Nationals or the US Commerce Department's Table
250-of Deny Orders.  By downloading the Software, you are agreeing to the
250-foregoing and you are representing and warranting that you are not
250-located in, under control of, or a national or resident of any such
250-country or on any such list.
250-
250-MIRRORING
250-Please don't mirror this software unless you are an educational
250-institution. If you want to mirror, or are uncertain about what to do,
250-please see http://home.netscape.com/comprod/mirror/
250-mirror_application.html or send email to mirror@mcom.com.
250-
250 CWD command successful.
ftp> ls
200 PORT command successful.
150 Opening ASCII mode data connection for file list.
readme.txt
license
n16e20b1.exe
n32e20b1j.exe
.message
n32e20b1n.exe
226 Transfer complete.
75 bytes received in 0.0032 seconds (23 Kbytes/s)
ftp> get readme.txt
200 PORT command successful.
150 Opening ASCII mode data connection for readme.txt (9566 bytes).
```

**Listing 5.1
(Continued)**

Pre-Netscape
FTP session via dialup
Internet account

```
226 Transfer complete.
local: readme.txt remote: readme.txt
9810 bytes received in 0.57 seconds (17 Kbytes/s)
ftp> bye
221 Goodbye.
$
```

Netscape has *greatly* simplified FTP sessions, as you can see in Figure 5.7. Now you enter a URL, click around a bit, and then move on to your next Web destination.

Figure 5.7

FTP in Netscape

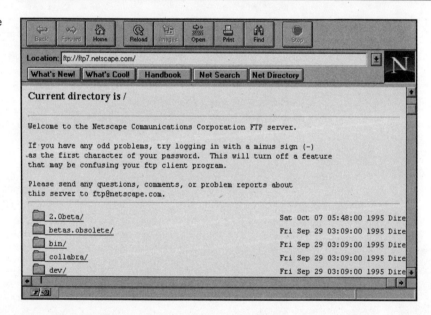

You may have FTP services available at your Internet access provider, or any other Internet site that requires a password using a URL of ftp://username:password@host/path. If you don't want to specify the password in the URL, use ftp://username@host/path. Netscape will pop up a window asking for your password to the machine.

The Monster FTP Sites List at http://hoohoo.ncsa.uiuc.edu/ftp/ lists many many FTP sites, offering all kinds of computer files.

Archie is an Internet service that lets you search FTP sites by keyword. You can do this through a WWW-Archie gateway, which is further described in this chapter's Gateway section below.

Popular FTP Sites, Mirrors, and Plain Ol' Courtesy

Popularity in this case means more users logged in at once; if you hit a popular FTP site (or Web site, for that matter) at the same time as teeming crowds, you may find it either filled to capacity and you'll be turned away at the door, or if you get in, find downloading incredibly slow. Sometimes an FTP site will be mirrored elsewhere, and even if the FTP site you were aiming for is too busy, the busy message may be accompanied by a list of sites that mirror the content of the site you were shooting for.

As in using any Internet resource, if there's a mirror site (a carbon copy of an FTP site residing on a different Internet site), it's for a reason. Be a good net.citizen and use the mirror site geographically closest to you to reduce traffic over the Internet. The closer geographically a site is to you, the fewer Internet sites the data has to travel over to get to you. Using a mirror site close to you instead of a main site situated farther away reduces strain on the already pretty crowded Internet, not to mention the wholly selfish effect of quicker access times. As someone's grandmother once said, it's nice to be nice.

Fabulous FTP Sites

A list of a few useful FTP sites appears in Table 5.4.

Table 5.4

Fabulous FTP Sites

FTP WEB SITE URL	DESCRIPTION
ftp://ftp.cica.indiana.edu/	The motherlode. More shareware and freeware Windows applications and files than you can shake a stick at.
ftp://ftp.netscape.com/	Latest versions of programs from Netscape.
ftp://ftp.microsoft.com/	Program patches and information about Microsoft and Microsoft products.
ftp://papa.indstate.edu/winsock-l/	Great collection of Internet software for use over your PPP connection.

■ Helper Application-Based Internet Services

Some Internet services require a separate program that acts much like a helper application. The two most prominent are Telnet and TN3270, which are listed in Netscape's Applications & Directories preferences tab.

Telnet and TN3270 Helpers

Using Telnet, you can log in to, and work on, remote computers. Telnet applications allow your computer to emulate what's known as a "dumb terminal"—one without a CPU or disk drive of its own, merely a screen, a keyboard, and a modem. You can log onto conferencing systems, information services (weather, for example), and bulletin board systems (BBSs).

Another popular form of Telnet service is MUD, or Multi-User Dimensions, which are online text-based environments. You can explore the world generally created by its users and converse with other users who are logged in. Check out the MUD FAQs at http://math.okstate.edu/~jds/mudfaqs.html for more info about MUDs and MUD-ding. Look for some MUDs to visit at http://www.yahoo.com/Recreation/Games/Internet_Games/MUDs__MUSHes__MUSEs__Moos__etc_/. (Those are *two* underlines in places.)

The Telnet application I use is the freeware program EWAN (Emulator Without A Name). It's available from the EWAN home page at http://www.lysator.liu.se/~zander/ewan.html. Download EWAN from this Web page, unzip it, and place it in the helpapps directory in your Netscape directory. Go to Netscape's Applications & Directories preferences tab, and click the Browse button next to the Telnet Application area. Locate EWAN on your hard drive and click OK.

Now let's go on a Telnet jaunt to shop for CDs. Open up EWAN and pull down the File menu to New. In the Network Address or Host Name field, type in cdnow.com and click OK. Follow the menus (type *P* for pop music, if you like) and type in the name of an artist. You'll get a listing of recordings like the one shown in Figure 5.8. You can also type *I* from this screen to get a brief biography of the artist.

EWAN suits my needs, but if you'd like to check out other Telnet applications, go to the Terminal Apps section of Stroud's Consummate Winsock Apps List at http://cwsapps.texas.net/term.html. A shareware TN3270 program, QWS3270 Extra, is also available from that page. TN3270 is used to log in to remote mainframe computers.

Several useful Telnet sites are listed in Table 5.5. To see a list of recently announced Telnet sites, check out Washington & Lee University's New Telnet Sites at gopher://liberty.uc.wlu.edu:70/11/internet/new_internet/new_hytelnet. To search the Web index Yahoo for Telnet sites, go to http://www.yahoo.com/search.html, use *telnet* as your keyword, and click the Search button. More about searching the Web in Chapter 6.

Figure 5.8

Telnet session in
progress in EWAN

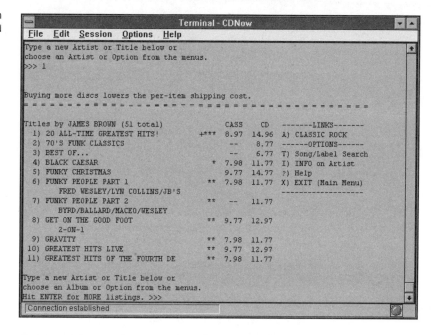

Table 5.5

Some Good Telnet Sites

TELNET SITE NAME	URL	DESCRIPTION
ECHO (East Coast Hang Out)	telnet://echonyc.com	New York-based conferencing system with 60 or so conferences about many subjects. Your humble author's home on the Internet (first month free).
LambdaMOO	telnet://lambda.parc. xerox.com:8888/	Multi-user explora-space (free).
CD Connection	telnet://cdconnection.com	Online CD store with good prices and 120,000 CDs listed (free).
Library of Congress	telnet://locis.loc.gov	Library of Congress Information System–Library of Congress Catalog, Federal Legislation, and Copyright Information, among other info (free).
The Well	telnet://well.com	Popular California-based conferencing system (pay service).

■ Gatewayed Internet Services

For those Internet services not directly accessible via Netscape, you can use completely Netscape-independent Windows client programs. These programs are available at Stroud's Consummate Winsock Apps List at http://cwsapps.texas.net/.

Archie FTP Searches

Archie is another Internet access service; more specifically, it's an FTP search service. If you're looking for a file or program you think is available via FTP, you can ask Archie to search its database of files available from FTP Web sites all over the world and tell you where the file is.

There's an Archie Request Form located at http://hoohoo.ncsa.uiuc.edu/archie.html. A list of other Web-based Archie servers is located at http://pubweb.nexor.co.uk/public/archie/servers.html.

Finger Gateways

The Internet service *finger* allows you to check the status of a user's e-mail account. A user can put various kinds of information in a text file called a .plan file that appears alongside information about the user's account, such as when he or she was last logged in.

For instance, Craig Copi uses his finger information to serve up a daily almanac of historical birthdays and events and sports information. Go to the U of Indiana Finger Gateway (http://www.cs.indiana.edu/finger/gateway) and type in copi@oddjob.uchicago.edu as the user to be fingered. The results are shown below.

Listing 5.2

Finger copi@oddjob.uchicago.edu

```
copi@oddjob.uchicago.edu

    Login name: copi                    In real life: Craig J Copi
Directory: /home/oddjob/copi            Shell: /usr/local/bin/tcsh
Last login Mon Aug 21 01:02 on ttyp2 from ntcs-ip13.uchica
New mail received Mon Aug 21 03:22:50 1995;
unread since Mon Aug 21 01:03:19 1995
Project: Learning that we are only immortal---for a limited time.
Rush, "Dreamline", _Roll_the_Bones_
Plan:
 Was it love or was it the idea of being in love?
        --- Pink Floyd, "One Slip"
           (current tally:  46 love, 63 idea of being in love)
              (Stand up and be counted, cast your vote today)


And you can analyze this situation.
```

Listing 5.2 (Continued)

Finger
copi@oddjob.uchicago.edu

```
                           To me it's all just mental masturbation.
                              --- Sammy Hagar, "There's only one way to rock"


            Information for today:


                                         Monday
                                   August 21, 1995

                           Day 233 and Week 34 of current year
                           126 shopping days until Christmas

                                   Day 25 of Av, 5755
                                  Year 17 of Machzor 302
                           119 shopping days until Chanukah

                                    For Chicago (CDT)
                        Sun rise: 6:05 AM, set: 7:43 PM (today)
                        Sun rise: 6:06 AM, set: 7:41 PM (tomorrow)

                               Phase of moon: waning crescent
                           Age of moon: 3 days (to next new moon)

                                  The year of the Pig

            **************** Special Events for 8/21 ******************
            **** Birth: Baron Augustin Louis Cauchy (206 years ago) ****
            ************ Birth: Count Basie (89 years ago) ************
            ************ Birth: Kenny Rogers (57 years ago) ***********
            ************ Birth: Jim McMahon (36 years ago) ***********
            * Death: Benjamin (Count Rumford) Thompson (181 years ago) *
            ***** Death: Claude Louis Marie Navier (159 years ago) *****
            *** Event: First Lincoln/Douglas debate (137 years ago) ****
            *** Event: First peace time nuclear death (50 years ago) ***
            **** Event: Hawaii became the 50th state (36 years ago) ****
            ***********************************************************

            Please email me event (mm/dd/YYYY) information to add to my list

            On the WEB 'the' source for sports info is . . .
                    http://www.netgen.com/sis/sports.html
```

You can also access the University of Indiana finger gateway directly from the URL. In Netscape's location field, type in the URL http://www.cs.indiana.edu/finger/gateway?spingo@panix.com. The list below displays yours truly's finger information (which, admittedly, is somewhat less informative than Mr. Copi's).

Listing 5.3

Finger spingo@panix.com

```
Login Name: spingo                    Full Name: James Barnett
Directory: /net/u/6/s/spingo          Shell: /usr/local/bin/ksh
Last login Sun Aug 20 15:45:05 on panix3.panix.com ttyq5 from 198.67.15.59.
No mail information available.
```

Delectable and Fancy Fingers

Some accounts to finger appear in Table 5.6.

Table 5.6

Fistful of Fingers
(Sorry, I Couldn't Resist)

SERVICE NAME	DESCRIPTION	URL
Coke machines	Describes the contents of a vending machine at the University of California at Berkeley. 24-hour beef jerky availability status.	finger coke@xcf.berkeley.edu
Trivia Time, by Cyndi Williams	Weekly trivia contest.	cyndiw@magnus1.com

◼ Finding Various Internet Services on the Web

Some of the places where you can find information about new Internet resources are Yanoff's List (http://www.uwm.edu/Mirror/inet.services.html), the Internet Resources List (Web page http://www.eit.com/web/netservices.html), and the InterNIC Scout Report (http://rs.internic.net/scout_report-index.html). Various types of Internet services are discussed in the Usenet newsgroup alt.internet.services. And you might also want to check out Neil Enns' Internet Resources on the Web page at http://www.brandonu.ca/~ennsnr/Resources/Welcome.html.

◼ Better Living through Distributed Networking

Armed with what you've learned in this chapter, you'll be ready to access just about anything on the Internet that Netscape can handle. In the next chapter, I'll show you some sites that will help you find what you need on the Web and talk about strategies for finding the information you need. Shall we? After you, I insist.

- *Web Searching Strategy*
- *Subject-based Web Indexes*
- *Keyword-based Web Indexes*
- *Geographically-based Web Indexes*
- *Indexes of Indexes*

6

Searching the Web

CONSIDERING THE DIZZYING RATE AT WIICH THE WEB IS EXPAND-
ing, you shouldn't be surprised to learn that some kind souls have
set up Web sites that either gather up Web pages and organize
them by subject, or sites that just index the whole darn Web into a
huge database so you can search by keyword. In this chapter, I'll
call the former Web-search tools *subject-based*, and the latter *keyword-based*. Keyword-based Web searching sites are also called
search engines, after the computer program on the Web site that
searches through all of its listings. Web search engines, such as Yahoo, double their usefulness by combining both tools, making for a
very helpful place indeed.

Let's use the following example to examine each Web site listed here. Say I'm watching a TV show about chimps. "Clever little fellas," I think to myself and decide to turn to the Web to further my education of our simian brothers and sisters.

■ Web Searching Strategy

As mentioned above, there are a couple different ways to go about looking for what you need on the Web. You can go to an index of Web sites and search through progressively more specific subjects. For chimp, I could go to a subject-based Web index and follow the hyperlinks from the general Science, down through Biology, to Mammals, to Primates, and then to Chimps.

Or I can go to a keyword-based Web index and search on *chimp*. In our current example, this strategy will be fairly straightforward. Searching for a more specific topic would entail using several keywords and what are called boolean operators. Deceptively simple little words like *and* or *not*, these operators let you combine keywords in different ways and exclude other kinds of information. For instance, if I was interested in what chimps eat, I might use the search phrase *chimp and nutrition*. If I wanted to know what they eat other than bananas, I might use the search phrase *chimp and nutrition not bananas*. The specific usage of operators varies from index to index; sometimes they're called query operators. Different sites handle this stuff differently; if your search brings up a lot of stuff that has nothing to do with what you're looking for, look around for the site's help Web pages.

Keep in mind also that computers are basically the machine equivalent of the dim-witted, villainous henchmen in the old "Batman" TV series. They're good at doing exactly as they're told but not particularly smart on their own. Search the Web like you would search the Yellow Pages. If you don't find anything under *Cabs*, look under *Taxi*, and if that doesn't work, try *Livery Services*. If your first attempt at a Web search has an unsatisfying end, try and think of related subjects or different ways of phrasing what you're looking for.

■ Subject-based Web Indexes

The Web indexes in this section all rely on some kind of subject framework to catalog Web pages into digestible chunks. For instance, in the "chimps" example given above, the Science subject area will probably contain many more listings than the Primates area. An advantage in using subject-based Web indexes is that you're more likely to stumble across related information within a subcategory that may not have appeared with a simple keyword search. Subject-based Web indexes are generally maintained by a staff that either checks out likely candidates for inclusion to their site and then adds the relevant Web pages to their listings, or by users who submit Web sites to the index's various subject categories.

Yahoo

Two former Stanford University grad students, David Filo and Jerry Yang, started the Yahoo Web index (http://www.yahoo.com/) in April 1994 as a hobby to categorize new sites that were popping up daily. Yahoo became wildly popular, in part due to sponsorship by Netscape Communications Corporation, and in 1995 they went pro, making Yahoo a company and selling (as-yet-unobtrusive) advertising on their excellent Web site. According to the Yahoo information available at the site, the name Yahoo! is supposed to stand for "Yet Another Hierarchical Officious Oracle" but Filo and Yang insist they selected the name because they "consider themselves yahoos." Yahoo is subject based and keyword searchable. It's invariably the first place I go to find something on the Web. See Figure 6.1 for a look at Yahoo.

Figure 6.1

Yahoo

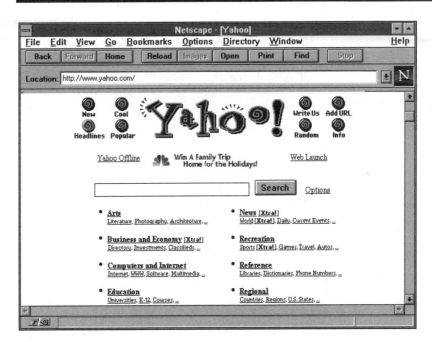

TradeWave Galaxy

Located at http://lmc.einet.net/galaxy.html, TradeWave Galaxy (see Figure 6.2) has been in existence since early 1994. Galaxy uses a slew of guest editors to maintain its subject areas, and it also categorizes gopher and telnet site information sources. Galaxy is also searchable, using the form at http://lmc.einet.net/search.html.

Figure 6.2

TradeWave Galaxy

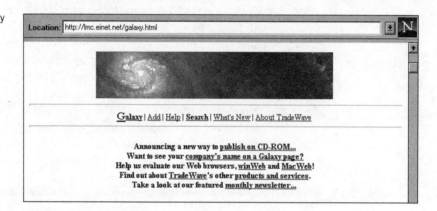

The Whole Internet Catalog

The Whole Internet Catalog is available at http://gnn.com/wic/ (see Figure 6.3). The Web sites contained here are handpicked by the WIC editorial team. You may not know that the *book* that spawned the Web version of the Whole Internet Catalog—Ed Krol's *The Whole Internet User's Guide and Catalog* (O'Reilly & Associates, Inc.)—is also an excellent introduction to the Internet. In fact, it's the very one that your humble author first read to gain entry to the world of the Internet what now seems like many moons (and dawns) ago.

■ Keyword-based Web Indexes

The Web indexes discussed below maintain internal databases of Web pages and their contents. The user requests keyword searches that result in a list of hits—that is, a list of Web pages that match the requested keyword and searching criteria. Keyword-based Web index databases are typically built by programs called Web robots that methodically search Internet sites for Web servers and then proceed to catalog all of the Web pages it can find.

Figure 6.3

The Whole Internet
Catalog

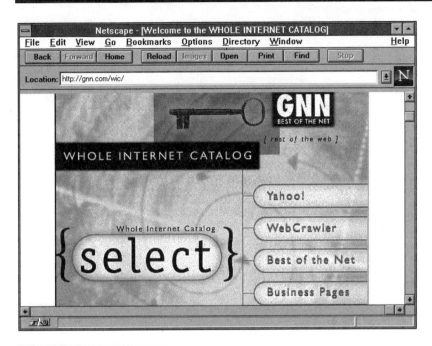

The Internet Sleuth

The Internet Sleuth, at http://www.charm.net/~ibc/sleuth/, provides not only an overall Web search engine but allows the user to access individual subject-based Web indexes elsewhere on the Web, letting you search many different indexes from one Web page. The Internet Sleuth is shown in Figure 6.4. In the past, I've used Lycos as my keyword-based Web index for those times when Yahoo's searches left me a bit short due to the smaller size of their database. But I'll seriously think about using Internet Sleuth in the future.

Lycos

Carnegie-Mellon's Lycos index at http://www.lycos.com/ (see Figure 6.5) allows the user to search a database of about five million individual Web pages. The Lycos search engine methodically scans the Internet (including FTP and gopher Web sites) daily, and indexes the results weekly. Lycos isn't the slickest keyword-based Web index I've seen, but it just may be the one with the most entries in its database, which comes in handy, especially when you're searching for Web sites on a particularly obscure subject.

Figure 6.4

The Internet Sleuth

Figure 6.5

Lycos in action

Find-It!

The Find-It! Web site at http://www.cam.org/~psarena/find-it.html (see Figure 6.6) lets you search an index that includes not only Web sites, but also Usenet news, Archie FTP indexes, WAIS databases, and several other types of Internet resources. Check it out!

Figure 6.6

Find-It!

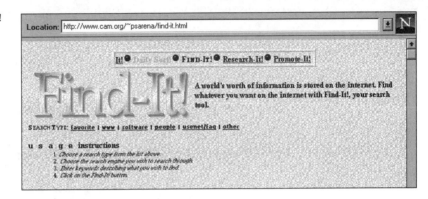

Magellan

The Magellan Internet directory at http://www.mckinley.com/ (see Figure 6.7) is keyword searchable and subject oriented, much like Yahoo. The difference is that 20,000 of Magellan's 80,000 listings add reviews of the listed Web site and ratings from one to four stars.

Figure 6.7

Magellan

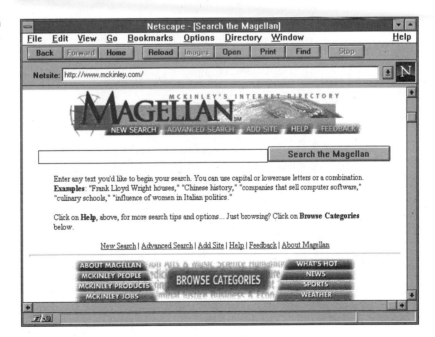

InfoSeek

InfoSeek is available from Netscape's Internet Search page at http://home.netscape.com/home/internet-search.html (and accessible from Netscape's Directory menu's Internet Search choice) or directly at http://www.infoseek.com/ (see Figure 6.8). InfoSeek's matches on a keyword tend to be pretty useful matches.

Figure 6.8

InfoSeek

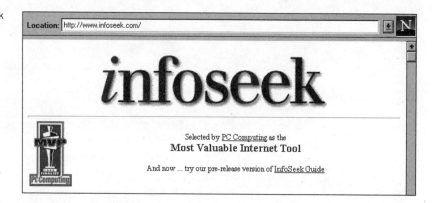

WebCrawler

WebCrawler, at http://webcrawler.com/ (see Figure 6.9), is an index of about 150,000 Web documents that's now owned and operated by the commercial service America Online.

Figure 6.9

WebCrawler

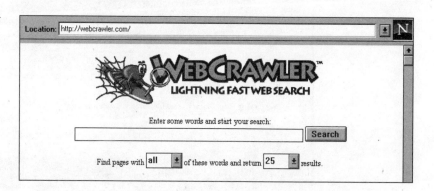

More Keyword-based Web Indexes

A few other notable keyword-based Web indexes are

- Harvest at http://harvest.cs.colorado.edu/

- Open Text Web Index at http://opentext.uunet.ca:8080/

- WWWWorm at http://www.cs.colorado.edu/home/mcbryan/WWWW.html

■ Geographically-based Web Indexes

Some of the Web's indexes are neither subject- nor keyword-based but deserve
mention here. They are structured geographically, organizing lists of Web servers by where they reside in the physical world. The global nature of the Web is,
on the whole, a good thing, but sometimes you may be curious about what
kind of information is available from a particular region of the world.

    The Virtual Tourist Web site at http://wings.buffalo.edu/world/ (see Fig-
ure 6.10) has Web sites organized by their servers' geographic location and is
accessible by way of maps of the world and its regions.

Figure 6.10

The Virtual Tourist

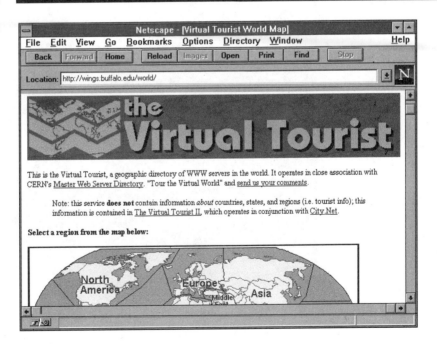

The World Wide Web Organization's Registry of WWW Servers page, at http://www.w3.org/hypertext/DataSources/WWW/Geographical.html, attempts to list all Web servers in the world (or at least those servers whose Webmasters register with the W3O), and it is also organized geographically. Warning! This Web page is 1.5MB long and may cause trouble if you run Netscape in a small amount of RAM. Prepare to up the memory you give to Netscape if you want to see it in full.

■ Indexes of Indexes

Some Web sites gather several Web indexes into one Web page to make for easier searching. A few of these are listed below.

All-In-One Internet Search is an amazing Web page that can submit search info to many of the Web's search engines from one Web page. It's at http://www.albany.net/~wcross/all1www.html and is shown in Figure 6.11.

Figure 6.11

All-In-One Internet Search

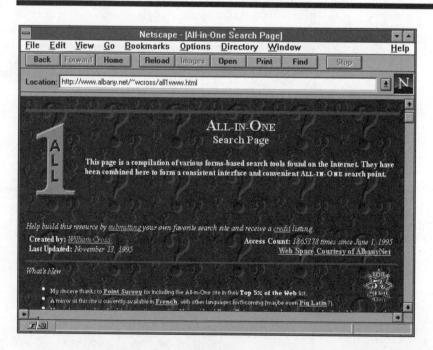

Other useful indexes of Web indexes include

- Yahoo-Reference: Searching the Web at http://www.yahoo.com/Reference/Searching_the_Web/

- W3 Search Engines Meta-Index at CUI at http://cuiwww.unige.ch/meta-index.html

- CUSI (Configurable Unified Search Interface) at http://Web.nexor.co.uk/susi/cusi.html

With the Web sites in this chapter firmly in hand, you'll be able to find your very own needle in the haystack that is the Web. In the next chapter, I'll show you some resources that will keep you up-to-date on new Web sites and developments.

- *What's New?*
- *What's Cool?*
- *What's News*
- *Abandon Sleep, All Ye Who Enter Here*

7

Keeping Up

New web sites pop up like roaches in a new york city apartment—the difference being you're happy to see the sites. A dizzying array of new Web tools and software is also appearing at an intoxicating rate. This chapter will point you to the newest Web sites, those others have deemed cool, and to the latest news about the Web. Consider these your starting points. What's here will help sate that deep-down new Web site hunger.

■ What's New?

Remember the NCSA from Chapter 1? This is the group that released Mosaic, the graphical browser that started the whole Web snowball. The NCSA What's New Page at http://www.ncsa.uiuc.edu/SDG/Software/Mosaic/Docs/whats-new.html (see Figure 7.1) is one of the first (and arguably the most comprehensive) of the "What's New" Web sites. Webmasters submit their new page information, and it eventually makes its way here. Prior NCSA What's New sites are archived at http://www.ncsa.uiuc.edu/SDG/Software/Mosaic/Docs/archive-whats-new.html.

Figure 7.1

NCSA What's New page

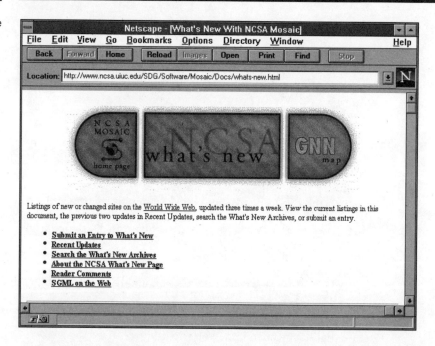

Some other What's New pages are listed in Table 7.1, with descriptions of noteworthy features.

Also remember to keep an eye out for sites mentioned in the Usenet newsgroups that cover your favorite topics; not all Web authors post notices of new sites in all of the places mentioned above.

■ What's Cool?

However fun or interesting they may be, the newest sites aren't always the best. "What's Cool" sites do the work of searching the Web for you, presenting

Table 7.1

What's New Sites

WEB SITE NAME	URL	DESCRIPTION
TradeWave's Galaxy: What's New	http://www.einet.net/about.html#NEW	
GNN's Whole Internet Catalog	http://nearnet.gnn.com/wic/nunu.toc.html	
Netlink Recent Additions	http://honor.uc.wlu.edu:1020/-rd%20-sd%20	
CUI's W3 Recent Changes	http://cuiwww.unige.ch/W3catalog/changes.html	
What's New Too!	http://newtoo.manifest.com/WhatsNewToo/	
Meta-List of What's New Pages	http://www.seas.upenn.edu/~mengwong/whatsnew.list.html	Big list of What's New pages.
What's New Pages	http://www.yahoo.com/Computers_and_Internet/Internet/World_Wide_Web/Indices_to_Web_Documents/What_s_New/	Even more What's New pages.
Announcement Services	http://www.yahoo.com/Computers_and_Internet/Internet/World_Wide_Web/Announcement_Services/	These sites are used for Web authors to publicize their pages and, well, the new information has to be announced on a Web page, now doesn't it?
What Snooze	http://digimark.net/mfu/whatsnoo.html	Cutting parody of the NCSA's home page, which savages the Web, the Internet, and pop culture in the process. Recommended!

you with sites for you to check out. Some of these Web sites are divided into subject areas, much like Yahoo, but contain fewer entries, are focused on a particular area or topic, and are somewhat less daunting to explore.

Cool Web Sites of the Day/Week/Month/Millennium/Etc.

The granddaddy of these is the Cool Site of the Day at http://cool.infi.net/ (see Figure 7.2). Cool Site of the Day presents a new site deemed hep by Glenn Davis, who thought up the pick-of-the-day idea before anyone else.

Figure 7.2

Cool Site of the Day

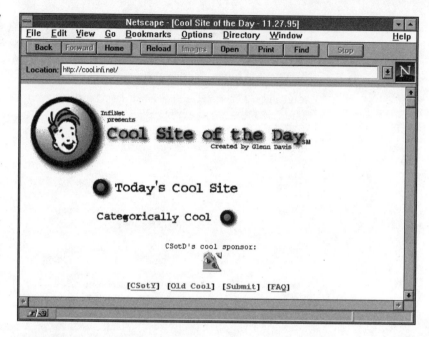

Some other What's Cool Web sites are listed in Table 7.2.

Table 7.2

What's Cool Sites

WEB SITE NAME	URL	DESCRIPTION
Web Site of the Week	http://www.duke-net.com/wsw/	Brief reviews of Web sites and interviews with Webmasters.
Gorski's Cool Site of the Day	http://www.city-net.com/~cgorski/coolsiteoftheday.html	
Funky Site of the Day	http://www.realitycom.com/cybstars/	
Geek Site of the Day	http://riceinfo.rice.edu:80/~indigo/gsotd/	This is the flip side of the Funky site. Really geeky.
Odin's Sighting of Today	http://www.oslonett.no/home/frodeni/odin/	"The Vikings' mythical allfather of Wisdom" chooses His favorites.

**Table 7.2
(Continued)**

What's Cool Sites

WEB SITE NAME	URL	DESCRIPTION
Web Hound	http://webhound.www.media. mit.edu/projects/webhound/ wwwface/homepg.html	This one recommends pages based on what you tell the Hound you like.
Yahoo Sites of the Day Index	http://www.yahoo.com/ Computers_and_Internet/Internet/ World_Wide_Web/ Indices_to_Web_Documents/ Sites_of_the_Day/	Hyperlinks to tons of cool Web sites as selected by the yahoos at a well-established search engine.

Random Web Sites

These pages hyperlink you to a random page each time you access them, culled from a list of Web sites that the maintainer thinks is cool or from a list of user-supplied URLs.

URouLette at http://www.uroulette.com:8000/ (see Figure 7.3) was probably the first of the random Web sites.

Figure 7.3

URouLette

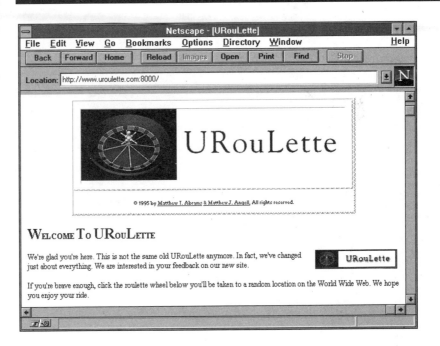

Another random Web site is MagicURL Mystery Trip at http://www.netcreations.com/magicurl/ (see Figure 7.4).

Figure 7.4

MagicURL Mystery Trip

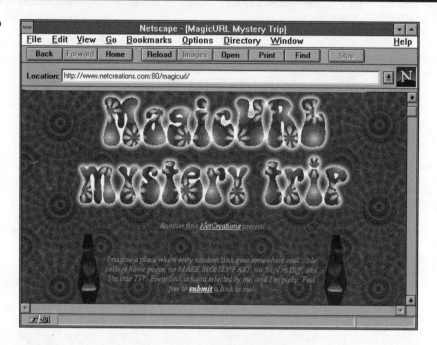

A list of other random Web sites is in Table 7.3.

Table 7.3

Random Web Sites

WEB SITE NAME	URL	DESCRIPTION
Get The Hell Out Of Dodge	http://www.fn.net/~roundman/jwz/rand/ran.html	
The Information Supercollider	http://www.eecs.harvard.edu/collider.html	
Random Yahoo Hyperlink	http://www.cen.uiuc.edu/cgi-bin/ryl	
A Thousand Points of Web Sites	http://inls.ucsd.edu/y/OhBoy/randomjump1.html	This one is not exactly random, but it's arranged kind of like a game of Concentration.

**Table 7.3
(Continued)**

Random Web Sites

WEB SITE NAME	URL	DESCRIPTION
Web Autopilot	http://www.netgen.com/~mkgray/autopilot.html	Instead of sending you to a single site, Autopilot uses Netscape's dynamic document capability to take you from one page to the next.
Yahoo Random Web Sites Index	http://www.yahoo.com/Computers_and_Internet/Internet/World_Wide_Web/Indices_to_Web_Documents/Random_Links/	As the name suggests, this is a listing of Web sites that'll randomly spin you back off onto the Web and to a random site. This list is updated as random-site Web authors and other Web denizens add their URLs to Yahoo's listings.

Selective Web Indexes

The sites in this section (see Table 7.4) all maintain a subject-oriented listing of Web pages, but they are smaller and more selective than a Yahoo or Web-Crawler. They don't represent themselves as being comprehensive.

Table 7.4

Selective Web Index Sites

WEB SITE NAME	URL	DESCRIPTION
NETLiNkS! What's Hot	http://www.interlog.com/~csteele/whathot.html	Selective Web indexes and Web site-of-the-day listings.
JUMP CITY	http://www.jumpcity.com/	Extensive listing of Web sites with handy reviews.
The Otis Index	http://www.interlog.com/~gordo/otis_index.html	
Loads-a-Links	http://www.aber.ac.uk:80/~ngd2/	Star-rated Web sites.
Where It's @	http://www.mistral.co.uk:80/wia/	
Webaholics Top 50 Web Sites List	http://www.ohiou.edu/~rbarrett/webaholics/favlinks/entries.html	
WEBsurf	http://www.crl.com/~whisper/	

WEB SITE NAME	URL	DESCRIPTION
The Sober Witness	http://itrc.on.ca/~jason/	This "hype-free guide to the Web."
Justin's Links from the Underground	http://www.links.net/	
WebCentral	http://www.tiac.net/users/ thorgan/home.html	
The Big Eye List	http://www.coolsite.com/ goodurls/bigeye.htm	
Scott Yanoff's Special Internet Connections	http://www.uwm.edu/Mirror/ inet.services.html	
The Spider's Web	http://gagme.wwa.com/~boba/ spider1.html	Check out Bob Allison's meta-site, with lots of paths to kids' collections of pages, funny pages, and more.
The League of Hyperlinks	http://www.tnet.de/cgi-bin/ league.pl	The League ranks each of its listed Web sites in popularity (by number of accesses from this Web page); users can add URLs.
The McKinley Internet Directory	http://www.mckinley.com/	This is a searchable index of sites including reviews and one- to four-star ratings, sorted by subject.
What We Learned on the Web Today	http://www.cio.com/ WebMaster/wmlearned.html	Here's a fun, small list of Web sites organized not by name, but by tidbits of information gleaned from them.
Kevin's Internet Encyclopedia	http://www.usask.ca/~lowey/ encyclopedia/	Kevin has organized this page alphabetically by topic, much like a 27-volume "encyclopedia" with an index. It also contains hyperlinks to non-Web Internet resources. From the creator of the popular Kevin's Prairie Dog Town gopher (gopher:// skynet.usask.ca/).

Another good source of good Web sites you haven't seen yet are people's personal bookmarks lists. Ask your pals for theirs; have a look at people's personal home pages. After all, one of the easiest (and most popular) ways to bulk up a personal home page is with a list of hyperlinks to your favorite Web sites.

■ What's News

These sites present you with the latest Web news, providing information on the latest Web trends and developments as well as new software and helper apps.

Web Week magazine presents a weekly update, Web Week Wednesday, at http://pubs.iworld.com/ww-online/wed/ (see Figure 7.5). The *Web Week* home page is at http://pubs.iworld.com/ww-online/.

Figure 7.5

Web Week Wednesday

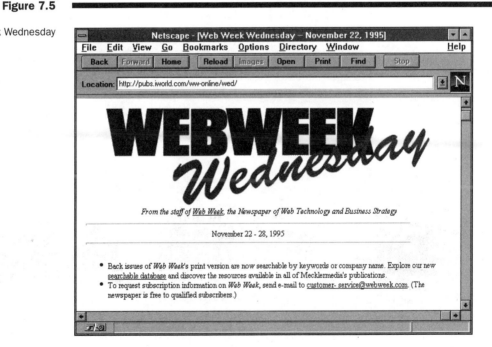

Interactive Age magazine presents a daily Web news roundup at http://techweb.cmp.com/ia/dailies/daily.htm (Figure 7.6). The Interactive Age home page is at http://techweb.cmp.com/techweb/ia/current/. Other good news sites appear in Table 7.5.

Figure 7.6

Interactive Age Daily

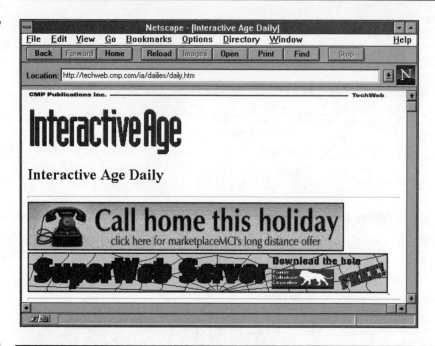

Table 7.5

Web News Sites

WEB SITE NAME	URL	DESCRIPTION
WebSight Newsflashes	http://websight.com/pages/news.html	
Weird Online World	http://www.dorsai.org/~tristan/MAG/mag.html	
NIC-News	http://www.washington.edu:1180/nic-news/	Written between January 1992 and June 1995 by Sheryl Erezat the University of Washington's Network Information Center.
The Web Word	http://www.euro.net/innovation/Web_Word_Base/Web.WordHP.html	
Simba Media Daily	http://www.mecklerweb.com/simba/internet.htm	

WEB SITE NAME	URL	DESCRIPTION
Internet World	http://www.mecklerweb.com/ mags/iw/iwhome.htm	
Internet World Friday	http://www.mecklerweb.com/ iwfriday/	This is a weekly Net news roundup.
Computer Mediated Communications Magazine	http://sunsite.unc.edu/cmc/mag/ current/toc.html	
.net's What's Happening Page	http://www.futurenet.co.uk/ netmag/Announce.html	The latest news from a British Internet magazine with a sense of humo(u)r.
Internet Resources	http://www.hw.ac.uk/libWWW/irn/ irn.html	
Netree	http://www.netree.com	This is an outline-format subject-based directory of Web sites with breaking news headlines from around the Web updated every five minutes, believe it or not.
Yahoo Internet Newsletters Index	http://www.yahoo.com/ Entertainment/Magazines/ Computers_and_Technology/ Internet/	This is an excellent roundup of news and commentary pages on Web and online developments in business and technology.
The Stick	http://www.vpm.com/tti/stick.html	
NetGuide Magazine's CyberGuide.	http://techweb.cmp.com/ techweb/ng/cybergui/cyber1.htm	
Wave Reviews	http://www.netwave.net/ wave_reviews/	
Web Review	http://www.gnn.com/wr/	

Web-Info Newsgroups and Mailing Lists

The Web isn't the only place to glean information about the Web. A few useful Usenet newsgroups and e-mail lists are described below.

Usenet Newsgroups

The main newsgroup to learn about new Web sites is comp.infosystems.www
.announce, which is moderated by M.L. Grant. The Charter FAQ is available
at http://www.halcyon.com/grant/charter.html.

According to Grant, comp.infosystems.www.announce covers "new
World Wide Web resources and Web sites, changes of URLs for existing Web
resources and sites, new Web resources and server, client, and supporting
software. Short summaries of monthly (or less frequent) changes to Web-
based magazines or journals." A searchable archive is available at http://
www.mid.net:80/ANNOUNCE/.

Web news, software, and technologies are also discussed in the Usenet
newsgroups alt.winsock, comp.infosystems.www.browsers.ms-windows,
comp.os.ms-windows.apps.winsock.misc. Other newsgroups of note are alt.in-
ternet.services, alt.culture.internet, alt.etext, and the rest of the 15 comp.info-
systems.www.* subgroups, whose FAQ files are located at http://
www.halcyon.com/grant/web-groups.html.

Mailing Lists

Gleason Sackman heads up the excellent Net-happenings mailing list, where
he passes along noteworthy news and developments about the Web and the
rest of the Net. I wholeheartedly recommend it!

To subscribe to Net-happenings, send e-mail to majordomo@lists
.internic.net, with no subject and "Subscribe net-happenings name@address"
(without quotes) in the body of the e-mail. The Net-happenings list is archived at http://www.mid.net/NET/.

You might also want to check out the Edupage mailing list, written by
John Gehl and Suzanne Douglas. Edupage is a summary of news items from
around the Net and the media covering information technology, delivered
three times a week. To subscribe, send e-mail to listproc@educom.unc.edu
with "subscribe edupage your name" in the body of the message. The latest
issue of Edupage is available at http://www.educom.edu/edupage.new and
the list is archived at http://www.educom.edu/edupage.old/.

There's a mailing list devoted to Netscape Navigator, where all aspects
of using Netscape are discussed. To join, send e-mail to listserv@irlearn.ucd.ie
with "subscribe NETSCAPE your name" in the body of the message.

Netsurfer Tools is an e-zine bringing news about online technology and
Web/Internet tools, accessible at http://www.netsurf.com/nst/ or via mailing
list. To subscribe, send e-mail to nstools-request@netsurf.com with "subscribe nstools-text" in the body of the message, or "subscribe nstools-html"
to receive Netsurfer Tools in HTML format.

The Winsock-L-Announce-Digest mailing list sends updates on new Winsock-based software and new versions of software available for downloading.

To subscribe to Winsock-L-Announce-Digest, send e-mail to List-Admin@ Papa.indstate.edu with the body "subscribe winsock-l-announce-digest." Back issues of the Winsock-L-Announce-Digest are available for anonymous FTP from ftp://papa.indstate.edu//winsock-l/digest/day.## (where ## is the day of the current month).

Netsurfer Digest covers Internet and Web topics and resources, as well as Web site and software reviews. To subscribe, send e-mail to nsdigest-request@ netsurf.com with "subscribe nsdigest-html" (for the HTML version, ready to be opened by Netscape from your hard drive), or "subscribe nsdigest-text." Netsurfer Digest back issues are available at http://www .netsurf.com/nsd/ or at ftp://ftp.netsurf.com/pub/nsd/ (see Figure 7.7).

Figure 7.7

Netsurfer Digest

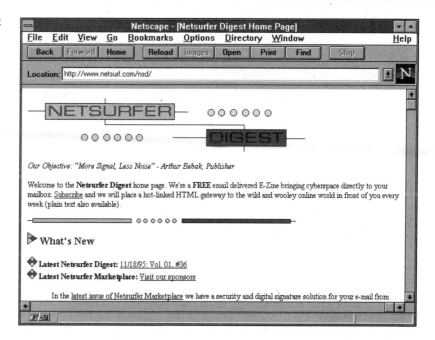

Another good mailing list for keeping up with selected new Web sites is the Scout Report, produced by Susan Calcari, InterNIC Info Scout. To join the mailing list and receive the Scout Report every Friday, send e-mail to majordomo@lists.internic.net, with the body of the e-mail containing "subscribe scout-report". Archives of the InterNIC Scout Report mailing list are available at http://rs.internic.net/scout_report-index.html.

The www-announce mailing list, brought to you by the 3WO (World Wide Web standards organization), is for "anyone interested in WWW, its progress, new data sources, new software releases." To join, send e-mail to listserv@w3.org with the single line in the body "subscribe www-announce your name," where your name is both first name and last name. The 1wwwannounce mailing list is archived at http://www.w3.org/hypertext/ WWW/Archive/www-announce, at http://www.cs.rochester.edu/u/ferguson/ announce.www/, and at http://sunsite.unc.edu/gerald/ciwa/.

The Internet Press is a guide to electronic journals about the Internet that will point you to more mailing lists covering the Web beat. The Internet Press is written by Kevin M. Savetz and John M. Higgins. To get the latest version once, e-mail ipress-request@northcoast.com with the subject "archive" and the body "send ipress." To get on the mailing list to receive new editions as they're released, send e-mail to ipress-request@northcoast.com with the subject "subscribe."

■ Abandon Sleep, All Ye Who Enter Here

The resources in this chapter are guaranteed to wreck any chance you may have had at getting a good night's sleep. But hey, if you weren't already intrigued, you wouldn't have read this far, right? In the next chapter I'll discuss new Web technologies that are expanding the limits of the Web, performing feats that the original team of HTML standards-makers never dreamed of, and I will preview some up-and-coming developments that will make the Web a much more powerful and amazing tool to use.

- *Tools and Multimedia*

- *Stretching the Internet*

- *Boxes and Servers and Modems, Oh My*

- *3-D, sans Silly Glasses*

- *It's a Small World, after All*

- *It's Made of People!*

- *The Palace*

8

Stretching the Web and the Future

IN THIS CHAPTER, YOU'LL LEARN ABOUT SOME THINGS THAT THE first wave of Web architects couldn't have foreseen, and I'll speculate a bit about where the Web is headed. Granted, I'm no Jeanne Dixon, but I do know that the Web of today and the Web of the future both hinge on two things: technology advances (no surprise there) and, more important, what people do with those advances.

New computer software and hardware is released daily. Faster computers, smarter software, and new multimedia formats come out all the time. Software companies have jumped on the Web bandwagon bigtime, and are making tools to create Web sites. Traditional programmers are also getting into the game. Some new programs are tangentially linked to the Web, offering hyperlinks to and from their environments and the Web. The important thing is that they're connected, not whether or not their multimedia files are displayed within the Netscape window itself.

The number of people using Web software is growing at a tremendous rate, too. The major online services now offer Web access, and new Internet providers are popping up all over the world, in the most remote places imaginable. New people are arriving on the Web at a dizzying rate, and they're writing Web pages, too—the number of Web pages is doubling every couple of months.

So let's take a quick spin through some of these trends and developments.

■ Tools and Multimedia

Netscape Navigator 2.0 offers new plug-in technology that allows viewing of multimedia files such as .PDF pages and QuickTime movies directly within Netscape's main window—without launching a separate helper application. Read more about plug-ins at http://home.mcom.com/comprod/products/navigator/version_2.0/plugins/.

HTML

HTML, the *lingua franca* of the Web, is an ever-changing beast, as new tags are constantly added. Work is progressing on version 3.0 of the language, which hadn't been finalized at this writing. The latest HTML 3.0 specifications are available at http://info.cern.ch/hypertext/WWW/MarkUp/html3-dtd.txt. See more about both the history of HTML and how to use it in the next chapter.

Java

Netscape has built-in support for Sun Microsystems's Java programming language, which is certain to shake up the Web and spawn all manner of advanced Web sites with increased interactivity and capabilities. You can read more about Java in the next chapter; and also at http: //java.sun.com/.

Streaming Audio (and Video)

Web users have been blessed (albeit in a mixed fashion) with a multitude of real-time "streaming" sound applications. Streaming is the process by which, instead of downloading a sound or video file, and then playing it back, the user clicks the hyperlink and the audio or video begins streaming to the client software. The flow of data runs through a player and begins playing after a brief delay. The file is not saved to your hard drive. Sound-streaming helper applications are currently available from:

- RealAudio at http://www.realaudio.com/
- True Speech at http://www.dspg.com/internet.htm
- Internet Wave at http://vocaltec.com:80/iwave.htm
- Xing Technology at http://www.xingtech.com/

Xing's StreamWorks will also display streaming video, though you'll pretty much be limited to sound over a modem and a PPP connection. Of course, the proliferation of streaming sound technologies without a single standard means that you'll have to download many more helper applications to be able to hear the various types of streaming-audio files you come across.

CDLink

Another technology depends on sound that comes not from the Web, but from a CD in the user's CD-ROM drive. Users with CDLink software installed and with Netscape correctly configured can click a hyperlink in a Web page to play a segment of a CD. For instance, in a Web review of a music album, there might be a mention of a particular passage from one of the songs on the album, with an accompanying hyperlink. The user clicks on the hyperlink and the passage discussed is played from the CD itself, with no downloading. CDLink was developed by the Voyager Company, makers of CD-ROMs, and is available from the Voyager Web site at http://www.voyagerco.com/cdlink/.

■ Stretching the Internet

The programs in this section don't necessarily have much to do with the Web per se, though sooner or later we'll probably see special URLs that tie the Web to them.

CU-SeeMe

CU-SeeMe (ftp://cu-seeme.cornell.edu/pub/cu-seeme/html/Welcome.html) is a free black-and-white video-conferencing program that allows users across the Internet to see and talk with each other. Anyone with the program can see other users, but you need a video camera and video-capture board in order to send a video image to others. Check out the Frequently Asked Questions

file at ftp://cu-seeme.cornell.edu/pub/cu-seeme/html/PC.faq.txt to see if your
board is compatible with CU-SeeMe.

More Internet person-to-person communications clients are available
from the Communications Clients page at Stroud's Consummate Winsock
Apps (http://cwsapps.texas.net/phone.html).

Hyper-G

Hyper-G is an Internet hypermedia system similar to the Web but containing
even more capability in multimedia, linking, and some other features. Hyper-
G browsers can read Web pages, but Web browsers are generally not able to
support some Hyper-G features. The Welcome to Hyper-G page is at http://
hyperg.tu-graz.ac.at:80/E20C556C/C0x811b9908_0x0013debd. The Windows
Hyper-G browser is called Amadeus. Amadeus requires that you have either
Windows 95, NT, or 3.11 with Win32s installed. Read more about Amadeus
at http://hyperg.tu-graz.ac.at:80/E20C556C/A0x811b9908_0x00069b28. A
sample Hyper-G database is shown in Figure 8.1.

Figure 8.1

Hyper-G database

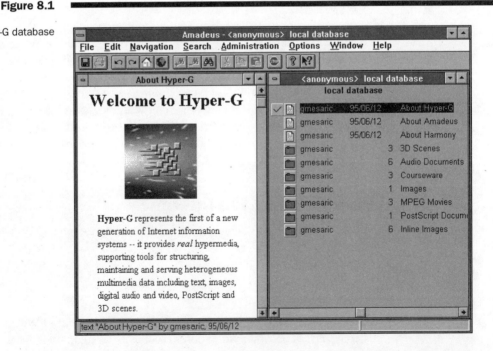

■ Boxes and Servers and Modems, Oh My

Of course, the power of the Web will only increase as home computers get faster and more powerful themselves. Faster modems (including those that use your cable TV line), larger monitors with increased dot-pitch, smaller subcompact notebooks, palmtops, Personal Digital Assistants (PDAs) that run Web browser software (possibly over cellular phone connections)—all these things will push the Web into places that it hasn't been to yet. All of these technologies are available in some form as this book goes to press. Some people think that the Web is destined to become what the media thought interactive TV would become a few years ago. I saw a cordless remote control mouse (that didn't require a desktop or mouse pad) advertised not long ago....

■ 3-D, *sans* Silly Glasses

Virtual Reality Markup Language (VRML) is a way of creating three-dimensional, browsable worlds that the user can visit and travel through over the Internet. VRML documents (which use the .WRL extension) are three-dimensional descriptions of spaces through which the user can navigate. The descriptions for these spaces—how far away objects are from each other, how big they are, and what colors or textures their surfaces are—are downloaded to your computer, along with texture files that are wrapped around the objects. As you move through a 3-D VRML space, your computer re-renders the scene based on this information.

There's a lot of information available about VRML. To join the standards discussion on the www-vrml mailing list, send e-mail to majordomo@wired.com with the following in the body of the e-mail: subscribe www-vrml yourname@ your.site. This list is archived at http://asearch.mccmedia.com/www-vrml/, and the goals of the list are available at http://vrml.wired.com/concepts/ list goals.html.

An interview with VRML developer Mark Pesce is at http://www.data-space.com/webbt/archive/95_07_28_vrml_w_mark_pesce.html. Some of his visions for the future of VRML are available at http://vrml.wired.com/ concepts/visions.html. Read more about VRML at the VRML Repository (http://sdsc.edu/vrml/) or at Yahoo's index to VRML-related Web sites at http://www.yahoo.com/Entertainment/Virtual_Reality/Virtual_Reality_ Modeling_Language__VRML_/. The following resources are also worth checking out:

- VRML Forum at http://vrml.wired.com/

- *New Type Gaming* Magazine's VRML Links at http:// Web.Actwin.Com:80/NewType/vr/vrml/

- ARC's VRML Hotlist at http://vrml.arc.org/vrmltools/hotlist.html
- alt.lang.vrml newsgroup
- sci.virtual-worlds newsgroup

Caligari's Fountain VRML browser is the most usable VRML browser I've seen so far. It's available from http://www.caligari.com/. A VRML scene as it appears in Fountain is shown in Figure 8.2.

Figure 8.2

Fountain

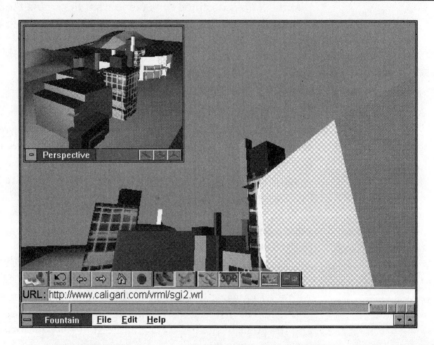

Another VRML browser, WebFX, displays VRML scenes directly within Netscape's main window. It's available at http://www.paperinc.com/.

Worlds Chat, by Worlds Inc., takes a slightly different approach to 3-D. They put people in the scene. Or fish, depending on the persona the user chooses. Users are first sent to the Avatar Gallery, where they pick their on-screen representation and then enter Worlds Chat, based on a space station of six rooms around a central hub. The program is kind of like DOOM with no guns, where the characters talk with each other instead of grunting or blasting each other to bits. We'll be seeing a lot of avatar applications like this coming anywhere that live online chat exists. You can find information about Worlds Chat and the Worlds Chat software at http://www.worlds.net/products/wchat/. A scene from Worlds Chat is shown in Figure 8.3.

Figure 8.3

Worlds Chat

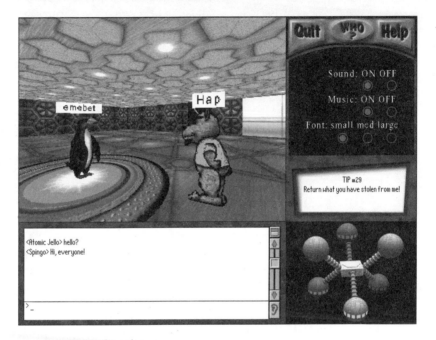

AlphaWorld, the next generation of Worlds Inc. products, allows users to build and maintain their own 3-D spaces. Information and the software are available from http://www.worlds.net/alphaworld/.

■ It's a Small World, after All

It used to be that people knew a lot about where they were from and not much about anywhere else. TV—especially CNN—has changed all that, but I'd like to think the Web can play as much of a role in our understanding of the world. In Usenet newsgroups and Internet Relay Chat (IRC) channels, you can converse with people from all over (well, those places with Internet access, anyway). On the Web, however, you can look up government and visitor information and local news, and *see* what different places across the globe actually look like, more or less live, without having to spring for a satellite dish or premium cable channels.

Virtual Tourist II at http://wings.buffalo.edu/world/vt2/ allows you to find local Web sites and hyperlinks to thousands of news sources from all over the world. You can also check out Yahoo's list of regional Web sites at http://www.yahoo.com/Regional/.

Government information on the Web is also becoming more and more pervasive. Check out some of the many government Web sites available from http://www.yahoo.com/Government/. And remember the Amazing Fish Cam? There are plenty of Web sites that offer a more or less real-time video feed from remote locations. Granted, a lot of the locations are indoors, but a few allow you an outside view of places around the world. The Web Voyeur at http://www.eskimo.com/~irving/web-voyeur/ lists many of these.

■ It's Made of People!

—Charlton Heston, Soylent Green, *1973*

Yes, the thing that makes the Web worthwhile is the people who use it; the people who create Web sites and who write the software and productivity tools that help others put up Web sites. Look at any magazine rack and what are the pictures on the covers? Human faces, that's what. You can talk all you want about this computer or that piece of software, but what makes the Web a vibrant and exciting place are its residents and makers.

Who's Out There?

A lot of people are "out there" on the Web. And more are on their way. More businesses are setting up Web sites for everything from real estate to book-selling to pet care to mathematics. And as the Web population increases, so does technology, allowing the greater possibility of communities connecting people across the world. What's the first creation of new Web authors? A personal home page, with their own information set out for the world to see. People are fascinated by each other. They want to see what others look like, know what books they read, and learn about their interests. They want to talk to each other, too, which is where the following resources come in. Many Web sites have put up chat rooms and bulletin boards (BBSs). Here's a few from a Web site that I helped create, Elektra.com (http://www.elektra.com/). To date, these two areas have met with mixed success. The browsing nature of the Web doesn't lend itself very well to people staying and chatting—most users tend to be in a bit of a hurry on their way to the next site.

Figure 8.4 shows the chat area and Figure 8.5 shows one of the bulletin boards available at Elektra's Web site.

And here are some resources for Web-based communication.

- The Sociable Web, by Judith Donath and Niel Robertson, at http://judith.www.media.mit.edu/SocialWeb/SociableWeb.html

- Yahoo's Web Communication Index at http://www.yahoo.com/ Computers_and_Internet/Internet/World_Wide_Web/Communication/

Figure 8.4

Elektra.com chat area

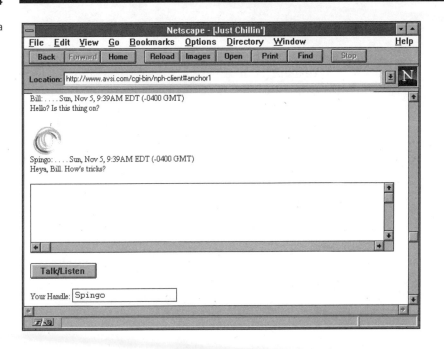

Figure 8.5

Elektra.com bulletin board

- Whimsy at http://monet.uwaterloo.ca/john/whimsy/start.htm

- Netscape Chat Information at http://home.netscape.com/comprod/chat.html

- Netscape Chat Download at ftp://ftp.netscape.com/pub/chat/

- Prospero Global Chat at http://www.propsero.com/

- Alamak's Internet Relay Chat at http://alamak.bchem.washington.edu/~sjohn/irc.cgi

■ The Palace

The Palace is the most promising development I've found on the Web. I really believe it's the greatest breakthrough on the Internet since, well, the release of Netscape. If VRML is like walking around inside a 3-D space, and Worlds Chat offers the appeal of live chat in a Doom-like environment, then Palace is like the CD-ROM *Myst* with a community and graffiti. Like *Myst*, you navigate through a Palace site by clicking hotspots on a two-dimensional screen. However, the skillful use of graphics, as in Palace's premiere Mansion site, can create a satisfying illusion of real 3-D space. Users can customize their avatars easily: Upon registration (and paying the registration fee), users can replace the default avatar with any graphic drawn with Palace's painting tools or with copied-and-pasted images from a graphics program. What Palace loses in authentic 3-D space, it gains in ease of use and creation.

It's relatively easy to create Palace sites with the authoring capabilities built into the program itself and by using its IPTSCRAE scripting language. Once the user pays the registration fee, servers are available for Windows, Macintosh, and UNIX platforms at no extra charge. Palace even has built-in MIDI capability. So go check out Palace, which is available from http://www.thepalace.com/.

A scene from Palace's Mansion is shown in Figure 8.6.

Figure 8.6

Palace

Palace demonstrates the most successful use of human-to-human inter-action software I've seen so far on the Net. Granted, the Mansion is silly fun. It probaby won't be used for many serious applications right away, but even so, users can draw on a communal screen while chatting, and the backgrounds can be photographs or 3-D renderings of existing spaces as well as fanciful creations. If you're looking for me, I'll be in Harry's Bar, with an Isaac Hayes avatar.

- *Spingo's Quick 'n' Dirty HTML Primer*
- *Medium-Strength HTML*
- *Industrial-Strength Web Authoring*
- *Java and Netscape Scripting Language*
- *Getting Your Page on the Web*
- *Serve 'Em If You Got 'Em*
- *Other Web Authoring Resources*

9

Rolling Your Own: Making Your Own Web Page

CHECKING OUT OTHER FOLKS' WEB PAGES IS FUN. PUBLISHING YOUR own can be even *more* fun. Why not write a page and serve it up? Now, I don't want to hear, "But I have nothing to *say* on my Web page!" If you've spent much time surfing the Web, you know *that* never stopped anyone. Your page could certainly be more interesting than many, and it's fun to try your hand at it.

You can pick up the basics of HTML, the Web-authoring language, pretty quickly. Of course, you have to keep a few design principles in mind, and though it's easy to get a basic Web page together, you can also get pretty complicated with authoring if you want to. Let's walk through the basics of how to write a page, and I'll point you to places where you can learn about more advanced Web authoring techniques and design principles.

■ Spingo's Quick 'n' Dirty HTML Primer

First, I'm going to let you in on a little secret. How do you create a Web page without knowing a single thing about HTML? You *swipe* one. You see, HTML lets you view the source code of pretty much any Web page you come across. You can copy the HTML layout of that page and save it as is, or rewrite to your heart's content. (How do you think I got started?) I've written a Web page just to show you how to get started. Fire up Netscape and your PPP connection, and pop over to http://www.echonyc.com/~spingo/Guide/swipeme.html, shown in Figure 9.1.

Figure 9.1

swipeme.html

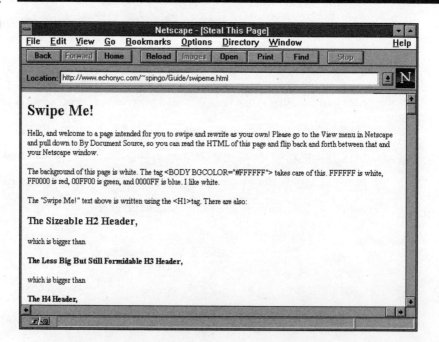

I created this page specifically for you to cannibalize from. If this page isn't available for some reason (the server's too busy, for instance), go to any Web site and save it to your hard drive, tinker with it, and save again. Voilà!

An (almost) instant Web page! Netscape can display Web pages from across the globe, but it's also capable of viewing HTML documents that sit on your hard drive.

In Windows File Manager, create a file in your Netscape directory called "htmlauth." Go on back to Netscape, and with my "swipeme.html" page (or any Web page in your Netscape main window), go to the File menu and pull down the Save As option (or hit Ctrl+S). Save the file (as swipeme.htm) to your Netscape directory. When you get into writing multiple Web pages or whole Web sites, you'll probably want to create directories for each project.

Open Windows Notepad and then the file you've just saved, which is shown in Figure 9.2. See the cryptic bits of text between the <>s? those are HTML *tags.* They look like this: <TAG> and they describe how the page will appear when viewed in Netscape or another Web browser. Some of them have matching closing tags that look like this </TAG>. At the top of the screen you'll see a pair of tags that read <TITLE> and </TITLE>. The text between them is the title of your Web page, and appears in Netscape's title bar when the Web page is being displayed. HTML tags work with either capital or lowercase letters: <P> does the same thing as <p>. HTML generally ignores extra spaces and returns (at least in the body of text; returns sometimes mess up the tags if you use them in between the brackets). < P > will work the same as <P>.

Figure 9.2

swipeme.html in Notepad

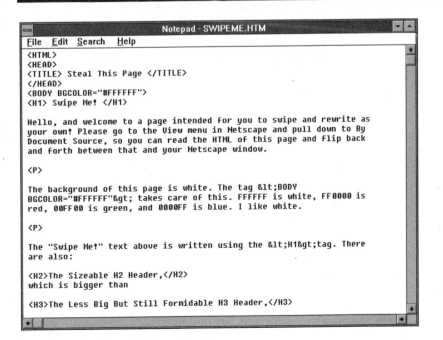

Now look at the text in between the <TITLE> tags. Where it says "Steal This Page," type in the title you want to appear. How about "(Your Name Here)'s First Web Page—yee-ha!"

Now save the file, and leave the Notepad program open. Go back to Netscape, and pull the File menu down to Open File. Locate it on your hard drive and click OK. You'll see the same file you saw when you swiped it, but there, the title in Netscape's title bar has changed to what you typed in. Switch back over to Notepad, and now look at the first round of <H1> tags, where it says "Swipe Me!" The <H1> tag tells the Web browser that the text between the tags is to be displayed in a larger, bold font, and that structurally it's an important headline in the document.

There are a series of header tags, <H-bomb>, where * can range from 1 to 6, in descending size and intended importance, all of which are included in swipeme.html for your perusal and edification. Think of HTML header tags as the equivalent of headlines and subheads on the front page of a newspaper.

Table 9.1 is a chart of some of the most basic HTML tags and what they do. These tags will work in any Web browser. As of this writing, there are other HTML tags that will only work properly within Netscape. More about these later in this chapter.

Table 9.1

Basic HTML Tags

TAG	EXAMPLE	EXPLANATION
<I></I>	<I> Italic words here</I>	Italicizes the words in between the <I> and </I> tags.
<B></B>	<B> Bold words here</B>	Makes the words in between the <B> and </B> tags bold.
<HR>		Draws a horizontal line across the width of the Web browser screen.
<P>		Inserts a full blank line between paragraphs. Similar to hitting Enter in many word processors.
 		Ends the current line and starts a new one. Similar to hitting Shift+ Enter in many word processors.

**Table 9.1
(Continued)**

Basic HTML Tags

TAG	EXAMPLE	EXPLANATION
<PRE> </PRE>	<PRE> Monospaced text here </PRE>	Displays the words in between the <PRE> and </PRE> tags in a monospaced font (which you designate in the Fixed Font setting in Netscape's Fonts Preference Tab, accessible from the General Options window).
<IMG SRC="/path-name/picturefile. extension">	<IMG SRC="Pix/pizza-guy.gif"> or <IMG SRC="pizzaguy.gif">	Displays an inline .GIF or JPEG image with the given path-name. If no pathname is given, looks for the picture file in the same directory of the HTML document.
<A HREF= "URL"> Hypertext link </A> or <A HREF= "URL"> <IMG SRC="picturefile"> </A>	Go to <A HREF="http://www.echonyc.com/~spingo/Spingo/"> Spingo's Home Page </A> or Click this picture of a donkey's butt to go to Spingo's Home Page: <A HREF="http://www.echonyc.com/~spingo/Spingo/"> <IMG SRC="donkeybutt.gif"> </A>	Creates a hyperlink from the text (or image) between the <A HREF=> and </A> tags. Clicking on the hyperlink takes you to that URL.

Open your swipeme.html document in Netscape. You'll notice that the places on the page where the pictures were are now either icons with question marks or broken icons. This is because the HTML document can't find the images. Grab the picture on the swipeme.html page and save it to your htmlauth directory by clicking on it with your right mouse button and pulling down to the "Save This Image As" menu choice. Now click the Reload button at the top of your Netscape screen and the pictures should pop into place. Handsome, isn't it? Go ahead and change swipeme.html's text and tags in Notepad as you like. Play around with it. Have fun! After all, no one else is going to see this page, unless you serve it on the Web. More about how to do that later in this chapter.

Introductory HTML Resources

A good place to start with HTML basics is at the Netscapen site, on the Creating Net Sites page (http://home.netscape.com/assist/net_sites/). Also check out the "Beginner's Guide to HTML" at http://www.ncsa.uiuc.edu/General/Internet/WWW/HTMLPrimer.html. One of the best guides to all existing HTML tags, including Netscape's, is the Sandia National Laboratories's

HTML Reference Manual at http://www.sandia.gov/sci_compute/ html_ref.html. The HTML overview available at http://www.w3.orhypertext/ WWW/MarkUp/ contains the latest official word on the constantly evolving HTML language. As for the latest HTML 2.0 specifications, they are available at http://www.w3.org/hypertexWWW/MarkUp/html-spec/html-spec_toc.html, and the most recent version of the proposed HTML 3.0 specifications can be found at http://www.w3.org/hyperext/WWW/MarkUp/html3/ Contents.html.

Netscape and Graphic Images on the Web

Netscape can display both GIF (Graphics Interchange Format) and JPEG (Joint Photographic Experts Group) image files. The weird blocky-picture-into-sharp-picture effect you sometimes see when Netscape loads an image is the way Netscape renders progressive JPEG and interlaced GIF picture files. These files are similar to plain old GIF and JPEG files you may have seen off the Web; here, the information is saved slightly differently—in layers. As you choose ether GIF or JPEG files in your Netscape window, they load a layer at a time. This process comes in handy if you're in a hurry—you can get the general idea of a picture as it downloads and not have to wait until the enire image comes into focus. Noninterlaced and nonprogressive JPEG files load from the top down, one line of pixels at a time. This process appears to make them load more slowly. To see a comparative duel of all four types of images at once, check out Netscape's demo at http://home.netscape.com/eng/mozilla/ 2.0/relnotes/demo/pjpegdemo.html.

The Bandwidth Conservation Society has put up a Web page of tips on how to get your Web images down to the smallest possible size. Check out their tips at http://www.infohiway.com/faster/. You can also find good information on preparing graphics for the Web in the newsgroup comp. infosystems.www.html.authoring.images.

Free Web Graphics Sites

In writing your Web page, you may want to add a lot more images, but find yourself wishing you'd taken some art classes. Fear not! Many people have geneously placed images on the Web intended for public use. Icons, clip art images of all kinds, and background textures (more about these in a bit) are available from the following sites:

- Yahoo Index of Icons at http://www.yahoo.com/Computers_and_Internet/ Internet/World_Wide_Web/Programming/Icons/

- Yahoo Index of Clip Art at http://www.yahoo.com/ Computers_and_Internet/Multimedia/Pictures/Clip_Art/

HTML-Authoring Programs and Converters

If you think that a lot of this HTML stuff can be automated, well, you're right. A number of commercial and share- or freeware HTML authoring programs are available, with varying degrees of usefulness. Some have a WYSIWYG (What You See Is What You Get) display, altering the text in the editor to match the tag used on it. For instance, bold text may be displayed as bold in the editor's window, where Notepad will display all the text the same. These programs make writing Web pages a little easier, but by no means make it automatic. You still have to know what each HTML tag does. If you want to try one of the HTML authoring programs, check out The Consummate Winsock Apps List's HTML Editors Web page at http://cwsapps.texas.net/html.html. More HTML Editors for a variety of platforms can be found on Yahoo!, at http://www.yahoo.com/Computers/World_Wide_Web/HTML_Editors.

Many programs also exist to convert existing electronic documents in a variety of formats into HTML. Yahoo's index of HTML converter programs is at http://www.yahoo.com/Computers_and_Internet/Internet/World_Wide_Web/HTML_Converters/. Of course, you can also use Make Your Own Home Page at http://www.goliath.org/makepage/. This is a forms-based tool that lets you create a very simple Web page.

■ Medium-Strength HTML

The HTML tags listed in Figure 9.2 and Table 9.1 are really only the basics. Netscape has introduced many extensions to HTML, and not all of them have been embraced by Web community or by the developers of other Web browsers. Since this is a book about Netscape and not a book about HTML authoring, I'll only point you to the pages in the list below and talk a bit about some of the more important Netscape-specific HTML extensions. When authoring Web pages, keep in mind that many of the HTML tags listed in the sites below will not work with browsers other than Netscape. See BrowserCaps at http://ichiban.objarts.com/cgi-shl/webmac.exe/browsercaps/ for a quick list of which tags are supported by which browsers.

- Netscape-Enhanced HTML 2.0 Extensions at http://home.netscape.com/home/services_docs/html-extensions.html

- Netscape HTML 3.0 Extensions at http://www.netscape.com/assist/net_sites/html_extensions_3.html

- Netscape's Release Notes: Pull down Help menu and select Release Notes

Backgrounds

Netscape has the ability to display Web pages that use colored as well as tiled-image backgrounds. You can also specify colors for your text and hyperlinks. Netscape's Web page on background color and image use is at http://home.netscape.com/assist/net_sites/bg/.

To make the background of a Web page a solid color, you have to put a special <BODY> tag into the top of the HTML document, after the </HEAD> tag. The HTML tag that makes the swipeme.html page white is <BODY BGCOLOR="#FFFFFF">. (At the end of the document, make sure to put in a closing </BODY> tag.) The characters inside the quotes, "#FFFFFF", are hexadecimal code for red, green, and blue, all turned all the way up—in hexadecimal numerals, 0 is the lowest and F is the highest. Divide FFFFFF into red, green, and blue segments and you get FF FF FF. If you remember this from art classes of yesteryear, you may recall that when you're dealing with light (like the light shined on the inside of a monitor's picture tube), as you turn up all the colors you get white. This is the opposite of painting, where all the colors together make black. To get pure red, you'd use the code FF 00 00. To get pure green, you'd use 00 FF 00, and to get pure blue you'd use the code 00 00 FF.

This may sound a little confusing (it sure was for me at first), but you really don't have to own a calculator to figure out which colors to use for the background of your Web pages. The best color selection tool I've found for choosing colors is ColorServe Pro, shown in Figure 9.3 (http://www.biola.edu/cgi-bin/colorpro/colorpro.html).

In much the same way that Windows's desktop uses BMP files as wallpaper, you can also make an image on your background. To do this, use the tag <BODY BACKGROUND="filename.extension"> (for example, <BODY BACKGROUND="parchment.gif">). The image repeats across and down to fill Netscape's content area. You can use either GIF or JPEG files as your background images. Remember to keep the images small (less than 10K in size), so that your Web page doesn't take forever to load. PatternLand (http://www.netcreations.com/patternland/) contains plenty of backgrounds for you to start with.

Tables

Netscape has already implemented a tables feature in HTML. Tables let you organize Web page information into neat little cells, as you can see in one of the Web pages of your author's alter ego, Mr. Bad Advice (see Figure 9.4). You can specify the width and spacing of the cells, or have no borders on them at all.

Netscape provides a helpful Web page about tables, with examples, at http://home.netscape.com/assist/net_sites/tables.html.

Figure 9.3

ColorServe Pro

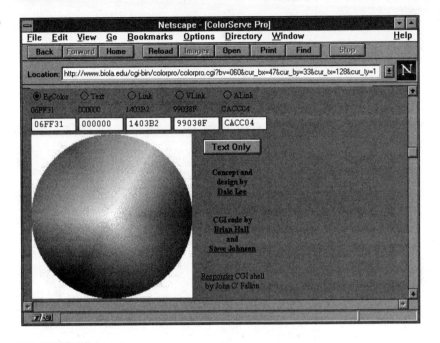

Figure 9.4

Ask Mr. Bad Advice!

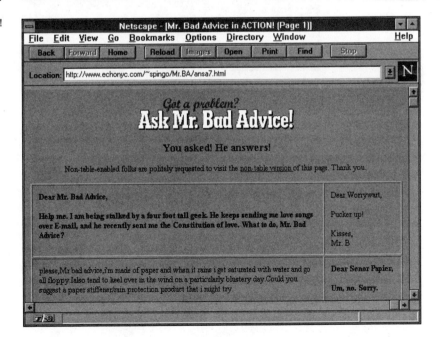

Frames

Frames allow the display of several Web pages in their own panes within one Netscape window, each independently scrollable and posessing its own URL. I've created a sample of frames at http://www.echonyc.com/~spingo/Frames/, shown in Figure 9.5.

Figure 9.5

Frames demo page

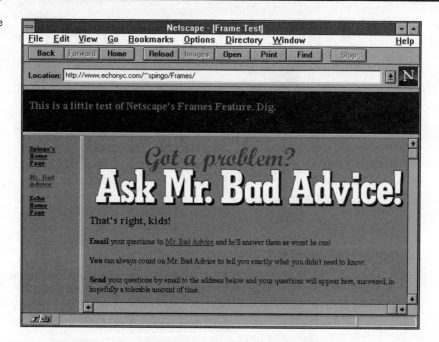

Netscape has several (somewhat more professional) Web pages showcasing the use of frames at http://home.netscape.com/comprod/products/navigator/version_2.0/frames/. To learn more about authoring Web sites using frames, go to http://home.netscape.com/assist/net_sites/frames.html.

■ Industrial-Strength Web Authoring

Note that I didn't say "industrial-strength HTML." The tools discussed here are mostly active *behind the scenes* of a Web page. Pages featuring these tools actually perform tasks and then generate the HTML *on the fly*, as opposed to most HTML pages, which are written once. With just a few exceptions, the sites I've pointed you to so far are fairly static, with standard text-and-graphics. Below I discuss a few of the tools that make for more dynamic Web pages.

Forms and CGI Scripting

On many Web pages, you'll come across fields which allow you to type in information, and one or more buttons that perform an action on what you've typed. The Madlibs page in Figure 9.6 (http://www.mit.edu:8001/madlib) is one of these.

Figure 9.6

Madlibs at MIT

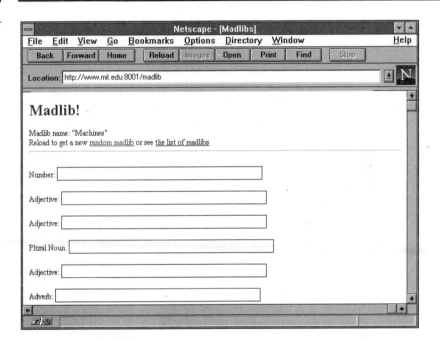

This page is based on the Madlibs books (you may have owned them as a kid; they were a staple of interstate rest-stop gift shops). You fill in the blanks (use the Tab key to move from one field to the next), hit the "Submit Madlib" button, and a little story with your chosen additions appears, undoubtedly causing uproarious laughter among your assembled friends and family.

Forms on pages use a system called Common Gateway Interface to perform actions using the server. CGI scripts are commonly written in the programming language Perl, though it's not unheard of to use other languages for CGI scripting. You can learn more about CGI scripting in the newsgroup comp.infosystems.www.authoring.cgi, and also at the places listed below.

- The Common Gateway Interface at http://hoohoo.ncsa.uiuc.edu/cgi/

- Learn to Write CGI Forms at http://www.catt.ncsu.edu/~bex/tutor/

- The CGI Frequently Asked Questions (FAQ) List at http://www.best.com/~hedlund/cgi-faq/faq.html

Dynamic Documents

Netscape allows Web authors to create pages with simple animations and other "live" information via a technique called client-pull/server-push. You can read more about these animations at http://home.netscape.com/assist/ net_sites/dynamic_docs.html.

Here are some Web pages which demonstrate dynamic documents:

- Mozilla at http://home.netscape.com/assist/net_sites/mozilla/

- Razorfish at http://www.razorfish.com/

You can read more about how dynamic documents work at the Dynamic Documents Explained Web page, and you can read about how to produce "live" documents at http://home.netscape.com/assist/net_sites/pushpull.html.

■ Java and Netscape Scripting Language

Java is a new programming language developed by Sun Microsystems which allows the development of Web pages with much greater interactivity than in the past. Mini-programs written in Java, called *applets,* are actually downloaded and run within Netscape. For instance, a Web page on chemistry might contain 3-dimensional rotatable models of the molecules of various compounds. Click on the molecule, move the mouse left or right, and the 3-D model of the molecule rotates in the direction of the mouse, in real time. With Java, there's no downloading of separate multimedia files.

For more information about Java and some sample applets, have a look at these resources:

- Java Home Page at http://java.sun.com/

- comp.lang.java newsgroup

- Java WWW Forum at http://www.pennant.com/java/

- Netscape's Java Applets Page at http://home.netscape.com/comprod/ products/navigator/version_2.0/java_applets/

- Gamelan Java Resource Registry at http://www.gamelan.com/

If you have a Java-capable version of Netscape (Windows 95 only as of this writing), see a demo at http://home.netscape.com/comprod/products/navigator/ version_2.0/script/. Pull Netscape's Help menu down to Release Notes to read more about the capabilities Java brings to Netscape.

Netscape also has its own scripting language, based on Java. For information about programming in the Netscape Scripting language, have a look at http:// home.netscape.com/comprod/products/navigator/version_2.0/script/script_info/

Design Resources

Now that you have a handle on how to write Web pages, you may want to have a look at some guides for the graphic design of pages. Remember what happened in the early days of desktop publishing, when everyone and their brother had access to a laser printer and 35 fonts for the first time? Remember how awful a lot of documents looked? You want to avoid that. These Web sites give some tips on how to best present your message to the world. David Siegel's page provides some exceptionally insightful tips for Web design.

- David Siegel's Web Wonk at http://www.best.com/~dsiegel/tips/ tips_home.html
- Yahoo Index of Web Design Sites at http://www.yahoo.com/ Computers_and_Internet/Internet/World_Wide_Web/ Page_Design_and_Layout/

◼ Getting Your Page on the Web

Once you write your Web page, you'll certainly want others to see it. Many Internet service providers (see the Appendix) offer subscribers access to their Web server as part of the monthly fee; they may charge extra for storing commercial pages. Ask your provider if they provide Web space, and if so, what the procedure is for setting it up. If you can't get access through your provider, you'll have to get it either by contacting a service that "sublets" space for Web pages (these services are known as "presence providers") or by serving the pages from your own computer. A list of presence providers is available at http://www.yahoo.com/Business_and_Economy/Companies/ Internet_Presence_Providers/.

Some kind souls and organizations offer free Web space for individuals; a list of these providers is at http://www.yahoo.com/Business_and_Economy/ Companies/Internet_Presence_Providers/Free_Web_Pages/.

And then there's Jon Pennycook, who maintains another list of Web sites offering free home pages, at http://metro.turnpike.net/J/JonsPage/freepages.html.

If you decide to serve your pages through a presence provider, you must get your files to the remote server using a devoted FTP program. Netscape allows you to download from—but not upload to—FTP sites. Check out any of several Windows FTP programs listed in Stroud's Consummate Winsock Apps directory at http://cwsapps.texas.net/ftp.html. You'll have to ask your presence provider for more information on where to upload your files and what steps you need to take once they are uploaded.

■ Serve 'Em If You Got 'Em

You can also serve up Web pages from your own PC. If you go this route rather than using a remote Web server, the PPP connection you use to access the Internet will be the same connection from which you'll be serving your pages, slowing things down in both directions (as well as consuming the power of your machine). Also, commercial providers generally serve up Web pages over a much faster connection than you are likely to have. If you do decide to serve Web pages yourself, download a Web server program from one of these sites:

- The Consummate Winsock Servers List at http://bongo.cc.utexas .edu/~neuroses/cwss.html

- Winsock Applications FAQ at http://www.lcs.com/faqhtml.html

Check Your HTML

Now you've got your Web pages created and on a server somewhere, the whole world can come 'n' get 'em. Before you announce your masterpiece to the world, however, you should submit it to an HTML validation service to check for errors and mistakes. Though they may look fine to you in Netscape, HTML mistakes may not allow other browsers to display your document properly. Like a spellchecker, HTML validators go through your document and catch any mistakes you may have made in your coding that might cause your Web page to display improperly in Netscape. Several of these validators are listed below.

- HaLSoft's HTML Validation Service at http://sunsite.unc.edu/boutell/ faq/checkinghtml.html

- Web Lint at http://www.khoros.unm.edu/staff/neilb/weblint.html

- Htmlchek at http://uts.cc.utexas.edu/~churchh/htmlchek.html

Publicizing Your New Web Site

Once you've written your pages, tweaked them until they're peachy-keen, checked and double-checked them, and uploaded them to your own server or a presence provider, it's time to tell the world about them. You'll want to get your site into the major Web search engines and subject-oriented indexes. Most, if not all, of the Web indexes listed in Chapter 6 have submission procedures that allow you to announce your new page.

   An excellent place to begin is Submit It! at http://submit-it.permalink.com/ submit-it/, which lets you unveil your new Web site to many indexes and search engines at once. You can also post a brief message describing your

page to the newsgroups comp.infosystems.announce and comp.internet
.nethappenings. If your page is about a particular subject, find a newsgroup
on relevant topics. Before posting, be sure to read the newsgroups for a
while to observe proper etiquette. Finally, don't forget to tell your friends
and associates. Word of mouth is very important.

■ Other Web Authoring Resources

Here are some other resources to check out in order to learn more about
authoring and serving Web pages.

Visit these Web sites:

- Virtual Library: WWW Development at http://WWW.Stars.com/Vlib/
  comp.infosystems.www.authoring.html

- Webmaster Reference Library at http://ic.corpnet.com/~aking/webinfo/

- Gang Cheng's Newsgroup and Mailing List Archive at http://asknpac
  .npac.syr.edu/ (You'll find archives to lots of Web-authoring related
  Usenet newsgroups and mailing lists here.)

- WWW-managers Mailing List Archive at http://asearch.mccmedia.com/
  www-managers/

These Usenet newsgroups are excellent resources:

- alt.binaries.sounds.d

- alt.binaries.sounds.utilities

- alt.corel.graphics

- alt.hypertext

- alt.graphics.pixutils

- alt.soft-sys.corel.draw

- alt.soft-sys.corel.misc

- comp.graphics

- comp.graphics.apps.photoshop

- comp.graphics.misc

- comp.infosystems.www.authoring.images

- comp.infosystems.www.authoring.html

- comp.infosystems.www.authoring.misc

- comp.multimedia

- comp.music

- comp.publish.electronic.developer

- comp.publish.electronic.misc

- comp.text.pdf

- rec.video.desktop

  You can also subscribe to this mailing list:

- Patrick Douglas Crispen's Advanced HTML List

  Subscribers to this list discuss advanced HTML-authoring topics and swap handy tips and tricks. Send e-mail to LISTSERV@UA1VM.UA.EDU with SUBSCRIBE ADV-HTML yourfirstname yourlastname in the body of the e-mail, replacing yourfirstname and yourlastname with your first and last name.

3

The World Wide Web Is Your Oyster

Welcome to the final part of the book, where you'll learn about Web sites we thought you might be interested in. We? Many of the pages we describe here were selected by Karen Wickre, co-author of ZD Press's *Atlas to the World Wide Web* (available at discriminating bookstores the world over, natch). Karen picked some of her favorite sites, and Spingo added some of his own, offered here for your browsing enjoyment. The best of the bunch have the Our Pick icon ([*]) next to them. Of course the sites here in no way represent a thorough listing of what's out there; they're a small sample of places you might enjoy exploring. Needless to say, there are plenty more where these came from.

■ Art

See also **Computing, Museums**

[*] Ansel Adams: Fiat Lux

**http://bookweb.cwis.uci.edu:8042/
AdamsHome.html**

This is an exhibition of photographs that Adams took throughout the University of California system for its centennial in 1968. His photos are of campus grounds, field stations, natural reserves, and other U.C. properties. This site includes links to a catalog, bookstore, and posters and note cards you can order electronically.

Art Crimes

**http://www.gatech.edu/desoto/graf/
Index.Art_Crimes.html**

This is a gallery of grafitti art from various cities. It's called "Art Crimes" because in most places, painting grafitti is illegal. Many of these pieces no longer exist in the real world since grafitti is often painted over by other grafitti or by building owners or other authorities. Pieces here come from such diverse places as Prague, Los Angeles, and Atlanta.

ArtServe

http://rubens.anu.edu.au

These pages reflect the varieties of image project work currently being undertaken by the Australian National University. It consists of an interactive student tutorial on the history of prints with over 2,800 digitized images, ranging from the fifteenth to the twentieth century; a survey of architecture and architectural sculpture in the Mediterranean basin; and a point-and-click system for the National Gallery of Australia.

ArtSource

**http://www.uky.edu/Artsource/
artsourcehome.html**

ArtSource is a gathering point for networked resources on art and architecture. The content is diverse and includes pointers to image collections, electronic exhibitions, art and architecture gopher sites, and electronic art journals, as well as original materials submitted by librarians, museums, art historians, and other art sources. A good overall art resource site.

Frida Kahlo

http://www.cascade.net/kahlo.html

This Web site contains not only images of paintings by famed Mexican artist Frida Kahlo, but also informative biographical information about the artist, presented alongside related paintings. Along with learning that Kahlo suffered polio as a child, was in a bus accident at 18 that left her in pain for much of her life, and was married to muralist Diego Rivera, we also learn that "Frida annoyed her family by wearing men's clothing at times to family functions."

You can access a self-portrait of Kahlo dressed in a black suit.

Kaleidospace

http://kspace.com/

Kaleidospace is a commercial service showcasing art over the Internet. Its philosophy of decentralized promotion and distribution helps individual artists and groups who otherwise would have difficulty reaching a mass audience. Artists advertise their works for purchase and pay a flat monthly rent for displaying their work on the Kalediospace server, which doesn't take any royalties or insist on exclusive distribution.

The Museum of Bad Art

http://mirror.wwa.com/mirror/orgs/moba/moba.htm

This Boston-based museum is dedicated to, well, lousy art. Art that was well-intentioned and created with effort (and sometimes talent), but somehow came out…wrong. Two shows are presented here with an almost straight face, along with information about the MOBA CD-ROM created by the Friends of MOBA.

OTIS General Information

http://sunsite.unc.edu/otis-bin/rndimg

OTIS (Operative Term Is Stimulate), at its most basic interpretation and intention, is a place for image-makers and image-lovers to exchange ideas, collaborate, and meet. OTIS is a collection of images and information open for public perusal and participation. People participate by giving artists feedback on their work or by joining in one of OTIS's collaborative art projects, held under the name SYNERGY, where artwork is created through a series of cooperative efforts by fellow conspirators. For example, one image can undergo multiple transformations by different SYNERGY participants. OTIS will provide you with a random image from its vast archive, and has also set up an e-mailing list for the discussion of net art, net artists, and the future of art itself.

Renaissance and Baroque Architecture: Architectural History 102

http://www.lib.virginia.edu/dic/colls/arh102/index.html

A large collection of images from a University of Virginia European renaissance and baroque architecture class. Images from fifteenth-century Italy, Florence, Venice, Rome, French classicism, and the English adoption of classicism. A very interesting tour through these different architectural periods of Europe.

WebMuseum, Paris

http://mistral.enst.fr/~pioch/louvre/louvre.html

Bienvenue au WebMuseum! Created and maintained by Nicolas Pioch, this page is a grand collection of well-known paintings, and a tour of Paris, the Eiffel Tower, and the Champs-Elysees.

You are even issued your own personal "ticket" to the museum. Merci beaucoup, Nicholas!

■ Business

CareerMosaic

http://www.careermosaic.com/cm/

CareerMosaic is a commercial Web page offering profiles of companies that have placed employment listings on their server, and informative articles and links to more career-related information on the Net. There is a library, where various employment resources are catalogd; reviews of those employers associated with CareerMosaic; and more. There's also information from the top 50 U.S. employment markets and the Consumer Price Index (CPI) for those cities. A list of government sources of labor information also appears in case you need more data on a market.

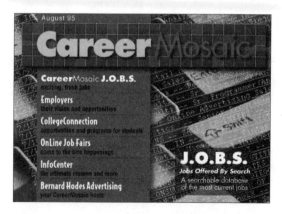

Consumer Information Center Catalog

http://www.gsa.gov/staff/pa/cic/cic.htm

You may remember all those commercials urging you to get your free "Consumer Information Center catalog" from Pueblo, Colorado;

here's the online version of same. While the center has a wealth of information on all sorts of topics, such as cars, children, employment, federal programs, and so on, it also has sections on money and small business. Some of the titles available online are "Basic Facts about Registering a Trademark," "General Information Concerning Patents," "Guide to Business Credit for Women, Minorities, and Small Businesses," "Invention Promotion Firms," "Starting and Managing a Business from Your Home," and the "Small Business Handbook." You can view the full text of the booklets and, if your browser has the feature, save the text to your local hard drive.

Economist Jokes

http://www.etla.fi/pkm/joke.html

An Adam Smith likeness heads up this page for the finance-minded, courtesy of Paul Kuoppamaki, a student at the Helskinki, Finland School of Economics. "How many Chicago School economists does it take to change a light bulb? None. If the light bulb needed changing the market would have already done it." Links not only the "wrecked humor page," (which happens to sport a whole collection of Top Ten jokes), but also "irony in economic theory."

Entrepreneurs on the Web

http://sashimi.wwa.com/~notime/eotw/ EOTW.html

This is a place to find useful business information and goods and services for entrepreneurial ventures. The business resources includes links to various business-related Internet resources such as the Internet Business Center and a FAQ on advertising on the Internet, as well as free national listings in directories of consultants and consulting firms. The goods and services section offers wares from other entrepreneurs, with everything from T-shirts, books, and CDs to computer sales and consulting.

Experimental Stock Market Data

http://www.ai.mit.edu/stocks.html

An experimental page created by Mark Torrance of the MIT Artificial Intelligence Laboratory, this page provides a link to the latest stock market information. There's general market news and quotes for selected stocks, which are updated automatically from an e-mail source in California to reflect the current day's closing information. The page contains stock charts of price and volume movement, mutual fund charts of price movement, the top stocks, the updated stock quotes, and links to other financial information available on the Web. This is the only free service on the Net to serve up stock quotes from the Washington Post business section.

FedEx

http://www.fedex.com/

Shipping and tracking software for Windows and Macintosh computers is available from the FedEx Web site, along with the service that really makes this Web site worth noting: the ability to track FedEx packages, even while they're in transit. Users can also inquire about service availability in their area and read the latest FedEx press releases.

The Internet Business Center

http://tsunami.tig.com/cgi-bin/genobject/ ibcindex

The Internet Business Center is a good, overall business oriented Web server. It covers Internet business resources, storefronts, traditional information brokerages like Dialog and the Lexis/ Nexis databases, travel, and government, as

well as financial, legal, and manufacturing services. There are also links to Internet statistics and Net information guides and resources.

Small Business Administration

http://www.sbaonline.sba.gov/index.html

The U.S. Small Business Administration (SBA) counsels, assists, and protects the interests of small business concerns and preserves free competitive enterprise. The SBA Web pages offer several different areas for the businessperson to explore, including current SBA events and information on starting, financing, or expanding a business. There is even a clickable regional resource map to find the SBA resources for your area. If you are involved with a small business in any way, visiting this server will probably be well worth your while.

Staples

http://www.harvardnet.com/staples/

And what business office is complete without office supplies? The Staples Virtual Office Superstore allows users to look up prices and product information on their most popular products, and then provides ways of ordering them via phone or fax. As futurists of the past would be somewhat irked to find, the paperless office still hasn't arrived.

■ Computing

See also Art, The Internet

Apple Computer

http:www.apple.com/

Apple's site includes information for both consumers and developers, as well the "special communities" Apple focuses on. There are resources here for the disabled, for libraries, and for school kids (K–12 and higher education).

IBM

http://www.ibm.com/

One of the largest computer manufacturers in the world with an active research and development wing, IBM remains a major force in the computing industry. IBM's server includes information on its activities on the Internet, the company's products and services, IBM-funded technology and research, and corporate information.

[*] Internet Computer Index

http://ici.proper.com/

A service of Proper Publishing, the ICI is a resource-locating service specializing in information on PC, Macintosh, and UNIX computer systems. ICI keeps links to popular archives of information such as Usenet newsgroups and popular FAQs, as well as ftp software archives. ICI is a good resource for tracking down information for the personal computer user.

Internet Font Archive

http://jasper.ora.com:80/comp.fonts/
Internet-Font-Archive/

Norman Walsh has attempted to collect in one place all of the shareware and freeware computer fonts available on the Internet, along with information about commercially-available collections of fonts available from several digital type foundries. Fonts are available in PC/UNIX and Macintosh formats, and best of all, each font is previewable via small thumbnail samples. A must-see for anyone looking for an extra kick for that memo or flyer.

Microsoft

http://www.microsoft.com/

Here's behemoth Microsoft—the largest software company in the world—offering links to information on its many programs (including Windows 95 and Windows NT developer resources), access to the Knowledge Base and Software Library, employment opportunities, and sales information, as well as information on Microsoft TechNet and Microsoft TV. Anyone who uses or develops software based on Microsoft products should take a moment to look through this site.

Mobile and Wireless Computing

**http://snapple.cs.washington.edu:600/
mobile/mobile_www.html**

A great collection of resources on mobile and
wireless computing, this page contains information on conferences, projects, labs and groups
conducting research, online journals and newsletters, and a list of wireless service providers.
Due to be a major growth area of computing as
the technology continues to shink in size and
grow in power, this will be a fascinating page to
watch over the next several years.

[*] OAK Software Repository

http://www.acs.oakland.edu/oak.html

The OAK Repository is the only place you'll
need to go to find tons of Windows, DOS, Windows NT and Windows 95 shareware and freeware. The handy Web interface makes it much
easier to find what you're looking for than if
you were using a conventional ftp archive site.

[*] Screensavers for Windows from A–Z

http://www.sirius.com/~ratloaf/

Someone by the name of, uh, *Rat Loaf* has collected over 200 shareware and freeware Windows screensavers (.SCR files) and made them
available for download. A Top 10 Downloaded
list is presented, and Mr. Loaf also can provide
custom screensaver development. Tired of
those flying toasters or "I Hate This Job" scrolling banners? This is the place for you.

■ Education

See also **Kids and Games, Reference and
Information, Language**

[*] AskEric

http://ericir.syr.edu/

An incredible resource for the K–12 audience,
AskEric offers a wide range of automated
access to its collection of education documents,
the Virtual Library. It includes over 700 lesson
plans, formatted Eric searches, listserv archives,
and pointers to other useful Internet services.
AskEric can also be accessed via gopher,
WAIS, ftp, and Telnet. From here you can also
access course guides for NASA's SIR-C education program, lesson plans, and other materials
for use with the popular PBS science series
"Newton's Apple," and the National Parent
Information Network. Resources like AskEric
will undoubtedly change the nature of education in the years ahead.

College and University Home Pages

**http://www.mit.edu:8001/people/
cdemello/univ.html**

This is an extensive list of colleges and universities around the world, and all of the info they
offer. The page also contains a geographical listing of its sites as well. Now when we said extensive, we meant it: There are nearly 1,000 unique
listings. Those shopping around for information
on university programs anywhere may not need
to go any further.

Educom

http://educom.edu/

A commercial Web page, Educom is aimed at
people interested in information technology for
higher education. The organization now boasts

approximately 600 higher education institutions and 100 corporations involved in its programs and projects. The page contains information on Educom information resources, its strategic development plan, upcoming conferences and events, memberships, and a variety of publications. Many of these services are also available through gopher, WAIS, and e-mail.

Globewide Network Academy

http://uu-gna.mit.edu:8001/uu-gna/
index.html

The Globewide Network Academy (GNA) is a consortium of educational and research organizations that provides a central organization where students, teachers, scholars, and researchers can meet, interact, and provide services and technical and administrative expertise to member organizations. GNA provides a meta-library of keyword-searchable indexes of information sources on the Internet, and GNA course specific resources. Our favorite is the Collaborative Textbook Project, where hypertext textbooks on a variety of different subjects are being created for their online coursework. For example, you can access textbooks on either Greek mythology, an introduction to the Internet, or a class on C++ programming language. This type of distributed education holds great promise for the future.

Janice's K–12 Outpost

http://k12.cnidr.org/janice_k12/
k12menu.html

Janice's Cyberspace Outpost specializes in resources for the K–12 crowd and has a fun, playful feel to its pages. Included here is much that's new within the K–12 Web community, gopher links, programs and projects, other K-12 metapages, virtual libraries, and information on the National Science Foundation's K–12 projects. Obviously geared to being used directly by kids as well as teachers, Janice's Outpost is most excellent!

Online Educational Resources

http://www.nas.nasa.gov/HPCC/K12/
edures.html

Part of the High Performance Computing and Communications program, the Online Educational Resources (OER) page fosters an increased use of new computer and networking technologies to help support accelerated learning programs in education. This is a good place to start your educational forays into cyberspace. In addition, OER provides links to museums and expositions, online libraries, collaborative technology resources and datasets, and links to the popular search engines on the Web.

Plugged In

http://www.pluggedin.org/

Pages like this reaffirm your faith in computers and humanity in general. This project helps kids from low-income communities work in a state-of-the-art multimedia lab where they do full-cycle multimedia projects and global video conferencing, and develop Web pages. In the process, they learn about communications, teamwork, and the creative process. You can tell by just looking at this page that the kids are having fun! While you're there, check out Nathan's thoughts and artwork and Daisy's "5 Minute Confusion," then e-mail them and let them know what you think.

The World Lecture Hall

http://www.utexas.edu/world/ instruction/index.html

One of our favorite pages from educational sites overall, this is a collection of links to pages created by faculty worldwide who are using the Web to deliver class materials. Here you can find course syllabi, assignments, lecture notes, exams, class calendars, and multimedia textbooks on a wide variety of subjects ranging from accounting and anatomy to computers, English, humanities, music, and even religious studies. With 38 categories in all and undoubtably more to come, the World Lecture Hall is an incredible educational tool. Whether you are brushing up on an old subject, augmenting your current studies, or learning something completely new, take advantage of the work created by instructors from all over the world.

■ Film

Buena Vista MoviePlex

http://bvp.wdp.com/BVPM/index.html

Welcome to Buena Vista MoviePlex, a commercial server and the home of Hollywood Pictures, Walt Disney Pictures, and Touchstone

Pictures. Organized as a sort of virtual theater using some very large clickable images, you can view samples from current films from any of these three production companies, get press releases on their current films, or play movie trivia games with the "Movie Brain." Very well done graphically and interesting to browse through. This is a good site to download JPEG or QuickTime snapshots of films.

[*] CineMedia

http://www.gu.edu.au/gwis/cinemedia/ CineMedia.home.html

Dan Harries is the intrepid searcher who created this cool Australian page with lots of links to many movie, TV new media, and even radio Web pages, plus many reference resources.

Entertainment Weekly

http://www.timeinc.com/ew/

This is the online version of the print mag covering movies, music, and television programs. The movie section features reviews of newly released films, profiles of directors, actors, and other film celebrities, and additional movie news. There's also "Critical Mass," in which film critics from around the country have rated current films. If you're headed to the movies and want a quick opinion, check out *EW*.

Hollyweb Online Film Guide

http://www.ingress.com/users/spease/
hw/hollyweb.html

Want to play critic, or compare notes with other moviegoers? You can e-mail your comments and have them posted for all in the Hollyweb Cafe to see: "I hated it! It should be banned to preserve people's mental health" or "What a total slab of mediocrity this was." Subscribe to e-mail magazine *Electronic Hollywood* for news of upcoming productions. National box office stats updated weekly.

Aspiring to be an online film Mecca!

Hollywood's Coming!

http://www.digimark.net/mfu/
hollywoo.html

You've been waiting for this: a cynical look at how the Big Studios are trying to cash in on the Internet with "15 upcoming or currently released films either directly about the Net, or 'with Internet retrofits.'" Read the capsule summaries "and save the price of admission."

The Hong Kong Movies Home Page

http://www.mdstud.chalmers.se/hkmovie/

Do the names Chow Yun Fat and Jackie Chan call up hours of action-packed fun for you? This definitive page may be for you and others who love those films from Hong Kong that always seem to feature humor, action, and acrobatics in varying proportions. There's a searchable database with information about H.K. movie actors, filmographies, alternative names, and pictures. There is also the Hong Kong Video

FAQ, Hank Okasaki's H.K. "Girls with Guns" movie list with over 250 movie reviews, a box office report, and much more. Heeeyaah!

[*] Internet Movie Database

http://WWW.MSState.EDU/Movies/

The mother of all movie databases, the IMD, also known as the Cardiff Movie Database, is an international volunteer effort coordinated via the Usenet newsgroup rec.arts.movies. This site provides useful and up-to-date movie information on over 39,000 movies with over 490,000 filmography entries, and it is expanding continuously. You can search titles by certificate, genre, country of origin, production company, locations, quotes, sound tracks, plot summaries, the year of release, or ratings. There is also an "on this day in history" page covering celebrity birthdays and deaths, the rec.arts.movies top- and bottom-100 films, some famous movie-made marriages past and present, and Academy Awards information. This site offers just about everything you could ever ask for in a movie home page. If you can't find it here, it may not exist.

Movielink

http://www.777film.com/?TP:National

"Hello, and welcome to Movie Link!" If you're a 777-FILM caller, check out this graphically-pleasing page, which lets you search by geography, schedules, and online ticket ordering up to a week ahead of showtime. Browse current movie listings or head to new releases. Search by title or theatre, or browse by genre.

[*] Mr. Showbiz

http://web3.starwave.com/showbiz/

Scoops, chat, movie and music reviews, and audience stats can be found here, all displayed very coolly with nonintrusive, quirky graphics. Daily Dose gives you birthdays and other significant dates (Christian Slater was born on the same day in 1969 that Genghis Khan died in 1227!) Be sure to check out Flash, which features movie silliness and articles on comparative reviews of genre or settings in films. And a link to current tabloid headlines!

Screenwriters and Playwrights Home Page

http://www.teleport.com/~cdeemer/scrwriter.html

We couldn't resist including this page, a resource for screenwriters and playwriters. There's information on dramatic structure, movie reviews, the business of screenwriting, scripts, plays, lyrics to musicals, and more. This is definitely worth a browse through for anyone in the industry and those who are just interested in reading up on plays from authors such as Goethe, Shakespeare, and Ibsen, or brand new plays from the burgeoning playwrights trying to get produced.

■ Food and Drink

Amy Gale's Recipe Archive

http://www.vuw.ac.nz/~amyl/recipes/

One of the things we like about the Web and the Net in general is the ability to access all kinds of wonderful information at any time. This recipe archive is a prime example of just that sort of thing. A collection of tasty and useful recipes all in one spot, it's essentially an online cookbook. Amy's Recipe Archive carries a wide range of recipes—everything from breads and casseroles to ethnic dishes, salads and soups (take a look at the recipe for vath-thalkozhambu, an Indian hot-and-sour soup). An active participant of the Usenet group rec.food.cooking, Amy has collected different recipes contributed from all over the Net.

Brew Sites on the WWW

http://www.atd.ucar.edu/homes/cook/beer/brewsites.html

Here are the basics to get you started: hotlinks to microbrewery beer recipes, mead making, the basics of brewing, and commercial supplies for making your own. And there are links to other brewski fans' pages, too.

Mostly Desserts and Other Culinary Atrocities

http://www.aus.xanadu.com/GlassWings/food/recipe.html

This is a good Web page in general and this section is truly icing on the cake. A tasty tidbit from their Web page: "Never judge a cookbook by its cover, judge it by its dessert recipes! I believe the most important part of the five basic food groups is the dessert group. As such this area is dedicated to some of the finer things in life." Could we have said it any better? This is the page for the more decadent pleasures in any foodie's life, including such treasures as "The Chocolate Biscuits of Doom" and "Really Gross Over-Sweet Popcorn Balls." They even have a recipe for wassail for those in Yuletide mode. Be careful though! Just reading this page may be enough to send you into insulin shock.

[*] Over the Coffee

http://www.cappuccino.com/

The ultimate in coffee pages on the Web, Over the Coffee has everything the coffee enthusiast could ever need. Compiled from Usenet coffee newsgroups, it contains a wide variety of coffee-related information, including: coffee by mail, gourmet coffee suppliers, and data about all sorts of coffee machines and paraphernalia. Be sure not to miss the list of retail coffee vendors, which includes both a listing for the "All Merciful Savior Russian Orthodox Monastery" on Vashon Island, Washington, (where the monks sell coffee by the names of "All Night Vigil" and "Angelic"), and the "Bad Ass Coffee Company" in Kona, Hawaii.

Rolling Your Own Sushi

http://www.rain.org/~hutch/sushi.html

Mark Hutchenreuther, a.k.a Hutch, has demystified the sushi-making experience for us. Here are schematic-like drawings, instructions on rice-making, equipment you'll need, food sup-

plies, and where to get them. Of course he has also described in painstaking detail how to create California rolls, stuffed tofu bags, sashimi, and other handmade, pressed, and rolled sushi of all kinds. There's a glossary, too.

Welcome to Pizza Hut!

http://www.pizzahut.com/

Here's the famed online ordering device. You can order, but only in the Santa Cruz, California area (and they don't tell you that on the page.) Second prize: you can send e-mail to P.H. or the Santa Cruz operation, which put up the page.

The Wine Page

http://augustus.csscr.washington.edu:80/personal/bigstar-mosaic/wine.html

From Washington state comes this page, which includes *The Wine Net Newsletter*, Virtual Tasting Group, a FAQ on wine, and a tasting archive. The site also features a hypermedia link to several other wine home pages.

■ Fun and Games
See also Kids and Games

AGD Antics and Mayhem

http://reality.sgi.com/employees/dbg/antics/

The boys in the Advanced Graphics Division at SGI have been rather creative with their lunch hours. Between setting off carbon dioxide bombs, creating surgical tubing slingshots, and melting SPAM cans with magnifying lenses, it's a wonder they get any work done at all.

Alex Bennett's World

http://www.hooked.net/alex/

This is the home of Live 105, KITS in San Francisco. Bennett, an "attitude plus" kind of guy, has a morning drive-time show best described as "television radio." Hot buttons send you to live events and the program schedule, information about the show's crew and special guests, and a link to Chuck Farnham's Weird World, which features "The Virtual Library" because "some of life's weirdest things are a matter of public record." Download comedy and video clips of performers including Roseanne and Jim Carrey. If you like interactivity, you'll want to make a sound file of your orgasm and send it in for the "events" page (really). Alex says it best: "If you find us rude, then we have done our job."

April Fools on the Net

http://sunsite.unc.edu/dbarberi/
april-fools.html

The "fine online tradition" of celebrating April Fools' Day on the Net now has a Web site. Never let it be said that hoaxers don't have a sense of tradition. "Silly postings" are arranged by year, from 1988–1994; mysteriously enough, there's also a button for 1984, but then a three-year break with tradition. The jokes are all text files which have been sent around the world, presumably, as e-mail. Special bonus: the press release announcing that Microsoft acquired the Catholic Church. It wasn't an April Fools' item,

but as Webmaster David Barberi says, "I'm sure you'll agree it fits in very well with this archive!"

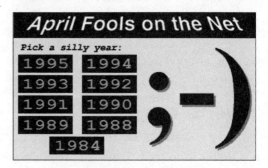

Ask Mr. Bad Advice

http://www.echonyc.com/~spingo/Mr.BA/

One of the jewels in the Spingo World Media crown, Mr. Bad Advice is one man's humble addition to the Web pages of the world that serve no good purpose whatsoever. E-mail delivers the pressing questions and Mr. B, well, he answers them:

"Dear Mr. Bad Advice,
How do we accomplish world peace?

Dear Fun-Killer,
Why should we? The newspapers would be empty and go out of business, and then I couldn't do the crossword puzzles.
Yrs,
Mr. B"

The Asylum

**http://www.galcit.caltech.edu/~ta/
cgi-bin/asylhome-ta**

In the finest tradition of the Internet's craziest
places, the Asylum is a great place to bounce
off the walls. Created by Joe "Madman Loose
in Disneyland" Cates and Aure "The Enforcer"
Prochazka, the Asylum features a host of fun
Web stuff. First check out the WWW Lite-Brite
art collection and create your own Lite-Brite
sculpture. Then there is the "Revolving Door,"
a great idea that allows people to create a self-
sustaining hotlist, where anyone can add or
delete a link at will. There is also the interactive
Asylum poll, sort of like Letterman's Top-10
list, where the readers can vote for their favorite items. Don't forget to visit the beloved "mascot," Wysiwyg, and be sure to share a little
twinkie with her while you're there.

David Gaxiola's Anime Resources
and Info

http://www.best.com/~gaxiola/Anime/

This MIT student is a total fan of Japanese animation, or anime. He's not alone: His meta-
page links to the anime favorites of his school
pals, along with Usenet, IRC (Internet Relay
Chat), ftp, and gopher sites about anime.
There's also a directory of anime fan clubs, CD
encyclopedias, "Anime's Most Disturbing
Home Videos," and more.

Funny Times

http://www.funnytimes.com/ft/

This funny monthly tabloid from Cleveland
now has a digital representation on the Web.
FT features a lot of political cartoons and syndicated columns by Dave Barry and other laugh-
mongers. The *FT* page offers weekly cartoon

updates and info on how to subscribe or order
sample copies.

[*] Games Domain

http://wcl-rs.bham.ac.uk/GamesDomain

A page dedicated to be the reference point for
all game-related information on the Net, the
Games Domain contains a variety of FAQs on
different games and various game "walk-
throughs" that will help you out of a tight spot
for a particular game. It also has downloadable
previews of different games. Additionally, there
are game-related ftp links, e-zines on games,
related commercial and personal game home
pages, and Usenet information. A large and
well put together site, the Domain has just
about anything an Internet gamer could want.
Be sure to check its list of the top 25 game
home pages on the Web.

Hyper-Weirdness by World Wide
Web

**http://www.physics.wisc.edu/~shalizi/
hyper-weird/**

Hyperlinks to as much kookiness as you can
stand from Cosma Rohilla Shalizi, who has cob-
bled together this gargantuan, freak-studded
compendium of Net oddities. Weird religion,
non-mainstream music, cyberpunk, paranormal
phenomena, and other kook sects are all represented here. While not exactly full of stuff you'd
want to use to demo the Internet to clients or
bosses, this Web site serves as a handy guide-
book to fringe culture in a big way.

Intrrr Nrrrd

http://www.etext.org/Zines/Intrrr.Nrrrd/
intrrr.html

Do you feel that the Net is here to foster ideas
and communication, despite the best efforts of
government, popular media, or established corporations to control, manipulate, or otherwise
bungle the Net's bandwidth? Well, then perhaps you'll like Intrrr Nrrrd. It's a combination
of punk do-it-yourself ideology, and how-to-use
technology to further freedom of expression
and thought for everyone. It carries artwork,
sound samples, and band reviews, and links to
other undergroundish pages.

Saving Souls with Punk Rawwwk Since August, 1994.

L.A. Cacophony Society

http://www.zpub.com/caco/caco-la.html

The Cacophony Society, which also has chap-
ters (and Web sites) in San Francisco, Seattle,
and Portland, is "a loose network of humans
devoted to the pursuit of experiences beyond
the mainstream…the bug under the rug, the ter-
mites in society's crutches, the bad egg at the
corporate picnic. You may already be a member!" A Rev. Al presides over the L.A. chapter,
and you can keep apprised of events at either
the "subscriber" or the "fanatic" level.

The Magic 8-Ball

http://www.resort.com/~banshee/Misc/
8ball/index.html

Remember those large plastic eight-balls with
the fortune that would drift to the top? You'd
shake it up, ask a question, and turn it over to
see the reply, like the mysterious "ask again
later." Here's the Web version. It's oddly reas-
suring to see how the eight-ball answers your
most soul-searching questions.

The MIT Hack Gallery

http://fishwrap.mit.edu/Hacks/
Gallery.html

This Web site is a wonderfully documented history of elaborate practical jokes committed by
MIT students. "Hack," in this case, "usually
refers to a clever, benign, and ethical prank
which is both challenging for the perpetrators
and amusing to the MIT community (and sometimes even the rest of the world!)." Check out
the Beer Shrine and the Biohazard Cafe for sure.

Plastic Princess Page

http://deepthought.armory.com/
~zenugirl/barbie.html

Of course Barbie has a Web page! Here's everything a collector and hobbyist could want: a
glossary of "Barbie collector-related terms," a
calendar of doll shows (starring vintage Barbies), links to Barbie periodicals and vendors,
and a photo gallery with downloadable images.
There's even a "Gossip and Rumor" page. You
can also buy and sell your Barbies here. And
don't forget to head to the other "Internet Barbie Resources" as well.

Sin City—The Web Home of Penn and Teller

http://www.sincity.com/

Paul Nielsen and friends have built a really entertaining site to the memorable anti-magicians who explain it all to you. Check out detailed floor plans and text descriptions of of Penn's new Vegas meta-house, The Slammer. Hear Teller speak! Order merchandise! Read smart-alecky remarks! Links to invaluable fortune cookie, Mofo, and food pages, too, if you want.

The Spider's Web Fun and Games Section

http://gagme.wwa.com/~boba/fun.html

The Spider's Web is an incredible collection of different "gimmicks, jokes, and other goodies," with over 2,000 links of various sorts. This Fun and Games page contains a plethora of entertainment from interactive games to just plain recreation and fun stuff. Like any good Web playground, the Spider's Web will keep you immersed and loving it for way too long!

The Straight Dope Archives

http://www.mcs.net/~krikket/html/tsd.html

Cecil Adams, who has his own newsgroup alt.fan.cecil-adams, presents his syndicated columns here for the edification of curious Internet folks. Ever wonder exactly what "keelhauling" is and where the term came from? So has someone else, and the ever-informative Cecil gets to the heart of things.

[*] Useless WWW Pages

http://www.primus.com:80/staff/paulp/useless.html

Useless WWW Pages is Paul Phillips's noteworthy collection of Web silliness and extemporanea, which naturally includes The Useless Statistics on the Useless Pages. Current links include Lyrics to 99 Bottles of Beer page, Stress Management Tape for Kids, and the World's Longest Domain Name Contest. Phillips was inspired by a Web page featuring a 30K file of a personal CD collection.

Video Arcade Preservation Society

http://www.vaps.org/

If stamps are too small and Barbies are too common, you might consider collecting coin-operated arcade videogames. VAPS is already five years old, and it boasts members who own multiple machines in most U.S. states. There are stats here on how many members own how many systems, and about the top 20 popular games collected (Tempest was number one when we looked). Check out the tips on how to buy from an operator or auction, an archive on the innards of game boards, and the home pages of serious arcade fans.

Wall O'Shame

http://www.milk.com/wall-o-shame/

Dan Bornstein has collected a really great page of bizarrely humorous true news stories which "characterize the erosion of our world," along with "tidbits that are just too nonlinear." You know the drill: bank robbers caught because they're handing out money to passers-by, the white supremacist who wants to change his name to "Hi Hitler"—that kind of thing. A great list of stories and news reports to make you wonder about the human condition in a big way. Be sure to stop in and sign the guest book.

Zarf's List of Interactive Games on the Web

http://www.cs.cmu.edu/afs/andrew/org/ kgb/www/zarf/games.html

A list of links to interactive games and toys available on the Web, Zarf's list will lead you to lots of fun. Games from Tic-Tac-Toe and Chess to the popular MUDs (multiuser dimensions or dungeons, depending on who you ask) and MUSHes to interactive fiction pages and other off-the-wall inventions are included. Definitely worth browsing through.

■ Government

The Capitol Steps

http://pfm.het.brown.edu/people/mende/ steps/

If satire inspired by current events is your thing, come hear The Capitol Steps. This group of Washington legislative staffers performs on National Public Radio and live at clubs. Their page features weekly news items they've fashioned into a songs, based on very familiar tunes, like the ode to Newt Gingrich's writing deal,

"Overpaid Writer" (from Lennon-McCartney's "Paperback Writer"). Then there's the plaintive "I've Grown Accustomed to This Base," referencing recent military installation closures, and "'Atsa Lawyer" ("That's Amore," what else?), on current House legal reform proposals. Download the song clips and link to related topical pages for more information on the subjects they skewer. Al Gore observes, "Some people in Washington are confused, but The Capitol Steps are not." And Newt Gingrich's assessment? "I think I like it better when you make fun of Clinton."

Charlotte's WWWeb

http://www.emf.net/~cr/homepage.html

This is a meta-page of resources and information from a third-party perspective, featuring the reminder that "our system of governance is an ongoing process, and never to be taken for granted." It includes links to pages like the current U.S. National Debt, the New World Order Page, and articles on government reform. There's a contest to pick the winning debt ceiling, a daily Treasury statement, and Will Rogers's line: "I don't make jokes. I just watch the government and report the facts."

Covert Action Quarterly

http://www.w2.com:80/docs2/c/ covertaction.html

This is a journal of investigative reporting "recommended by Noam Chomsky; targeted by the CIA." It includes extensive foreign coverage. Allen Ginsberg, Howard Zinn, and Dave Dellinger are contributing writers. You can read the table of contents of the current issue and you can also subscribe via this page.

The English Server: Government, Law, and Society

http://english.hss.cmu.edu/Govt/

This page is part of the English Server, a cooperative project at Carnegie-Mellon University which has been publishing a variety of texts on the Internet since 1990. This topic aims to integrate political contexts into common reading texts, and to show the impact of politics on daily life. Subjects covered include Congress, courts, economics, education, feminism and gender issues, history, international politics (with a Noam Chomsky archive), law and legislation, periodicals, political theory texts, and race relations writings. This is a very good place to get a broad overview of politics throughout history and globally, both theoretical and in the day-to-day lives of people around the world.

[*] FedWorld

http://www.fedworld.gov/

Created by the National Technical Information Service (NTIS), FedWorld was introduced in late 1992 to offer access to U.S. government information online. And we are talking about a lot of information! FedWorld provides access to more than 130 government dial-up bulletin boards, most of which are not available via the Internet. There are links to U.S. Government World Wide Web servers and other government resources, sorted into subject categories. In addition, FedWorld adds 700 new information listings each week. Don't let these numbers scare you; FedWorld is well organized and makes it easy to find any government information you seek.

National Archives Information Server

http://www.nara.gov/

Did you ever wonder who is keeping track of official government proceedings and historical documents? Well it's NARA—the National Archives and Records Administration—which preserves and makes available for research the records of the federal government from its beginnings in 1774. We're talking treaties, contracts, journals, inventories, maps, photographs, and films by the carload. On NARA's Web page you can find information on the Federal Records Centers, the Presidential Libraries, the Regional Archives, Washington D.C. area sites, NARA's publications, papers, grants, and more. Also be sure to take a look at the genealogy holdings: They even have lists of the micro-fiches of the U.S.'s major immigration centers.

The Political Participation Project Home Page

http://www.ai.mit.edu:80/projects/ppp/home.html

Developed by MIT's Artificial Intelligence Lab in conjunction with Harvard's Kennedy School of Government, this is a nonpartisan research program about global political activism and Internet resources on that subject. This site is a very good overview of political pages on the Net (ftp and gopher sites, too). It also has a hotlink to a directory of grassroots organizations from ACT UP to the World Federalist Association.

Political Science Resources

http://www.keele.ac.uk/depts/po/psr.htm

Here is a large offering of topics and categories for the politically-minded. Maintained by Richard Kimber in the U.K., this page contains information on a list of government-maintained Web pages, constitutions, treaties, and official declarations, elections and electoral systems, political parties, interest groups and other political movements, political thought, and international relations. It provides links to major international organizations such as the EU, NATO, and the UN, collections of social, and economic and other data, journals, magazines, newspapers, and useful politics servers.

STAT-USA

http://www.stat-usa.gov/stat-usa.html

An amazing governmental resource, STAT-USA is part of the Economics and Statistics Administration of the U.S. Department of Commerce. It provides economic, business, social, and environmental program data produced by more than 50 federal sources. Here, you can access four major databases: the Trade Data Bank, comprising more than 160,000 documents; the Economic, Social, and Environmental Data Bank, on U.S. socioeconomic programs and trends; a database on economic trends, education, health issues, criminal justice, and the environment.

There's also an Economic Bulletin Board, via Telnet, which provides government-sponsored business data. A huge compendium of accessible information, these databases are valuable conduit of info from the U.S. government back to us taxpayers. We've paid for it—let's use it!

Thomas: Legislative Information on the Internet

http://thomas.loc.gov/

A service of the U.S. Congress through its library, this site includes full text of legislation, full text of the congressional record, information on how U.S. laws are made, and house gopher and e-mail addresses. You can also access the C-SPAN (Cable-Satellite Public Affairs Network) gopher, which provides program schedules, press releases, and Congressional election results. This is a great tool for perusing the American ideal of democratic rule and involvement in the political process.

U.S. Bureau of the Census

http://www.census.gov/

The Census Bureau collects data about the people and economy of the United States and produces a wide variety of statistical data, including printed reports and briefs. The page also contains original radio broadcasts created by the Bureau to inform the public of its findings, graphics from censuses, and a fascinating list of publications on the different aspects of American culture. All are available for downloading in Postscript directly to your computer.

U.S. Department of Education

http://www.ed.gov/index.html

This page makes us feel like our tax dollars are well spent in this case. Here you'll find a number of resources, including the DOE's mission statements and national education goals, a Teacher's and a Researcher's Guide to the department and its staff and facilities, and special projects such as GOALS 2000. There's a link to the main gopher server, newsletters, press releases, funding opportunities, and hypertext versions of recent publications. While you're here, be sure to take a look at the *Community Update* newsletter, which serves school and community organizations involved in grassroots efforts to address critical issues in school reform. Like we said, money well spent.

U.S. House of Representatives Home Page

http://www.house.gov/

The House page provides public access to legislative information as well as information about members, committees, and organizations of the House and other government information resources. There's information on the legislative process, legislative schedules, a Who's Who list of House members's names and contact information, committees, and House leadership. There are details about visiting the House, and links on how to improve the government via citizen input, among other things. More and more of them have e-mail access, too.

Welcome to the White House

http://www.whitehouse.gov/

This is the President's page, an "Interactive Citizen's Handbook," with greetings from the president and vice president, information on the Executive Branch, the First Family (including Socks), tours of the White House, publications, comments, and a guest book for you to sign. Get access to daily press releases from the White House, presidential speeches, information on the U.S. budget or the National Information Infrastructure, major international treaties, and historical documents.

■ Health and Medicine

AIDS Resource List

http://www.teleport.com/~celinec/ aids.shtml

AIDS information has a great presence on the Net. Here is an ever-growing list of links of individual pages, search engines, government reports and resources, and publications. It includes links to the CDC (Center for Disease Control) WHO (World Health Organization), Usenet groups, as well as individual pages and safe sex information.

Alternative Medicine Homepage

http://www.pitt.edu/~cbw/altm.html

Charles Wessel has built a meta-page covering all kinds of information on "unorthodox, unproven, innovative" health treatments. There are links to various studies supporting alternative healing practices, jumps to many pages on acupuncture, homeopathy, chiropractic, and herbal treatments. Look for a list of paper newsletters, mailing lists and newsgroups you can subscribe to, and a FAQ directory. This is a great starting point.

The Good Health Web

http://www.social.com/health/index.html

A compilation of daily health newsbits, a library of articles on health issues, and links to relevant newsgroups (alt.hypnosis, sci.med.nutrition, misc.health.diabetes). There's a page of FAQs, e-mail lists, and discussion areas.

HyperDOC: National Library of Medicine

http://www.nlm.nih.gov/

The NLM houses a huge collection of materials on the history of medicine. These include online exhibitions, downloadable images, detailed instructions on how to search, and a full description of the archives. There's even a suggestion box.

The Medical Education Page

http://www.primenet.com/~gwa/med.ed/

Compiled by medical student and "net.addict" Greg Allen, this page links to newsgroups and discussion lists, FAQs, and a long list of indexes, learning tools (online texts), reference guides to Medline and the National Library of Medicine, as well as a long list of links to hospitals and medical schools. Don't miss the link to the Whole Brain Atlas, a pro-doctor article by columnist Mike Royko, and a medical school ratings list.

Medical Matrix: Guide to Internet Medical Resources

http://www.kumc.edu:80/mmatrix/

This meta-list is geared to medical professionals interested in finding information on the Internet. There are links to pages containing information categorized by disease, by medical specialty, and clinical medicine. You can also link to health care policy information, clinical practice issues, resources for allied health care workers, patient education, medical images, and multimedia sites. The page was created by the Internet Working Group of the American Medical Informatics Association.

National Health Information Center

http://nhic-nt.health.org/

NHIC offers referrals to health information and agencies across the U.S. Link to a huge list of toll-free numbers, agencies, and associations for virtually every ailment. The page also offers keyword searches of the Health Information Resource Database with its 1100 entries for organizations and agencies, publication lists and contact information. Go from here to the U.S. Department of Health and Human Services (HHS) or the Public Health Service.

National Institutes of Health

http://www.nih.gov/

The National Institutes of Health (NIH) home page, maintained by the Division of Computer Research and Technology, contains a great deal of information for the general public on NIH funding and research. Of special interest to biologists, a section of the page offers biomedical information relating to health issues, clinical protocols, and molecular biology.

OncoLink

http://cancer.med.upenn.edu/

This page, from the University of Pennsylvania, provides an immense amount of information about cancer. There are links for specific diseases and specialties, for psychosocial support and cancer organizations, clinical trial news, book reviews, and a rotating gallery of pictures from pediatric cancer patients. An especially helpful area is a Q&A section on billing information, where OncoLink professionals demystify and offer strategies for dealing with insurance bills and lingo for laypeople.

The University of Pennsylvania Cancer Resource

Personal Health and Fitness Resources on the Net

http://none.coolware.com/health/ health.html

Here are links to pages with information on preventive health, Oncolink ("one-stop shopping for people concerned about cancer"), and the relationship between computers and health. There are FAQs about topics ranging from communicable diseases to stretching and flexibility to tinnitus and smoking.

Stress Space on the Web

http://www.foobar.co.uk/users/umba/
stress/#talk3

"Warm up and chill out" is the advice you'll
find on this page about stress—the symptoms of
which we're all familiar with. There are articles,
exercises, and lots of advice about managing
stress in our lives. Take that self-assessment
quiz now and start to work on it!

The Virtual Hospital

http://indy.radiology.uiowa.edu/
VirtualHospital.html

Created by the University of Iowa Radiology
Department, VH is a medical multimedia database stored on computers and available for
access 24 hours a day. It offers patient support
and "distance learning" to practicing physicians.
Information can be used to answer patient care
questions or for continuing medical education
credits. You'll see multimedia textbooks on a
variety of materials that are searchable, with
the ability to display high-resolution images.
Information is split between data for health
care providers and data for patients.

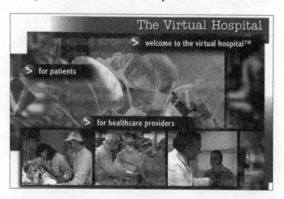

Women's Health Resources on the Internet

http://asa.ugl.lib.umich.edu:80/chdocs/
womenhealth/toc.html

Two University of Michigan library students
have created a page of links to Net resources
including gopher sites and Usenet groups on
the emotional, physical, and sexual aspects of
women's health. This is a good starting point
for topics like breast cancer.

■ History

See also Education, Reference and
Information

[*] American Memory

http://rs6.loc.gov/

This is a project of the Library of Congress for
its "National Digital Library." AM lists an
impressive list of manuscripts and documents,
photos and sound or film clips by title and
topic. This site is a rich stew featuring very early
motion pictures (1897–1916); life history manuscripts from the Federal Writers' Folklore
Project, 1935–1939; early (1897–1916) motion
pictures; and color photos from the Farm Security Administration, 1938–1944.

The Historical Text Archive

**http://www.msstate.edu/Archives/
History/index.html**

Based at Mississippi State University, this page
supports the oldest ftp site geared to historians.
Text files of documents and scholarly papers
are here, along with GIF/JPEG image files, various scholarship resources, database and library
search programs, diaries, and bibliographies.
Click on icons for resources covering history in
Canada, Africa, Asia, Mexico and Latin America, and the U.S. Be sure to check out the pointers to other historical archives at http://
www.msstate.edu/Archives/History/more.html.

The History Network Source

**http://history.cc.ukans.edu/history/
hnsource_main.html**

This is a University of Kansas index to historical databases, a global news site, and an electronic full-text library. Search for historical
reference and database information by epoch
(antiquity to twentieth century), country
(within Europe, the Americas, Asia, Africa,
Australia, and the Pacific) or by information
type (Dewey Decimal, subtopics, and research
location).

History of Science, Technology, and Medicine

**http://www.asap.unimelb.edu.au/hstm/
hstm_ove.htm**

Created by Tim Sherratt at Australian National
University, this handy page is now housed at
the WWW Virtual Library. A great overview of
a huge subject area, it links you to general history of science collections and bibliographies to
get started. It also provides links to special collections and topics within the history of science,
including astronomy, computers and informa-

tion processing, physics, medicine, and more.
You'll find a biographical dictionary, links to science museums and exhibits, electronic journals
and publications, and e-mail discussion lists and
newsgroups.

Selections from the African-American Mosaic

**http://lcweb.loc.gov/exhibits/
African.American/intro.html**

This is a special library-wide research project of
the Library of Congress's Study of Black History and Culture. Rich information is within
each link, which denotes a period: colonization,
abolition, migrations, and the WPA (Work
Projects Administration). Within each section,
you can view photos, historical summary information, and go to referenced documents.

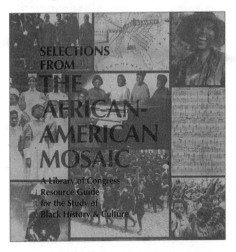

Usenet Alternate History List

**http://thule.mt.cs.cmu.edu:8001/
sf-clearing-house/bibliographies/
alternatehistories/**

As the name suggests, this page links to an
impressive two-year-old Usenet annotated list

of essays, stories and novels on "allohistory," the study of alternative history themes. Two of the most common are "What if the Nazis won World War II?" and "What if the South won the Civil War?" These speculative queries are also known as "what-ifs" or "uchronias."

■ The Internet

See also **Computing**

The Awesome List

http://www.clark.net/pub/journalism/awesome.html

Compiled by well-known Internet trainer John S. Makulowich, the Awesome List is his view of scores of sites of interest on the Net. (He suggests that the lists are most useful to trainers, journalists, and speakers.) A straightforward alphabetical listing links to sites of all different kinds, this is a great place to start a tour through Cyberspace proper (versus Webspace only, that is). Here you will find places like Comet/Jupiter Impact, the Electronic Cafe, gopher sites, mailing lists, NSFNet Backbone statistics, the Games Domain, and much, much more. Searchable via Lycos, too.

CharmNet

http://www.charm.net/

Deceptively small on its surface, CharmNet holds many precious treasures for those who are willing to dig just a little. The areas of special interest for those looking for more info on the Net are the Big Trees section, which contains a variety of Web links; the Learning section, with its array of tutorials, books and hints on how to get around the Net; the Deep Wells section, a list of monster ftp sites for all types of platforms; Search, with a variety of search engines available; Technophile, offering new

and hot sites on the Net; and the Connect section, with its Personal IP page, where there's a load of information on TCP/IP, PPP, and SLIP connections. Many new gems to be found here!

[*] CyberWire Dispatch

http://cyberwerks.com:70/1/cyberwire

Brock Meeks, a journalist for *Communications Daily*, *Wired*, and other publications, maintains a page he describes as a "take-no-prisoners news service that concentrates on issues related to Cyberspace." He covers technology policy, the telecommunications industry, and the politics of the Internet in an irreverent and savvy style. There's a link to another page he maintains with John Makulowich (see other Makulowich pages below), "Scoop d'Jour," with late-breaking newsbits for others to pursue. You can join his e-mail dispatch list here.

[*] EFF's Extended Guide to the Internet

http://www.eff.org/papers/eegtti/eeg_toc.html

Here's the table of contents for a project created by the Electronic Frontier Foundation in conjunction with Apple. There are statewide listings of public access Internet providers; e-mail resources and detailed sections on Archie, Usenet, Telnet, ftp, WAIS, and gophers, IRC, MUDs; and a very good glossary.

Gopher Jewels

http://galaxy.einet.net/GJ/index.html

Sponsored by EINet, this is a Web page cataloging hundreds of the best gopher sites by category. Before the onslaught of the Web, gopher was often the easiest and quickest way of accessing and indexing the Net's vast information repositories. Created and maintained by David Riggins of the Texas Department of Commerce, the page offers over 2,300 pointers to information by category, the ability to (jughead) search all menus in Gopher Jewels, and an archive of the Gopher Jewels mailing list, as well as tips, help, and other gopher-related information.

Internet Resources

http://www.eit.com/web/netservices.html

This page, from Enterprise Integration Technologies, is a guide to the different services available on the Net organized by both the type of information provider and subject category. It includes links to gopher sites, veronica (a method of searching gopher space), ftp, Telnet, music and image files, multimedia, various news, and educational and governmental services, a number of searchable indices and reference works, and other miscellaneous tools and resources. Easy to read with a small summary by each type of serivce, this page is good for browsing through a number of different links to Internet information.

The Internet Society

http://info.isoc.org/

The Internet Society is the international organization for global cooperation and coordination of the Internet and its technologies and applications. The Society's Web page includes information on the structure and activities of the Society, its publications, and ongoing develop-ment and operations around the world—including regional and national developments, Internet technologies, applications, issues, user communities, conferences, and publications. While visiting, take a quick look at the Global Connectivity Map to see who's on the Net or not, around the world.

An Introduction to Usenet News

http://ocf.berkeley.edu:80/help/usenet/ trnint-3.3.html

This is a scholarly how-to resource on Usenet, including a detailed tutorial. Subscribing, cross-posting, using signature files, guidelines for saving and canceling articles, beginning new discussions, and screening articles are among the many helpful topics that are covered here.

John December's Internet Web Text

http://www.rpi.edu/Internet/Guides/ decemj/text.html

Another well-known Net resource is John December's Internet Text. It's an ideal place to begin exploring the Net, starting with a number of well-written tutorials and guides to using the Net, and proceeding to lists of information sources and Internet tools, and then to a variety of gopher, Hytelnet and WWW-based resources and exhibits. Concise and well-written, yet very comprehensive, this list has become one of the standard references for exploring the Net.

Patrick Crispen's Internet Roadmap

http://www.brandonu.ca/~ennsnr/
Resources/Roadmap/Welcome.html

Still wish you had a map to guide you through the Net? Well, Patrick Crispen's Internet Roadmap may be just for you. Patrick's course is an entertaining, step-by-step tutorial on how to use and navigate the Internet. Originally distributed as a listserv mailing list, and then HTML-ized by Neil Enns, the roadmap course teaches the basic skills that you need to travel on the Net, and also tells you whom you can turn to for help if you ever get lost. Lessons in the workshop cover the subjects e-mail, listservs, Internet connectivity, the ever-infamous netiquette, Usenet news, spamming and Internet security, using Telnet to connect to remote sites, and using ftp, archie, gopher, veronica, and, of course, the World Wide Web. The workshop even includes guest lectures and topics such as advertising on the Internet.

Scott Yanoff's Special Internet Connections

http://www.uwm.edu/Mirror/
inet.services.html

Started in fall 1991 as a short personal list, Scott Yanoff's list has grown both in size as well as notoriety, and is now very widely distributed. A large subject-oriented guide, it covers a wide range of topics from argiculture and art to employment, food, law, literature, movies, religion, software, sports, travel, weather, and a whole lot more. While large in breadth, the list is easy to look through and you'll have no trouble finding the resources you are interested in. Often a reference point for navigating the Net, this list will provide you with many hours of cruising pleasure.

USENET FAQs

http://www.cis.ohio-state.edu/hypertext/
faq/usenet/top.html

What listing on the Internet could really be complete without something on Usenet news? This page contains a list of all Usenet FAQs (frequently asked questions) found in the news.answers group, alphabetized by topic. If you haven't seen this yet, you'll find an amazing collection of technical, professional, and folk knowledge gathered via FAQs, the consummate collection of "all-you-ever wanted-to-know-but-were-afraid-to-ask" Q&As. Browsing through this list illustrates the Net's strength: bringing together all kinds of people from all over the world to discuss, ask, and answer questions on just about every topic under the sun.

■ Kids and Games

See also Fun and Games, Education

Children's Literature Web Guide

http://www.ucalgary.ca/~dkbrown/
index.html

This site offers a helpful set of links, including lists of children's book award winners and best-sellers, as well as author, publisher, and book-seller information on kids' titles. Also available are links to discussion groups and resources for teachers and storytellers. You can go from here to resources including movies and TV shows based on children's books, and children's writings and drawings.

Classroom Internet Server Cookbook

http://web66.coled.umn.edu/Cookbook/contents.html

The University of Minnesota offers this how-to treat: how to create pages, build a mail, ftp, or Web server in the classroom, and what "utensils" you'll need. Excellent for teachers.

Kids Web

http://www.npac.syr.edu:80/textbook/kidsweb/

Very simply a Web-wide digital library for school kids, this page offers a simple point-and-click Web interface to Web sites on the arts, sciences, computers, government, history, literature, math, music, sports, and weather. Turn the kids loose to have fun for hours.

Riddle du Jour

http://www.new3.com/riddle/

"While I was walking down the lane,/From the dead the living came,/Six there were, seven to be,/Solve this riddle and I'll set you free." If you like untangling this kind of puzzler, you're bound to win the daily prize and join The Sphinx's Hall of Fame.

■ Language

See also **Education**

American Dialect Society

http://www.msstate.edu/Archives/ADS/

Natalie Maynor manages the ADS page, which provides information on this 100+ year-old association devoted to the study of English in North America. E-mail lists, publications, meetings, and news from ADS are here, along with ftp and gopher sites.

[*] The Human-Languages Page

http://www.willamette.edu/~tjones/Language-Page.html

Tyler Jones of Willamette University has compiled a terrific page of language resources from around the world. Ongoing projects of his include locating copyright-free translating dictionaries to put on the page, and the translation of all information into multiple languages. There are links to many ftp, gopher, and Web resources, and sites for languages from Aboriginal to Welsh. Also includes links to linguistics labs, commercial sites for linguistic software, books and archives, and a host of multilingual resources. Check out the Glossary of Computer Terms in Vietnamese, Tibetan Tools for Windows, or the Rasta/Patois Dictionary.

Learning Japanese on the Internet

http://www.twics.com/~kenbutler/butlerconsulting.html

Ken Butler, a business consultant living in Tokyo, has put together a ten-unit "cybertutorial" for learning Japanese. You can also order a CD-ROM version, and be sure to check out "Ten Differences between Japanese and English That Make Japanese an Easy Language to Learn."

Linguistics Links

http://www.us.itd.umich.edu/~clunis/ linguistics.html

Kevin McGowan offers hot buttons to tutorials and language-learning pages for Gaelic, Serbian, Slovak, Tagalog, Arabic, French, and Hindi. There are also links to phonetics resources and various e-mail lists for linguists. For tutorials, go to Foreign Languages for Travellers. There are sound files included for trilingual (English, German, and French) training in a variety of languages.

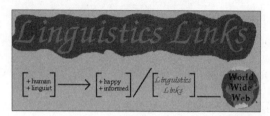

[*] Twists, Slugs, and Roscoes: A Glossary of Hardboiled Slang

http://www.io.org/~buff/slang.html

We couldn't resist William Denton's all-text dictionary of tough-guy talk, which he culled from the works of Raymond Chandler, Dashiell Hammett, David Goodis, and Mickey Spillane. The intriguing list references specific uses he found in books identified by title. What is "tooting the wrong ringer"? ("Asking the wrong guy," of course.) Then there's "grab a little air" ("put your hands up"). Sorry, not responsible for crimes committed after you've absorbed the lingo.

■ Law

LawInfo Legal Referral Service

http://www.lawinfo.com/~netlaw/index.htm

LawInfo is a U.S.-based service and directory offering legal advice (downloadable articles) and referral information for legal support services and individual attorneys. There's an employment center and self-help legal information, too.

Law Marks

http://www.iwc.com/entropy/marks/ bkmrkjsm.html

A very handy *uber*-page that can take you to scores of Web sites including legal directories, reference sources, federal documents, court opinions, law libraries, journals, law schools, and more. The "human rights/civil liberties" button is excellent.

LawTalk

http://www.law.indiana.edu:80/law/ lawtalk.html

This page from the Indiana University Law School contains lectures on various topics: amendments to the U.S. Constitution, business and personal finance law, civil law, criminal law, and others. All are sound files that are about 5MB each; you'll need a sound player to listen to them. LawTalk is available on the Sun, NeXT, Windows, and Mac platforms.

■ Literature

British Poetry 1780-1910: Hypertext Archive of Scholary Editions

http://www.lib.virginia.edu/etext/britpo/britpo.html

From several universities come selected texts including ones by Coleridge, Lewis Carroll, Rossetti, Tennyson, Keats, Shelley, Wilde, and Wordsworth. You'll find links to earlier periods of British poets (Marvell, Milton, Spenser) and the University of Virginia's huge English poetry database, A.D. 600–1500, which is a full text database of thousands of poems.

Electronic Archives Home Page

http://www.georgetown.edu:80/tamlit/tamlit-home.html

Essays, syllabi, and bibliographies about teaching a wide range of American literature topics and areas are featured in this project sponsored by Georgetown University and publisher D.C. Heath. Literature and culture studies are covered; e-mail lists, discussion groups, and online journals are here, as well as pointers to campus servers in American Literature and American Studies.

Internet Poetry Archive Home Page

http://sunsite.unc.edu/dykki/poetry/

A project of the University of North Carolina, this ongoing page will feature selected poems from living poets around the world. The first selections are from Czeslaw Milosz and Seamus Heaney. Audio clips will be another feature on this new page. It was created and is edited by Paul Jones at UNC.

Online Books Page

http://www.cs.cmu.edu/Web/books.html

This page indexes many online books, journals, bibliographies, and catalogs. It's linked to Banned Books Online. You can search by author, title, new listings, or some subject listings. It points to several common repositories of books and other documents.

The Professor's Guilt List

http://www.next.com/~bong/books/GuiltList.html

We may never know the name of the San Jose State University prof who turned out this list of the books graduating English majors are expected to know. It's long, and you're bound to feel like a slacker. Bruce (our page creator) tells us he gave up and took the engineering route instead. Naturally enough, you can link to Bruce's own reading page, which isn't half bad for an engineer. Just a few links here, but the list is great for information and comparison.

Project Gutenberg

http://jg.cso.uiuc.edu/PG/welcome.html

"Fine literature digitally republished" is the motto of this page, a huge alpha listing by title and author of classical fiction, essays, and other writings available online. You can find hundreds of classics by Twain, Wharton, Thoreau, Hawthorne, James, Maugham, and many other European and American writers. The list indicates file sizes and instructions for downloading the entire text.

Shakespeare Web

http://www.shakespeare.com/

This young site "aims to provide a one-stop shopping center for all your bard-related desires." There's a link to "today in Shakespeare History," Shakespeare quotation contests, queries from Web-surfers, a FAQ list, and links to let you search the complete works of Shakespeare.

The Shiki Internet Haiku Salon

http://mikan.cc.matsuyama-u.ac.jp/ ~shiki/

This is Masaoka ("Kim") Shiki's home page about the practice and history of haiku, including an e-mail list to discuss and share poems with him. This page supplies links to several other poetry and literature pages Kim likes.

■ Museums

See also Art

ExploraNet

http://www.exploratorium.edu/

San Francisco's Exploratorium science museum was a pioneer in the analog world, and its virtual presence is also groundbreaking. Besides all the standard museum information—hours, cost, list of exhibits, and schedule of events—there's a digital image library of some favorite exhibits and a library of sounds from Exploratorium demos and experiments. ("Click here to hear the doppler effect. Volvo blowing horn at 30 miles per hour.") Check out the links to Exploratorium artists-in-residence pieces, which include cool phenomena like plasma sculpture, LED images, wave-activated acoustics, the fluvial storm globe, and a six-foot vortex.

The Field Museum of Natural History Server

http://www.bvis.uic.edu/museum/

Chicago's famous museum features "DNA to Dinosaurs," an interactive Web tour of a popular exhibit. You can study a host of images and specimens from the museum collection, or discover a beautiful collection of Javanese masks.

Museums, Exhibits, and Gardens

http://white.nosc.mil/museum.html

The Webmaster of the Planet Earth Home Page has created a reference page of museum and gallery servers, gardens, selected exhibits, and some museums around the world. Go to the Australian botanical gardens, see a twelfth-century map of the Kremlin, take in an Ansel Adams exhibit, or head for the Whitney Museum of Art. It's doubtless this page will grow as more institutions come online.

Natural History Museum of Los Angeles County

http://cwis.usc.edu:80/lacmnh/default.html

This Web site describes the holdings and programs of the Los Angeles County Museum of Natural History. There's a virtual tour you can take (the floor-by-floor maps are hotlinks to specific exhibit information), a guide to museum services, information on museum travel programs, and mail-order gifts. Plus, a bonus dinosaur JPEG because you just couldn't resist hitting the "Here Abide Monsters" hotlink.

Rome Reborn: The Vatican Library and Renaissance Culture

http://sunsite.unc.edu/expo/vatican.exhibit/Vatican.exhibit.html

An exhibit at the Library of Congress presents some 200 of the Vatican library's most precious manuscripts, books, and maps—many of which played a key role in the humanist recovery of the classical heritage of Greece and Rome. The exhibition presents the untold story of the Vatican library as the intellectual driving force behind the emergence of Rome as a political and scholarly superpower during the Renaissance. The exhibit is divided into nine sections: The Vatican Library, Archaeology, Humanism, Mathematics, Music, Medicine and Biology, Nature Described, A Wider World I: How the Orient Came to Rome, and A Wider World II: How Rome Went

to China. Each section contains exhibit text and separate image files for each object.

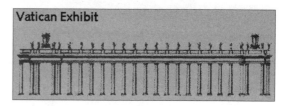
Vatican Exhibit

Smithsonian Institution

http://www.si.edu/

The mother of all museums, at least in the U.S., has a meta-page containing links to its many museum, research, and archival offshoots. This makes the What's New button at the top of the page especially helpful. Here you'll find links to museums in the SI family including the National Air and Space Museum, the Natural History Museum, the National Museum of the American Indian, the Freer Gallery of Art, the Center for Earth and Planetary Studies, and the Harvard-Smithsonian Center for Astrophysics.

Welcome to the Natural History Museum's WWW Server

http://www.nhm.ac.uk/

Located in London, this museum page features descriptions of the exhibits and public programs. There's also a handsome photo-essay about the scientific research and curatorial work that goes on behind the scenes. And for further research, there are hotlinks to the museum's gopher server and huge library catalog.

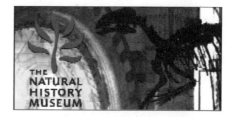
THE NATURAL HISTORY MUSEUM

■ Music

BluesNet Home Page

http://dragon.acadiau.ca/~rob/blues/

This is a scholarly page maintained by Rob Hutten. There are brief bios of some blues greats (Albert King, Howlin' Wolf), and a picture page. The best part is "Blues Mentors." Hutten writes, "These people are willing to answer your every question about their area of blues expertise." Included are artist name, name of mentor, and the e-mail address. Have a question about Bobby Blue Bland or T-Bone Walker? How about gospel groups or jug band performers? These folks are just an e-mail away.

[*] CDNow! The Internet Music Store

http://cdnow.com/

This is the most fun way to shop on the Net for music of every persuasion. CDNow lists over 100,000 CDs, tapes, and videos. It's fun to browse and easy to buy, especially if you have a forms-based browser. Hot buttons take you to pop, and classical music listings, music magazines, and your current account information. (Pop, incidentally, covers everything that's not classical: C&W, R&B, klezmer—you name it.) There's a Telnet address, too.

Country Music

http://galaxy.einet.net/EINet/staff/
wayne/country/country.html

Wayne Allen has put together a great overview, including issues of magazines like *Twangin'* and

links to the 100 most popular country and Western songs, the Country Music Fan Page, concert reviews, and clips from featured artists. Fan club listings are here, too.

Definitive Anime Song Archive Store

http://chatlink.com/~khollis/welcome.cgi

If you want to know more about Japanese pop music, Ken Hollis has made this site for you. There are lengthy lists of songs by artists and the text of the songs.

[*] Dotcom

http://ringo.sfc.keio.ac.jp/~yasaka/
dotcom/dotcom.html

This Web site emulates the Roland TR-909 drum machine, popular among dance-music practioners the world over. Users set the BPM (beats per minute) and enter a drum pattern and bassline via a grid of check boxes and radio buttons. Dotcom then serves up a rhythm loop that's clickably downloadable in AIFF, WAV, or mulaw sound formats, in either 8 bit or CD-quality 16 bit! If you're proud of your creation, you can add your pattern to the "List of Saved Sounds," for the edification of future visitors.

FolkBook: An Online Acoustic Music Establishment

http://web.cgrg.ohio-state.edu/folkbook/

Whether you prefer the classics or contemporary artists, FolkBook can link you there. Concert info, record labels, coffeehouses and clubs, radio stations, regional, and calendar information are on these pages. The Resource Database has detailed info on folk publications, radio and TV slots, and clubs. Newsgroups and e-mail lists are here by area of interest, and there's a great reference page: Acoustic Music on the Web. Stephen Spencer at Ohio State University maintains FolkBook.

[*] Internet Underground Music Archive

http://www.iuma.com/

IUMA, "the first free hi-fi music archive," is a well-designed, stylish, and appealing site, sporting some of the best graphics and hot buttons we've seen. This is the place to download music clips or browse the newest list of independent bands. Go to Fresh Catches to download stereo or mono samples of new cuts by new groups. Also download the MPEG CD sound utility to help you launch and hear clips quickly through your browser. There are links to music e-zines, and of course you can choose between the "heavy graphics" and "dull text" versions of the page.

The Jazz Photography of Ray Avery

http://bookweb.cwis.uci.edu:8042/Jazz/jazz.html

An exhibit of text and Avery's photographs of performers at jazz clubs and festivals in Los Angeles and the South dating from the 1950s. You'll find black-and-white JPEG files which you can download. An index of musicians and a bibliography are also available.

Music Resources on the Internet

http://www.music.indiana.edu:80/misc/music_resources.html

This is an immense page compiled by the Indiana University School of Music. It consists only of links (but hundreds of them!) covering all musical styles and artists, as well as meta-pages created by individuals and fan clubs. There's a helpful index at the top which can send you to sites maintained by users. The page has links to gopher, Telnet, and ftp. The largest category by far is "maintained by users," which includes home pages and others from Abba to ZZ Top. But you'll also find Ali Akbar Khan, Gustav Mahler, the Kronos Quartet, and Robert Johnson here, too.

[*] OLGA (On-Line Guitar Archive)

http://www.umn.edu/nlhome/m161/schn0170/olga.html

OLGA is the Web front door to a worldwide network of ftp sites containing guitar tablature for all kinds of songs, duly transcribed by Internet denizens and frequenters of various guitar-centric Usenet newsgroups. Alternative and Top 40 music are the best-represented styles. OLGA is a great resource for both the beginning guitar player and people like me, who are too lazy to figure out notes and chords for themselves.

The Ultimate Band List

http://american.recordings.com/
wwwofmusic/ubl.html

This is the Web's largest interactive list of music links, and only on the Net could it exist. Click on a genre, search by artist, and you'll find every citation of a Net resource on your performer(s). You'll find gopher sites, newsgroups, FAQs, lyrics files, digitized songs, e-mail lists, Web pages, and related links. There's also a "hits" list, which tells you the bands/groups that have had the most Web accesses. (Lately, Pearl Jam, Nirvana, Pink Floyd, Aerosmith, REM, Tori Amos, Nine Inch Nails—and the Beatles!—top the list.) And UBL boasts 3,044 links for 1,107 performers, including 911 Web pages.

Welcome to the World of Classical Music

http://classicalmus.com/

This page from Catalyst Records contains extensive video and audio clips complete with technical instructions for downloading them, a Beginner's Guide to Classical Music (with an excellent timeline, glossary, and chronological guide), as well as a large catalog of CDs.

■ News and Media

The Daily News—Free Internet Sources

http://www.helsinki.fi/~lsaarine/
news.html

One of the best overall listings of news sources available on the Web, the Daily News is Sam Sternberg's catalog of those sites on the Internet that provide significant news daily without charge. It contains a healthy listing of the commercial news services that are publishing on the Web, some good journalism links such as John December's Communication List and The Journalism List by John Makulowich, and other news-oriented links. This is a great example of how one person can gather diverse resources on the Web into one collection.

The Electronic Telegraph

http://www.telegraph.co.uk/

The online version of the *London Daily Telegraph* is nicely laid out with hot buttons taking you to the front page, city and world news, sports, features—even e-mail to the editor. It's free, but you register once to receive a PIN (personal identification number), which you use for subsequent access.

[*] FEED

http://www.emedia.net/feed/

Feed is a beautiful 'zine: nonintrusive, distinctive design; clear, original writing and thinking. *Feed* is what the Web can be when it really tries. It features threaded discussion and departments including Beltway Watch, Digital Thinking, and Technopolitics, along with book, music, film, and lowbrow culture reviews. Check out

Jaron Lanier's critique of Newt Gingrich's use of the word "virtual."

[*] HotWIRED

http://www.hotwired.com/

You can't talk about 'zines on the Web and not talk about *HotWIRED*. This online spinoff of *Wired* magazine has forged a new style and perspective. Topics covered include media, technology and communication, new consumer toys, and netsurfing; there are personal essays and articles; live chat and threaded discussion areas; an art section containing QuickTime clips, images, music, and more.

The Journalist's Toolbox

http://studentpress.journ.umn.edu/ toolbox/journ.html

Hot buttons link you to John Makulowich's journalism list; there are also Web and gopher pointers to online school papers and academic programs. And there's a pointer to excellent Internet searching tools any journalist would want to keep handy.

[*] The Mercury Center Web

http://www.sjmercury.com/main.htm

Based on the *San Jose Mercury News*, this is one of the best Web papers, offering continually updated news coverage, the complete text of each day's final edition, and classified ads. One of the most interesting features is NewsHound, a news-filtering service that scans about 2,000 daily articles for keywords you have specified, and mails them to you. (NewsHound is a paid subscription service.) It's great for anyone following a particular topic, product, or service.

[*] The Nando Times

http://www.nando.net/newsroom/nt/ nation.html

The Raleigh, North Carolina *News and Observer* has created a multilayered Web site with a wide variety of newsworthy and entertaining information about North Carolina as well as a daily (national and world) news page. Click on the headlines to read the stories.

Pathfinder

http://www.pathfinder.com/

This is the meta-magazine page for Time, Inc. There are links to their entire family publications, including *Time, Money, Vibe, Entertainment Weekly, Sports Illustrated*, and *People*. It's a great example of linking information between sources and offering virtual updates and variations of the paper editions. You can find reviews and cross-publication information, post on discussion boards, and search for topics.

Spunk Press

http://www.cwi.nl/cwi/people/
Jack.Jansen/spunk/Spunk_Home.html

Put together by Jack Jansen of Amsterdam, Spunk Press collects and distributes literature with an emphasis on anarchism and anarchist resources. Spunk has a large collection of articles, excerpts, quotations, and prose from a wide variety of writers of political theory. These include Mikhail Bakunin, William Godwin, Emma Goldman, Abbie Hoffman, Henry David Thoreau, George Orwell, Noam Chomsky, Kropotkin, and many, many more. There is even a recipe for anarchist pumpkin pie—something to chomp on while reading your Chomsky.

ZDNet

http://www.ziff.com/

Ziff-Davis, publishers of *PC Week*, *PC Magazine*, *PC Computing*, *MacWeek*, *MacUser*, *Computer Shopper*, and more, has its own Web page. Each Ziff publication is represented separately, with articles, reviews, and columns from each. You'll also find *Internet Life*, which reviews Web sites, and *Inter@ctive Week*, covering the online business world.

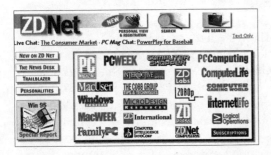

■ People

The Archimedes Project

http://kanpai.stanford.edu/arch/arch.html

The Archimedes Project is a great use of today's technology to improve access to information for people with disabilities. Its founders aim to influence the early design stage of technology by educating developers about the obstacles and opportunities that technology presents for people with disabilities.

Feminist Activist Resources on the Net

http://www.igc.apc.org/women/
feminist.html

Sarah Stapleton-Gray maintains this page which includes current feminist news and issue discussions (domestic violence and reproductive rights, among others), links to women's organizations, general resources for political activists, and an event calendar. There's "feminist fun and games" and Ellen Spertus's wry commentary on women in computing.

The Genealogy Home Page

http://ftp.cac.psu.edu:80/~saw/
genealogy.html

One of the most comprehensive genealogy
resources on the Web, this page is compiled by
Stephan Wood, and it offers a wide variety of
genealogical information on resources on the
Net. There's information on libraries, contacting other genealogists, North American
resources, a collection of geographic, national,
ethnic, and religious resources (such as German, Irish, and Jewish), genealogy software,
maps and geography, and more.

The Human Factor

http://www.human.com/

Located in Santa Cruz, California, the Human
Factor offers free pages to "anyone doing worthwhile nonprofit types of things." Lots of nonprofit
and social service information can be had here.

Native American Resources on the Internet

http://hanksville.phast.umass.edu:80/
misc/NAresources.html

This page links to a host of topics and sites,
including the National Museum of the American Indian, Ojibwa language and culture, a
guide to the Great Sioux Nation, the California
Indian Library Collections, and more. You can
also find the text of bills on Indian policy, and a
link to IndianNet, an Internet resource.

Nonprofit Organizations on the Internet

http://www.ai.mit.edu/people/ellens/
non.html

Maintained by Ellen Spertus of MIT, this is one
of the largest collections of nonprofit and charita-
ble organizations we found anywhere on the
Net. There are links to nonprofit organizations
and their Web pages. This provides such a
diverse grouping of organizations that both the
Bethany Christian Fellowship and the Cannibis
Action Network are listed, along with more well-
known organizations such as Amnesty International and the ACLU. This page is well worth a
look as a guide to nonprofits on the Web.

Women Homepage

http://www.mit.edu:8001/people/
sorokin/women/index.html

This site provides a collection of online writings
and resources by, about, and for women. It
includes women in computer science and engineering, women's studies programs and centers,
details on women in academia, industry, and
health care; gender and sexuality studies; various
information clearinghouses and resources; and
even "unclassified cool information."

■ Pets

Canine Directory

http://www.acmepet.com/canine/
canine.html

This site offers links to a variety of Web sites
for dog enthusiasts: services and products, pet
classifieds, canine newsgroups, clubs, shelters,
and rescue operations. There's a glossary, breed-
ing and boarding info, and links to personal dog-
lovers' pages. "On the Internet, no one knows
you're a dog" was never truer.

Cat Fanciers' Home Page

http://www.ai.mit.edu/fanciers/ fanciers.html

This page was created by a group of cat breeders, exhibitors, and other ailurophiles via an Internet mailing list called Fanciers. There are links to FAQs on cat colors, feline leukemia virus, and breed descriptions. You'll even find FAQs on specific fancy breeds including Maine Coon Cat, Bombay, and Chartreux. You can also join the CF from this page, or check out various Online Cat Clubs.

Cat Fanciers' Home Page

[*] Fish Information Service (FINS)

http://www.actwin.com:80/fish/index.html

There's lots of information here: a glossary of aquarium terms, catalogs of marine and freshwater fish, archives of "interesting discussions" on a variety of aquarium topics, disease diagnosis tools, how to build an aquarium…. There are also lots of underwater and fish images, a directory of public aquaria, local clubs, online pet stores, and vendors of aquarium products. You'll find cross-links to amphibians and reptiles, wildlife protection law, and even scientific trivia about fish. Mark Rosenstein created this

page. Check out the Waterlily Cam and the venerable Fish Cam from here, too.

Herpetocultural Home Page

http://gto.ncsa.uiuc.edu/pingleto/herp.html

Mike Pingleton, reptile enthusiast from NCSA (National Center for Supercomputing Applications), has created a meta-page featuring "herp pictures" and a growing list of other herp home pages. It includes a link to Pingleton's current collection of snakes, turtles, lizards, frogs, and toads.

Internet Vet Column Home Page

http://www.zmall.com/pet_talk/tittle/ pets/ivc/homepage.html

Written by Jeff Parke, D.V.M., this page indexes the 1994–1995 issues of his column, with its detailed answers to questions about diseases that dogs and cats are susceptible to, vaccinations, infection information, and neutering.

■ Reference and Information

See also **Education, History**

Bartlett's Familiar Quotations

http://www.columbia.edu/~svl2/bartlett/

It's the best—and it's searchable! It has a huge link list to hundreds of the primary authors cited. You can also link to other trusted Bartlett's sources like the Old and New Testaments and the *Book of Common Prayer*.

Hypertext Webster Interface

http://c.gp.cs.cmu.edu:5103/prog/webster

Bennet Yee of Carnegie Mellon University offers this searchable link to various *Webster's Dictionary* services on the Net.

[*] The Library of Congress

http://www.loc.gov/

The parent of all U.S. library collections, the Library of Congress page offers mega-information on Congress and the government, of course, including publications and online exhibits. More importantly, you can access the Library of Congress online systems via Telnet, or go to several digitized LC collections (historical and Americana).

List of USENET FAQs

http://www.cis.ohio-state.edu/hypertext/ faq/usenet/

Thomas Fine wrote the software that allows you to search a list of thousands of USENET FAQs found in the <news.answers> newsgroup.

You can search alphabetically, by alpha topic, or by newsgroup name.

Roget's Thesaurus

http://tuna.uchicago.edu/forms_unrest/ ROGET.html

Full-text and head-word searching from the latest edition of *Roget*.

Spider's Web References

http://gagme.wwa.com/~boba/ref.html

Bob Allison's meta-page contains a huge catalog of links to references all over the Net, including the Library of Congress, various *Yellow Pages*, the Consumer Information Center, *The Complete TV Guide*, Congressional e-mail list, and many more. He has also created a section of "desk references," searchable dictionaries, thesauruses, directories, and calendars. Then there's the zip code server, census information, fat-free recipes, even a dinosaur link. You get the idea. Just put this page on your hotlist and you'll do just fine in the reference department.

U.S.P.S. Address Quality and Zip Code Lookup

http://www.usps.gov/ncsc/aq-zip.html

The post office has kindly entered a look-up form for zip codes by city and state. You can also link to state abbreviations, street suffixes, if you're rusty on those, and a postal service area map.

The Virtual Reference Desk

http://thorplus.lib.purdue.edu/reference/ index.html

Make this a bookmark and you'll have all you need to link to many dictionaries and thesauruses, maps, phone books, area code listings, historical documents, scientific tables, and time and date sites. Courtesy of Purdue University Libraries, and what a wonderful service it is.

■ Science

See also **Weather**

Biology

http://info.er.usgs.gov:80/network/science/biology/index.html

The U.S. Geological Survey maintains a registry of Web and gopher servers related to biology—from biodiversity and biological collections to biological research labs around the world. There are also listings for bioinformatics, biocomputing, and genomes.

California State University Biological Sciences Web Server

http://arnica.csustan.edu/

Probably one of the best indices available for bioscience information on the Internet, this page categorizes many Web links to all of the sciences. Topics that have been indexed are agriculture, biological molecules, biochemistry, molecular biology, biophysics, biodiversity and ecology, entomology, evolution, fish and other aquatic animals, developmental biology, genetics, herpetology, medicine, anesthesiology, microbiology, and virology. There are links to multimedia materials, too—images and sound files.

Colorado State Entomology

http://www.colostate.edu/Depts/Entomology/ent.html

Giving new definition to the term "computer" bugs, this entomology server contains a great deal of information for the professional or amateur bugmeister. Among its resources are upcoming events in entomology, job positions in entomology, educational opportunities, collections of insect graphics, selected publications, and links to other entomology resources on the Internet. With all that's here, folks will undoubtedly swarm all over the page.

Earth Science and Geology Links

http://jacobson.isgs.uiuc.edu/earthsci_links.html

Part of the Earthnet Info server maintained by Russ Jacobson, the Earth Science and Geology Links page contains a listing by category of over 200 links. Some of the categories covered include earthquakes, geochemistry, geology departments and schools, geological surveys, geophysics, hydrogeology, meteorology, mineralogy and crystallography, museums, paleontology, resources and mining, satellite images and digital data, stratigraphy and sedimentation, and societies and volcanology, among others.

Don't miss "Dino Russ's Lair" on dinosaurs, too: http://jacobson.isgs.uiuc.edu/

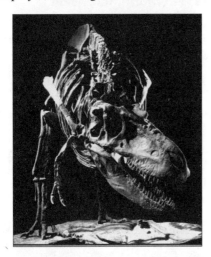

General, Organic, and Biochemistry

http://odin.chemistry.uakron.edu/genobc/

Here are class notes, articles, and animations based on general, organic, and biochemistry classes taught at the University of Akron. Read all about chemical reactions, organic compounds, body fluids, and lots more. Of course, you can also link to the periodic table from here.

Missouri Botanical Garden

http://straylight.tamu.edu/MoBot/ welcome.html

The Missouri Botanical Garden operates one of the world's most active research programs in tropical botany. Scientific research at the garden focuses on exploration of the tropics, which encompass the earth's least known, most diverse, and most rapidly vanishing ecosystems. The botanical garden also coordinates the Florae of North America, China, Mesoamericana, and Missouri projects. For each of these, there are information and databases available.

Images and data are also available for various educational programs at the botanical garden and the history of the garden itself.

National Aeronautics and Space Administration

http://hypatia.gsfc.nasa.gov/ NASA_homepage.html

This is NASA's home page, with news and subjects of public interest, R&D, policies, public affairs, online educational resources, and information sources by subject. There is even a clickable map of NASA centers around the country. Check out the navigable global map of Mars. You can check on the recent activity of the space shuttle, or maybe just browse through NASA's collection of space sciences resources with everything from high-energy astrophysics to space radiation and space physics.

Physics Servers and Services around the World

http://www.physics.mcgill.ca/deptdocs/ physics_services.html

McGill University in Montreal has created a meta-page on physics Web sites and other Internet resources using various search engines. There's a searchable database which you can search by keywords. You'll also find links to physics departments and companies, conferences, summer programs, software and computing resources, books and journals, and more.

Science and Technology

http://white.nosc.mil:80/science.html

This compilation page is a very helpful overview with links to physical science servers, NASA online resources, ecology, and more. Information can be linked by category: who's who in science, science servers, science disciplines (from astronomy to photonics), and technology sites (NIST, National Technology Transfer Center). Other topics include science museums and exhibits, NASA, science news clips, and science fairs. Created by the San Diego-based Planet Earth Home Page.

"Whole Frog" Project

http://george.lbl.gov/ITG.hm.pg.docs/
Whole.Frog/Whole.Frog.html

Remember those frog dissection classes in high school biology? The smell of the formaldehyde and the cries of "eewww, gross!" Well, now you can experience a no-muss, no-fuss virtual frog dissection via the Web. The "Whole Frog" project is intended to introduce the concepts of computer-based 3-D visualization, while demonstrating the power of whole-body, 3-D anatomy imaging as a curriculum tool. The project's goal is for classes to explore the anatomy of a frog using data from high-resolution MRI and mechanical sectioning. Currently available is the ever so fabulous 3-D reconstruction of a frog's anatomy, interactive frog dissection, and a big favorite, the rotating-transparent-frog movie.

■ Science Fiction

See also Literature, Television

Feminist Science Fiction, Fantasy, and Utopia

http://www.uic.edu/~lauramd/sf/
femsf.html

This text-based outline page links you to a host of writers of feminist sci-fi, including Margaret Atwood, Suzy McKee Charnas, E.M. Broner, Joanna Russ, and Marge Piercy. There are hotlinks to several feminist retellings of traditional myths.

Feminist Science Fiction, Fantasy, & Utopia

The Lysator Science Fiction and Fantasy Archive

http://sf.www.lysator.liu.se/sf_archive/
sf_main.html

Here's a Swedish home page from Mats Ohman that sports a collection of Usenet information on science fiction and fantasy. There's a fan art area and links to fiction and electronic fanzines with names like Quanta, MTVoid, Other Realms, Cyberspace Vanguard, and Dargonzine.

Science Fiction Resources

http://www.arisia.org:80/sf.html

This is a topical collection of sci-fi information on the Web and Net. It's helpfully categorized by archives, bookstores, animation, authors, comics, conventions, cyberpunk, film, interactive games, subsets of Star Trek and Star Wars pages and FAQs, TV shows, and 'zines.

Sci-Fi Channel: The Dominion

http://www.scifi.com/

This is the home page of the Sci-Fi cable channel. There's cool art here and links to the full channel schedule. "The Edge" is where you find news about upcoming specials and programs. "Pulp" is for articles, reviews, and excerpts from dogeared favorites in print. There's a "Board" for posting and flaunting "all of the useless factoids you've gathered," and of course places to download graphics, audio, and video clips. You can buy sci-fi wear and gear, natch. Go to Original Series to get the full details of the channel's various special-topic programs like Inside Space and FTL Newsfeed, the Sci-Fi Channel's fictional news feature from 150 years in the future.

The Klingon Language Institute

http://www.kli.org/KLIhome.html

This page promotes the use and further development of Klingon, and endeavors to bring together Klingon enthusiasts. See it written! Hear it spoken! Back issues of the KLI newsletter and a browsable index of the Klingon mailing list are here.

Star Trek Page

http://www.cosy.sbg.ac.at/rec/startrek/index.html

Maintained by Brigette Jellinek in Austria, this fan's collection has a handy summary of Star Trek resources all over the Internet, including detailed episode guides—and parodies!

Star Trek: The Next Generation (ST:TNG)

http://198.147.111.30/st-tng/sounds/welcome.au

This graphic-intensive page is linked to trivia, information about the cast, the episodes, and even Star Trek science info. There are also inks to a lengthy Gene Roddenberry bio. Compiled by Andrew Tong, this site is also mirrored in Australia.

■ Sex and Sexuality

Gender and Sexuality

http://english-server.hss.cmu.edu/Gender.html

That incredibly useful reference, the English Server, comes through again with a very long page of links to Web pages, gopher, and ftp sites covering all viewpoints and more kinds of information than you'd think would fit under this topic. You can go to Concerned Women of America, a distinctly conservative group, or to

Girl's Guide to Condoms. Read a scholarly paper called "Madonna's Revenge" or an informational article on "More Than You Wanted to Know about Clothespins." There are links to topics and places addressing virtually all points on the sexual spectrum.

[*] Good Vibrations

http://bianca.com/shack/goodvibe/index.html

Bianca Troll, an individual Web creator, has included in her home page some descriptions and graphic images of products from "her favorite sex store," Good Vibrations, which has been a San Francisco landmark since 1977. (Apparently GV is in the process of establishing its own page.) Stop by Bianca's Pillow Talk Lounge, or jot a note and send it to her Dream Book.

[*] Queer Resources Directory

http://www.qrd.org/QRD/

This is the mother of all gay/lesbian/bisexual/transgender information pages on the Internet. Originally created by Ron Buckmire, QRD is a meta-library of information from many sources, including a specific hot link to health and sexuality issues. There you'll find safe sex and AIDS information. At QRD you'll also find nonsexual information: business, legal, and political topics, a calendar of events, and a host of organizations.

The Safer Sex page

http://www.cmpharm.ucsf.edu/~troyer/safesex.html

This useful page was created by John Troyer at the University of California atSan Francisco. It offers brochures and articles about conducting safer sexual practices which can prevent the spread of HIV and other sexually-transmitted diseases. The page also includes a forum for

your comments and questions, information for counselors, photos, audio and video clips in a multimedia section, and links to other sexuality resources on the Net.

Yellow Silk

http://www.dc.enews.com/magazines/yellow_silk/

This is a quarterly journal of erotic literature. "All persuasions, no brutality" is the *YS* slogan. *Yellow Silk* offers poetry and short stories, photographs, and graphic arts. Information on how to subscribe, how to read the archives, and current issue details are available here.

■ Sports

The Baseball Server

http://www2.nando.net/SportServer/baseball/

News on- and off-season, with a link to the 1994 Baseball strike. There are major and minor league reports, AL and NL game details by division, standings, transactions by league, and a

More Stats page. Latest news and game reports and World Series Guides, too.

Dan's World of Skateboarding

http://web.cps.msu.edu:80/~dunhamda/ dw/dansworld.html

This page showcases Dan Dunham and some pals maneuvering. It features a paper on the history of skateboarding, press clips on the sport, a gossip page, and cool photos of 'boarders in action.

[*] ESPN SportsZone

http://espnet.sportszone.com/

SportsZone is a well-designed resource catering to fans of most any major sport. RealAudio and .WAV sound bites are available to hear the players and coaches talk about the big game in their own words. Nonsubscribers only get access to the top stories of the day; the monthly $4.95 subscriber fee gives you access to the serious sports-nerd information.

Mountain Biking

http://xenon.stanford.edu:80/~rsf/ mtn-bike.html

This useful compendium, created by Ross Finlayson at Stanford University, links you to TV shows ("Fat Tire Journal"), the Women's Mountain Biking and Tea Society (WOMBATS), photos, and a germane "Calvin & Hobbes" cartoon. Official rules are here, and recent race results, along with news and descriptions of races in Canada, Europe, and New Zealand. There are trail details from Northern California, and, yes, there's even a group of fanatical mountain bikers in the vertically-challenged city of Chicago.

NBA Team Home Pages

http://tns-www.lcs.mit.edu/cgi-bin/ sports/nba/teams

A starting point for locating information on the teams in the NBA, their schedules, seasonal and cumulative stats, rosters and, of course, bios.

The 19th Hole

http://www.sport.net/golf/home.html

A compiled golf page by Jimbo Odom IV, the 19th Hole features daily golf news, an 800-number directory of golf companies, and a list of Net golf resources. The page also features an almanac of events (PGA, LPGA, Senior Golf, USGA, European and Australian tourneys) and classified ads for equipment. At the bottom, Jimbo has even collected links to other Jimbos.

Professional Football Server

http://www.netgen.com/sis/NFL/NFL.html

A Best of the Web winner, this page has it all: NFL team histories, the current year's season schedule, and season schedule by team. You can find stats on players in the League Leaders section. After a game is played, you can link to particulars such as scoring by quarter and scoring summaries by player.

Professional Hockey Server

http://maxwell.uhh.hawaii.edu/hockey/
hockey.html

Not only does this page contain information on the current NHL season, but it also shares space with the University of Hawaii's professional football team and the UH Physics/Astronomy Home Page. On the hockey side, there's a link to the Stanley Cup Playoffs, the most recent two seasons' standings, and Maxwell's Hockey Archive. Created by Richard Crowe.

Sports Information Server

http://www.netgen.com/sis/sports.html

An Internet service company, Net.Genesis, has created a good overview page for hockey, bas-

ketball, football, and international sports. There are team schedules, player stats, and game summaries, with more in the works as they continue to build the page.

The Tennis Server Home Page

http://arganet.tenagra.com/
Racquet_Workshop/Tennis.html

This page offers tennis-related e-mail and newsgroups, the FAQ on rules and codes of tennis, players and equipment tips of the month, and links to other tennis sites on the Net and the Web. Daily tennis news wrapups from the U.S. and Australian Opens, and .GIF files of Graf, Seles, Sabatini, and others. You may learn how to treat sprained ankles, and how to get to tennis information on the commercial online services (America Online, Prodigy, CompuServe, and GEnie).

Ultimate Frisbee

http://pipkin.lut.ac.uk/~scott/
ultimate.html

Ian Scotland's page from the U.K. is a very good pointer to a variety of international Ultimate activities in the U.S., Europe, and U.K. It links to articles including "The Disc Commandments," "Ultimate in 10 Simple Rules," and "Teaching Forehand." Then there's the History of the Frisbee Disc, rules, and an ongoing "spirit of the game" discussion. Check out the usage stats of all the Ultimate Frisbee Web pages, too.

World Wide Web of Sports

http://tns-www.lcs.mit.edu/cgi-bin/sports

Photos and links to NBA, NCAA basketball, football, baseball, sailing, tennis, hockey, soccer, and then the not-so-usual: frisbee, cycling, rugby, rowing, skating, cricket, and equestrian events. You can customize your page by selecting a sport and entering its URLs in your hot-list. You can also choose the master World Wide Sports page to receive regular updates.

■ Television

***See also* Science Fiction**

Comedy Central's Totally Free Web Site

http://www.comcentral.com/com-menu.htm

Schedules, spoofs, shopping, E-therapy with Dr. Katz, and a host of funny bits, all slyly delivered. Get your "Ab Fab" T-shirts here.

Corporation for Public Broadcasting

http://www.cpb.org:80/

This page for the U.S. CPB features news releases, funding guidelines for productions, a

CPB job line, and text and graphics from CPB Today, a monthly newsletter. K–12 teachers may also find useful information from CPB on its EdWeb page, along with guidelines for applying to the Annenberg Higher Education Project.

[*] English Server—Film and Television

http://english-www.hss.cmu.edu/filmandtv.html

A page of many links, listed alphabetically, including articles like "The Centrist Ideology of the News Media," and "90210 as Nostalgia TV." Go from here to specific TV show pages, the Movie Database Browser, and sites for Patrick McGoohan, Monty Python, and The Simpsons. Letterman's Top Ten lists are here.

Guide to Film and Television Resources on the Internet

http://http2.sils.umich.edu/Public/fvl/film.html

Lisa Wood and Kristen Garlock of U-Michigan have compiled a lengthy, no-frills list of links to a huge number of newsgroups and sites about specific films or genres (alt.cult-movies.monty-python, or alt.asian-movies) with sketches of newsgroups, how to reach them, volume of messages. Film reviews, filmographies, and bibliographies are here, too. Obviously a graduate school project—and a terrific one. Updated bimonthly.

TV Net

http://tvnet.com/misc/abouttvnet.html

"1,236 links for 405 shows, including 495 WWW pages!" Search TV programming by alpha title, genre, or Internet resource (FAQs, episode guides, newsgroups, and more). David Cronshaw has done a yeo-person-like job of compiling lists of US local TV stations, international broadcasters, polls, and his Ultimate TV List.

■ Travel

Business Traveler Online

http://www.biztravel.com/guide/

This online mag features articles on topics like the high cost of AirFone calls, frequent flyer programs, site visits to U.S. cities, airline stats, and fare wars. A good stop for the restless air jockey who logs too many miles. Book reviews, hotel summaries, all dedicated to "making your next trip work."

The CIA World Factbook

http://www.odci.gov/cia/publications/95fact/index.html

An amazing resource, *The World Factbook* is produced annually by the Central Intelligence Agency for the use of U.S. government officials. It contains information on most countries, with info provided by a wide variety of federal agencies. There are maps, atlas information, and demographic data. Whether you are a geographer, tourist, government offical, schoolteacher, or student, the *Factbook* probably has something that you'll find fascinating and educational.

CityNet

http://www.city.net/

Probably one of the most comprehensive guides to cities around the world, CityNet provides access to information on travel, entertainment, local business, government, and community services for virtually all parts of the world. Information either by region—even Antarctica—or by country. Two favorite spots are the Real Time Traffic Report for Los Angeles, where sensors provide the speed of the traffic throughout the Los Angeles area, and Nicolas Pioch's Walk about Paris. Kevin Altis and Nancy Tindle have edited a nice set of links. Be spontaneous and link to one of their random destinations!

GNN Travelers' Center

http://nearnet.gnn.com:80/meta/travel/index.html

Global Network Navigator's travel page is a fine collection of travel links. Research a trip for health and weather info, languages, packing tips, phone numbers, visas/passports, currency and converters. Learn about traveling by air, ocean, rail, and/or for free. Travel guides listed by country, state, city. Link to travel newsgroups and newswires, or find travel magazines. The top link is to a fine article by GNNer Allen Noren: "Using the Internet to prepare for a trip." Don't miss it.

Japanese Information

http://www.ntt.jp/japan/

Available in both English and Japanese, this server contains a wealth of information on Japanese geography—including a clickable map of Japan—and weather information. You can also investigate Japanese national holidays, an incredible "Living Manua" of Japanese customs and habits compiled by the Nippon Telegraph and Telephone Corporation, and a fascinating collection of Japanese idioms. "Your Traveling Companion Japan" has information on planning, airport arrival, accommodation, dining, touring, shopping, and information on Japanese government and law, Radio Japan, and more. Then there's the Japanese national anthem, the "Kimigayo" (only 400,419 bytes!)

Moon Publications Online

http://www.moon.com/

The publisher of well-known "handbooks" about places in Asia, Central and Latin America, Mexico, the Caribbean, and the Pacific Islands. You can read about and order Moon's travel guides from here. Check out Travel Matters Newsletter (paper or e-mail), and the exhibits area, featuring recommended reading lists and sources for traveling cross-culturally in Asia and the south Pacific, and staying healthy in the third world.

Route 66

http://www.cs.kuleuven.ac.be:80/~swa/ route66/main.html

This page pays homage to the old U.S. route from Chicago to Los Angeles. A Belgian man, Swa Frantz, put the page up as thanks to all the Net help he received in preparing to drive Route 66. There's a link to the Route 66 Association, information from books and magazine articles about the road, state-by-state road descriptions, area maps, short stories featuring the road, and an interactive advice page for others to contribute their impressions and tips.

Shoestring Travel E-Zine

http://metro.turnpike.net/eadler/ shoe1.html

The Traveler's Diary offers info on events and calendars in Europe via a searchable database (choose country, month and kind of events). There are some links to French and Parisian pages, and American Roadtrips links to routes and driving tips. You can also go to inexpensive travel information for Mexico, Thailand, Sweden, Hong Kong, Germany, and Turkey. There are clips from newsgroups for cheap lodging, hostels, airline 800 numbers, and home exchange groups.

Subway Navigator

http://metro.jussieu.fr:10001/bin/cities/ english

You can find routes for subway systems around the world on this page, from Calcutta to Paris to New York, Hong Kong to Berlin to Montreal. Searchable by city, station name for departure, and destination. You will get a list of the stops along the way, and estimated travel time.

The Travel Log

http://web2.starwave.com:80/outside/
online/travellog/index.html

Outside magazine has a great feature in the Log, which is a list of recent trips by readers/ viewers to places (mostly in the U.S., but also to Mexico, Australia and the Caribbean). If you want to find a good hiking, biking, kayak or canoe trip, mountaineering or snow sport adventure, check here. You can also add your own tale, of course. There is a link to National Park trips as well.

Travel Unlimited Newsletter

http://nexus.datawave.net/travel/
travel.html

A full-text newsletter, available on the Web, by e-mail or fax, that lists inexpensive courier flights, unannounced special fares, and travel tips. If you're scouting for bargains or adventurous flights, head here.

[*] The Virtual Tourist

http://wings.buffalo.edu/world/

The Virtual Tourist offers a clickable world map of Web servers throughout the globe so you can explore the Web with a regional, rather than subject-oriented, focus. Let your fingers do the walking!

Web Travel Review

http://webtravel.org/webtravel/

Philip Greenspun is known on the Web for his personal travel journals and beautiful photographs. His first, *Travels with Samantha*, was a 1994 Best of Web winner. The WTR features all of Greenspun's work to date—over 600 pages of text and 2,000 photographs to a wide variety of places around the world. Terrific armchair traveling. Link to an annotated bibliography on travel and other Net resources too.

■ Weather

***See also* Science**

Global Network News Weather Page

http://gnn.com/news/weather.html

Featured at this site are U.S. weather maps, earthquake information, auroral activity sightings, satellite images, and a searchword function.

Weather Map: Current US Weather

http://www.mit.edu:8001/usa.html

From its home at M.I.T., this hypermedia weather map gives current weather conditions and forecasts for the U.S. Just click on any spot on the map.

WeatherNet

http://cirrus.sprl.umich.edu/wxnet/

The Weather Underground at the University of Michigan runs WeatherNet, an exhaustingly comprehensive guide to online world weather information—over 250 Web sites' worth. Forecasts and warnings, satellite maps and hyperlinks to other weather resources are here, as well as a good-sized archive of weather-related software.

Weather World Satellite Imagery Menu

http://www.atmos.uiuc.edu/wxworld/ html/satimg.html

All the infrared and visible images (not to mention water vapor images) you could want from the University of Illinois are here. There are links to other university satellite image servers. You can also download animations and watch the weather travel across your screen.

■ Appendix: Internet PPP Providers

Without an Internet connection, even the finest Internet software in the world is completely useless. What do you do if you buy this book before you have an Internet PPP Provider? You find one!

Send e-mail to one of the automated Internet provider lists (such as POCIA's below) or go see a pal who has Web access and check out one of these Internet provider Web sites:

The List

http://thelist.com/
This is the big one, searchable by area code.

Providers of Commercial Internet Access (POCIA) Directory

http://www.celestin.com/pocia/
Indexed by area code (for the U.S. and Canada) and by country (for the rest of the world). The POCIA directory is available by e-mail—send a blank message to info@celestin.com with the subject "SEND POCIA.TXT."

List of Provider Lists

http://www.tagsys.com/Provider/ListOfLists.html

Peter Harrison's Access Provider (PHAP)

http://www.well.com/user/peterh/phaphome.html
List of North American Internet providers.

Providers around the World

http://www.earth.org/~lips/

The Internet Society's Network Service Providers Around the World

http://www.isoc.org/~bgreene/nsp-d.html

UWEC International Free-Net/Community Net Listing

http://www.uwec.edu/info/freenets.html

The Internet Society's "How to Find a Service Provider"

http://www.isoc.org/~bgreene/nsp-c.html
A helpful place to start your search, with hyperlinks to other Internet provider resources.

Additionally, Prodigy, CompuServe, and America Online now all offer Web access, and have local access numbers all over North America—and in CompuServe's case, the world. (Pretty much any magazine published in the last year or so came with an America Online disk—you may be using one as a coaster as we speak! The others advertise in magazines you probably already have around the house or at work.) You want to get a dedicated Internet provider, though, if you can find one—connecting to the Web over one of the commercial online services is just too expensive.

Check the FreeNet list above—you may have a community network in your backyard. Another option, of course, is the Netscape Navigator Personal Edition (http://home.netscape.com/comprod/netscape_personal_edition.html) that's available at your local software chain, such as Egghead or Software, Etc., and possibly via your favorite mail-order catalog. The Personal Edition package comes with software to sign you up easily to one of several Internet providers. You can also buy one of the various Net-in-a-Box packages available at the same stores to get connected.

Included here is contact information for at least one Internet provider in each nation a provider could be located in. If there was a choice between academic providers, such as universities and private providers, the latter is presented. If you have access to an academic connection you should use it first—hey, it might be free.

All of these providers were in business at press time, but because this is a very fast-paced field, company names, status, and offerings may change. In some cases the companies listed are the only Internet providers in the nation, but in many cases they are not. Many of these firms maintain local-access nodes in cities or regions other than the one in which they are physically located. Check with the provider geographically closest to you; you may be surprised. Please also note that you may need an additional country or city code or access number to reach some of these firms by telephone or fax, depending on your location.

By the way, neither I nor Ziff-Davis Press are expressing support or endorsement for any company or service by including it in this list. Thanks again to Karen Wickre and Bob Powell's *Atlas to the World Wide Web* (which, if I may remind you, is available at a fine bookshop near you) whence this list comes.

■ Africa

Many areas in Africa are served only by FidoNet, if at all. If the providers below don't meet your needs, download "Connectivity with Africa by Randy Bush" via gopher from rain.psg.com:70/00/networks/connect/africa.txt.

Algeria

Algeria Net

06 Rue Frederic MISTRAL Telemly
Algiers
Phone: (213) 2-612-715

Burkina Faso

ORSTOM

01 BP 182—Ouagadougou
Phone: (226) 30 67 37 or 30 67 39
Fax: (226) 31 03 85

Cameroon

ORSTOM

BP 1857
Yaounde
Phone: (237) 20 15 08
Fax: (237) 20 18 54

Congo

ORSTOM

BP 181
Brazzaville
Phone: (242) 83 26 80
Fax: (242) 83 29 77

Egypt

EUnet Egypt

E-mail: ow@estinet.uucp
Phone: (20) 2 3557253
Fax: (20) 2 3547807

Ethiopia

Pan African Development Information System (PADIS)

Box 3001
Addis Ababa
E-mail: sysop@padis.gn.apc.org
Phone: (251) 1 511 167
Fax: (251) 1 514 416

Ivory Coast

ORSTOM

15 B.P. 917
Abidjan 15
Phone: (225) 24 37 79
Fax: (225) 24 65 04

Kenya

ELCI

E-mail: sysop@elci.gn.apc.org
Phone: (254) 2 562 015

Madagascar

ORSTOM

BP 434—101
Antananarivo
Phone: (261) 23 30 98
Fax: (261) 23 30 98

Mali

ORSTOM

BP 2528
Bamako
Phone: (223) 22 43 05 or 22 27 74
Fax: (223) 22 75 88

Niger

ORSTOM

BP 11 416
Niamey
Phone: (227) 73 20 54
Fax: (227) 72 28 04

Senegal

ORSTOM

BP 1386
Dakar
Phone: (221) 32 34 76 or 32 34 80
Fax: (221) 32 43 07

Seychelles

ORSTOM

Seychelles Fishing Authority Headquarters
Rue des Frangipaniers—BP 570
Victoria-Mahe
Phone: (248) 247 42
Fax: (248) 245 08

South Africa

Commercial Internet Services (CIS)

P.O. Box 395
Pretoria, 0001
E-mail: info@cis.co.za
Phone: (27) 12 841-2892
Fax: (27) 12 841-3604

Togo

ORSTOM

BP 375
Lome
Phone: (228) 21 43 44 or 21 43 46
Fax: (228) 21 03 43

Tunisia

EUnet Tunisia

E-mail: mondher@Tunisia.EU.net
Phone: (216) 1 787757
Fax: (261) 1 787827

Uganda

MUKLA

Makerere University
Kampala, Uganda
E-mail: sysop@mukla.gn.apc.org
Phone: (256) 41-532-479

Zambia

ZAMNET Communication Systems Ltd.

Box 32379
Lusaka
E-mail: sales@zamnet.zm
Phone: (260) 1-293317

Zimbabwe

MANGO

Department of Computer Science
University of Zimbabwe
P.O. Box MP-167
Harare
E-mail: Rob_Borland@mango.apc.org
or johnux@zimbix.uz.zw

■ Asia

China (People's Republic of)

China Resaerch and Education Network (CERNET)

Contact: Wu Jian Ping, head of the CERNET Technical Board and professor
of the computer engineering department
Tsinghua University
Beijing 100084
E-mail: jianping@cernet.edu.cn
Phone: (86) 1-2595931
Fax: (86) 1-2595933

Hong Kong

Hong Kong Supernet

HKUST Campus
Clear Water Bay, Kowloon
E-mail: info@hk.super.net or postmaster@hk.super.net
WWW: http://www.hk.super.net/~rlowe/bizhk/bhhome.html
Phone: (852) 358-7924
Fax: (852) 358-7925

Internet Online Hong Kong Ltd.

P.O. Box 47165
Morrison Hill, Post Office
Hong Kong
E-mail: info@iohk.com
Phone: (852) 768-8008

India

aXcess Online Services

Business India Information Technology Ltd.
3-10 Phoenix Mills Compound, Bombay—400 013, India.
E-mail: sharad@axcess.net.in or postmaster@axcess.net.in
Phone: (91) 22-493 7676
Fax: (91) 22-493 6578

UUNET India Limited

270N Road No. 10
Jubilee Hills
Hyderabad, A.P. 500 034
E-mail: info@uunet.in
Phone: (91) 842 238007
Fax: (91) 842 247787

Indonesia

University of Indonesia, Department of Computer Science
Jl. Salemba Raya 4, P.O. Box 3442
Jakarta 10002
E-mail: postmaster@UI.AC.ID
Phone: (62-21) 727-0162

Japan

Japan has a rapidly growing demand for Internet access, and new firms are springing up to meet it seemingly overnight. For a fresh update, send the message "subscribe" (without the quote marks) to efj-request@twics.com, or have a look at ftp://neoteny.eccosys.com/pub/efj/efj-faq.txt.

Cyber Technologies International K.K.

Otake Bldg. 304, 4-6 Daikyocho
Shinjuku-Ku, Tokyo 160
E-mail: sales@cyber.ad.jp
Phone: (81) 3-3226-0961
Fax: (81) 3-3226-0962

Global Online Japan

Oshima Building 302
1-56-1 Higashi Nakano
Nakano-ku, Tokyo 164
E-mail: info@gol.com (to receive information automatically) or
sales@gol.com (to ask specific questions)
Phone: (03) 5330-9380
Fax: (03) 5330-9381

Malaysia

JARING/MIMOS

7th Floor, Exchange Square
Off Jalan Semantan, Bukit Damansara,
50490 Kuala Lumpur
E-mail: noc@jaring.my or mal@mimos.my
Phone: (60) 3-254-9601 or 3-255-2700, ext. 2101
Fax: (60) 3-253-1898

Nepal

Mercantile Office Systems

E-mail: kgautam@mosnepal.ernet.in
Phone: (977) 1 220773
Fax: (977) 1 225407

Pakistan

Brain Computer Services/Brain NET

730-Nizam Block
Iqbal Town, Lahore-54570
E-mail: info@brain.com.pk
Phone: (92) 42-541-4444
Fax: (92) 42-758-1126

Philippines

Email Centre

108. V. Luna Road, Sikatuna Village
Quezon City
E-mail: sysop@phil.gn.apc.org
Phone: (63) 2 921 9976

Phillippine Network Foundation Inc.

Phone: (63) 2 633-1956

Singapore

SingNet

Gopher: gopher.technet.sg
Phone: (65) 751-5034

South Korea

DACOM Corporation

140-716 DACOM B/D.
65-228, 3-Ga, Hangang-Ro
Yongsan-Ku, Seoul
E-mail: help@nis.dacom.co.kr
Phone: (82) 2-220-5232 or 2-220-5233
Fax: (82) 2-220-0771

Sri Lanka

Lanka Internet Services, Ltd.

IBM Building, 5th Floor
48 Nawam Mawatha
Colombo 2
E-mail: info@lanka.net
WWW: http://www.lanka.net/
Phone: (94) 1-342974
Fax: (94) 1-343056

Taiwan (Republic of China)

Hsinchu Service Center

E-mail: service@shts.seed.net.tw
Phone: (035) 773311, ext. 512
Fax: (035) 788031

Pristine Internet Gateway

3F, No. 2, Alley 2, Lane 244, Roosevelt Rd. Sec. 3
Taipei, Taiwan
E-mail: robert@pristine.com.tw
WWW: http://www.pristine.com.tw/
Phone: (886) 2 368-9023
Fax: (886) 2 367-0342

SeedNet

Taipei Service Center
E-mail: service@tpts1.seed.net.tw
Phone: (02) 733-8779
Fax: (02) 737-0188

Thailand

Thaisarn Internet Service at NECTEC

E-mail: sysadmin@nwg.nectec.or.th
WWW: http://www.nectec.or.th/
Phone: (66) 2 248-8007
Fax: (66) 2 247-1335

Vietnam

NetNam

E-mail: admin@netnam.org.vn
Phone: (84-4) 346-907
Fax: (84-4) 345-217

■ Canada

Many U.S. providers, notably Portal and IAT, also serve many parts
of Canada.

UUNET Canada

1 Yong Street, Suite 1400
Toronto, ONT, M5E 1J9, Canada
E-mail: info@uunet.ca (to automatically receive information) or
support@uunet.ca (to ask specific questions)
FTP: ftp.uunet.ca
WWW: www.uunet.ca
Phone: (800) INET-123
Fax: (416) 368-1350

HookUp Communications

1075 North Service Road W., Suite 207
Oakville, Ontario L6M 2G2
E-mail: info@hookup.net
FTP: ftp.hookup.net/pub/info/Info-Brochure
Phone: (905) 847-8000
Fax: (905) 847-8420

■ Caribbean

Bahamas

CUNET

IBM Bahamas Ltd.
P.M.B. SS-6400
Nassau
E-mail: KBETHEL@UBAHAMAS.ORG.BS
Phone: (809) 322-2145
Fax: (809) 322-4649

Barbados

CUNET

Computer Center
University of the West Indies
Cave Hill Campus
P.O. Box 64
Bridgetown
E-mail: WILLIAMS@UWICHILL.EDU.BB
Phone: (809) 425-1310
Fax: (809) 425-1327

Bermuda

Internet Bermuda Limited

P.O. Box HM 2445
Hamilton HM JX
E-mail: info@ibl.bm
WWW: http://www.ibl.bm
Phone: (809) 296-1800
Fax: (809) 295-7269

Cuba

CENIAI

Instituto de Documentacion e Informacion Cientifica y Tecnica
Jefe de Departmento Tecnico Red CENIAI
Industria y San Jose Capitolio Nacional
Apartado 2213
Habana
E-mail: jemar@ceniai.cu
Phone: (537) 62-6565 or 62-0757
Fax: (537) 33-8237

Dominican Republic

REHRED (Academic and Research Network)

E-mail: sjb@acn.miami.com or pimienta!daniel@redid.org.do

Grenada

CUNET

Granada National College Tanteen
St. George's
E-mail: LINDY@GNC.EDU.GD
Phone: (809) 465-2090
Fax: (809) 465-5202

Jamaica

CUNET

University of the West Indies, Mona Campus
Kingston 7
E-mail: MANISON@UWIMONA.EDU.JM
Phone: (809) 927-2781
Fax: (809) 927-2156

Puerto Rico

Corporacion para la Red Cientifica Cientifica y de Investigacion Nacional de Puerto Rico (CRACIN)

Secretario de Relaciones Internacionales
P.O. Box 195355
San Juan 00919-5355
E-mail: ERivera@mxruc.clu.net
Phone: (809) 759-6891
Fax: (809) 759-8117

St. Kitts and Nevis

CUNET

College of Further Education
P.O. Box 295
Horsford Road, Basseterre
E-mail: IDM@CFE.EDU.KN

Santa Lucia

CUNET

ISIS
P.O. Box GM 717
3 Castries
E-mail: ADANIEL@ISIS.ORG.LC
Phone: (809) 452-3702
Fax: (809) 453-7690

Trinidad and Tobago

CUNET

4 Serpentine Place
St. Clair
E-mail: SLAURENT@CARIRI.GOV.TT or
LARS_J@NIHERST.GOV.TT
Phone: (809) 628-8523
Fax: (809) 622-7880

■ Central America

Belize

CUNET

University College of Belize
P.O. Box 990
Belize City
E-mail: OLDA@UCB.EDU.BZ or brian@ucb.edu.bz
Phone: (501) 232732
Fax: (501) 230255

Guatemala

MayaNet

Universidad del Valle de Guatemala
Apartado Postal #82
Guatemala City 01901
E-mail: furlan@uvg.gt
Phone: (502) 2-690791
Fax: (502) 2-380212

Mexico

Internet de Mexico, SA de CV

Paseo de Echegaray 3—206
Nauclapan, Estado de Mexico
E-mail: info@mail.internet.com.mx
WWW: http://www.internet.com.mx
Phone: (525) 360-2931
Fax: (525) 373-1493

RepCom de Mexico, S.A. de C.V.

Av. Nuevo Leon 67 Despacho # 601
Col. Hipodromo Condesa, CP 06140
Mexico City, Mexico Distrito Federal
E-mail: staff@seinet.net.mx
Phone: (525) 211-2282
Fax: (525) 211-2391

Sistema Profesional de Informacion (SPIN)

Cuenca 87-4 Alamos 03400
Mexico City, Mexico Distrito Federal
E-mail: info@spin.com.mx
Phone: (525) 628-6220
Fax: (525) 628-6210

Nicaragua

Nicarao CRIES

Iglesia El Carmen, 1 cuadra al lago
Apartade 3516
Managua
E-mail: ayuda@nicarao.apc.org
Phone: (505) 2 621312
Fax: (505) 2 621244

Panama

Universidad de Panama
Vicerectoria de Investigacion y Postgrado
Ciudad Universitaria Octavio Mendez P
Panama City
E-mail: barragan@huracan.cr
Phone: (506) 64 4242
Fax: (506) 64 4450

■ Eastern/Central Europe

Along with commercial online services, such as CompuServe and Europe
Online, there are companies that provide connectivity across national borders in Europe, including Euro telecommunications pioneer EUnet. The
company below does them all one better by sweetening the deal with low-
cost dial-up access to the U.S. as part of their all-Europe service package.

Pan-European

I-COM

4, rue de Geneve B33
B-1140 Bruxelle
Belgium
Phone: (32) 2 215 71 30
Fax: (32) 2 215 8999

Azerbaijan

InTrans

370000 Azerbaidjanskaya respublika
g. Baku, ul. Hagani, 18
E-mail: postmaster@insun.azerbaijan.su
Phone: 7 8922 930832

Belarus

EKSPO

210001 g.Vitebsk, ul. Kosmonavtov 4
E-mail: lav@ekspo.vitebsk.by
Phone: 7 0212 370898

Bulgaria

EUnet Bulgaria

E-mail: postmaster@bulgaria.EU.net
Phone: 359 52 259135
Fax: 359 52 234540

Croatia

CARNet

E-mail: Predrag.Pale@carnet.hr
FTP/Gopher: carnet.hr
Phone: 385 41 629 963

Czech Republic

EUnet Czechia

E-mail: prf@Czechia.EU.net
Phone: 42 2 3323242
Fax: 42 2 24310646

Estonia

Ants Work

Deputy Director
Institute of Cybernetics
Estonian Academy of Sciences
Akadeemie tee 21
EE 0108 Tallinn
E-mail: ants@ioc.ee
Phone: 007 0142 525622
Fax: 007 0142 527901
(Note: also serves Latvia and Lithuania)

Georgia

Omega

380056 g.Tbilisi, pr. G. Robakidze, 3 kv., 5 korpus
Kazarova Narine Georgievna
E-mail: postmaster@aod.ge
Phone: 7 8832 985647

Hungary

EUnet Hungary

1518 Budapest PoB 63
E-mail: info@Hungary.EU.net
Phone: 36 1 2698281
Fax: 36 1 2698288

Latvia

(See also entry for Estonia)

Versia Ltd.

Kleistu 5
Riga, LV-1067
E-mail: gene@vernet.lv, voll@vernet.lv
Phone: 371 2 417000 or 428686
Fax: 371 2 428937

Lithuania

(See also entry for Estonia)

Amber Software Technologies, Inc., LT Branch

Litovskaya Respublika, G. Klaipeda 5800, a/ya 49
E-mail: root@mes.lt
Phone: 7 01261 99926

Romania

LOGIC

Calea Grivitei 136, 78122 Bucharest, Romania
E-mail: Tudor.Panaitescu@alliance-partners.sprint.com
Phone: (4-01) 617-6333
Fax: (4-01) 312-8443

Russia

GlasNet

Ulitsa Sadovaya-Chernogryazskaya, 4-16a
RU-107078 Moscow
Phone: 7 095 262 7079
Fax: 7 095 207 0889

JSV Relcom

123060, Moscow, ul.Raspletina, d.4, korp.1
E-mail: postmaster@kiae.su or support@kiae.su
Phone: 7 095 943 4735
Fax: 7 095 198 95 10

Slovakia (Slovak Republic)

EUnet Slovakia

MFF UK Computing Centre
Mlynska dolina
842 15 Bratislava
E-mail: info@Slovakia.EU.net
WWW: http://www.eunet.sk/
Gopher: gopher.eunet.sk
Phone: (42) 7 725306
Fax: (42) 7 728462

Slovenia

Histria

Ziherlova 43 61
Ljubljana
E-mail: support@histria.apc.org
Phone: 386 (61) 211 553
Fax: 386 (61) 152 107

Ukraine

Apex Network Centre

17/315 pr. Gagarina
320095, Dniepropetrovsk
Phone: 7 0562 476995
Fax: 7 0562 410911
E-mail: vaget@apex.dnepropetrovsk.ua

Uzbekistan

Firma Kompyuternye Kommunikacii

700000 Tashkent, 1 Ulxyanovskii per., 3
E-mail: postmaster@ccc.tashkent.su
Phone: 7 3712 687956

■ Middle East

Egypt

EUnet Egypt

E-mail: ow@estinet.uucp
Phone: (20) 2 3557253
Fax: (20) 2 3547807

Israel

DataServe Ltd.

E-mail: info@datasrv.co.il or register@datasrv.co.il
Phone: (972) 3-647-4448
Fax: (972) 3-647-3833

■ Pacific

Australia

You can find a more extensive list of Australian service providers at http://www.cs.monash.edu.au/~zik/netfaq/org.html.

APANA

E-mail: info@apana.org.au or propaganda@apana.org.au
WWW: http://www.apana.org.au/apana/
Phone: (03) 571-0484

AUSNet

E-mail: tom@kakadu.com.au
WWW: http://www.ausnet.net.au/
Phone: (089) 483-555
Fax: (089) 480-232

Drasnian Technologies

12 Guinevere Way
Carine 6020, Western Australia
E-mail: admin@drasnia.it.com.au
WWW: http://drasnia.it.com.au/
Phone: (09) 447-6261 (a/h)

Spirit Networks

Canberra
E-mail: info@spirit.com.au
WWW: http://www.spirit.com.au/
Phone: (06) 281-3552
Fax: (06) 281-3552

New Zealand

You can get a FAQ on New Zealand connectivity that includes a larger list of public and private service providers from the Web page at http://www.cis.ohio-state.edu/hypertext/faq/usenet/internet-access/new-zealand/faq.html.

IBM Global Network

E-mail: bowden@vnet.ibm.com
Phone: 0800 105-765

PlaNet

E-mail: support@ak.planet.co.nz
Phone/Fax: (09) 3786006

■ South America

Argentina

Proyecto Wamani

Centro de Comunicacion de Informacion (CCI)
Talcahuano 325—3F
1013 Buenos Aires
E-mail: carlos@wamani.org.ar or eduardo@wamani.org.ar
Phone: 54 (1) 382-6842 / 793-1502

Bolivia

Academic and Research Network

Av. Mariscal Santa Cruz, No. 1175 (Obelisco)
Facultad de Ingenieria, Tercer Piso
La Paz
E-mail: clifford@unbol.bo
Phone: (591-1) 314990
Fax: (591-1) 314990

Brazil

Rua Vicente de Souza, 29 Botafogo

Rio de Janeiro, RJ
E-mail: saff@ibase.br or iyda@ibase.br
Phone: 55 021 286-4467/286-0348
Fax: 55 021 286-0541
Telex: 2136466 BASE BR

Chile

REUNA

Bernarda Morin 550-A
Providencia, Santiago
E-mail: postmaster@reuna.cl
Phone: (56) 2 274-0403
Fax: (56) 2 209-6729

Colombia

SAITEL - ITEC - TELECOM

Bogota
E-mail: hcaballe@itecs3.telecom-co.net or jserrano@itecs3.telecom-co.net
Phone: 571 334 8149
Fax: 571 613 1814

Costa Rica

Red Nacional de Investiacion CRNet

Universidad de Costa Rica
San Jose
E-mail: gdeter@ns.cr
Phone: (506) 255911
Fax: (506) 2255911

Ecuador

Corporacion Ecuatoriana de Informacion–ECUANET

P.O. Box 988
Guayaquil
E-mail: xbaquero@ecnet.ec
Phone: (593-2) 433-006, ext. 1410
Fax: (593-2) 437-601

Paraguay

LEDNET

P.O. Box 1718
Campus Universitario, Barrio Santa Librada.
Asuncion
E-mail: gbellas@ledip.py or postmaster@ledip.py
Phone: (595 21)334650
Fax: (595 21)310587

Peru

Red Cientifica Peruana

Alonso de Molina, 1698
Monterrico, Lima
E-mail: js@rcp.net.pe
Phone: (54) 14 35-1760
Fax: (54) 14 36-4067

Uruguay

Chasque

Miguel del Corro 1461
Montevideo 11200
E-mail: apoyo@chasque.apc.org
Phone: 598-2-496-192
Fax: 598-2-419-222

Venezuela

CONICIT

Sistema Automatizado de Informacion Cientifica y Tecnologica (SAICYT)
Edificio Mapioca
v. Ppal. Lops Cortijos de Lourdes
Caracas 1071
Phone: (58) 2 239-0577
Fax: (58) 2 239-8677
Telex: 25205

■ United States

I concentrated on the larger national or regional firms here; it's entirely possible that a smaller local company might be able to provide you with better prices or services.

Many of the companies here are accessible from Canada and/or Mexico as well, and most are accessible via the CompuServe Packet Network (CPN) or Sprintnet. Some maintain local access numbers through other dial-up services (which have additional fees).

East Coast

Clark Internet Services

E-mail: info@clark.net
WWW: http://www.clark.net
Phone: (800) 735-2258 or (410) 730-9764
Fax: (410) 730-9765

Echo

179 Franklin Street, 4th floor
New York, NY 10013
E-mail: info@echonyc.com (to receive information automatically)
or help@echonyc.com (to ask specific questions)
WWW: http://www.echonyc.com/
gopher: echonyc.com
Phone: (212) 292-0900
Fax: (212) 292-0909

Phantom Access Technologies Inc. (MindVox)

E-mail: info@phantom.com
Phone: (800) 646-3869 or (212) 989-2418
Fax: (212) 989-8648

Public Access Unix and Internet (PANIX)

E-mail: info@panix.com (to receive information automatically) or
staff@panix.com (to ask specific questions)
Phone: (212) 787-6160

Midwest

APK Net, Ltd.

1621 Euclid Ave, Suite 1216
Cleveland, Ohio 44115
E-mail: info@apk.net (to receive information automatically)
or support@apk.net (to ask specific questions)
WWW: http://www.apk.net
Phone: (216) 481-9428
Fax: (216) 481-9425

Msen Inc.

628 Brooks Street
Ann Arbor, MI 48103
E-mail: info@mail.msen.com
WWW: http://www.msen.com
Phone: (313) 998-4562
Fax: (313) 998-4563

Ripco Communications Inc.

E-mail: info@ripco.com (to receive information automatically) or
sysop@ripco.com (to ask specific questions)
WWW: http://www.ripco.com:70/1/ripco
Phone: (312) 477-6210

Northwest

Eskimo North

P.O. Box 75284
Seattle, WA 98125-0284
Phone: (206) 361-1161
E-mail: nanook@mail.eskimo.com
WWW: http://www.eskimo.com

Teleport Inc.

319 SW Washington Street #803
Portland, OR 97204
Phone: (503) 223-4245
Fax: (503) 223-4372

South

Interpath

P.O. Box 12800
Raleigh, NC 27605
E-mail: info@interpath.net
gopher: gopher.interpath.net
WWW: http://www.interpath.net
Phone: (800) 849-6305

Southwest

Crossroads Communications

E-mail: info@xroads.com
Phone: (602) 813-9040

Illuminati Online

P.O. Box 18957
Austin, TX 78760
E-mail: info@io.com
WWW: http://www.io.com
Phone: (512) 447-7866
Fax: (512) 447-1144

West Coast

Information Access Technologies (IAT)

46 Shattuck Square, Suite 11
Berkeley, CA 94704-1152
E-mail: info@iat.mailer.net (to receive information automatically) or
support@holonet.net (to ask specific questions)
WWW: http://www.holonet.net
Phone: (510) 704-0160
Fax: (510) 704-8019

The Little Garden

3004 16th Street #201
San Francisco, CA 94103
E-mail: info@tlg.org (to receive information automatically) or
sales@tlg.org (to ask specific questions)
FTP: ftp.tlg.org
WWW: http://www.tlg.org/
Phone: (415) 487-1902
(Note: The Little Garden is building a network of affiliates in other areas;
contact them for information about one in your area.)

Portal Information Network

20863 Stevens Creek Blvd, Suite 200
Cupertino, CA 95014
Phone: (408) 973-9111
Fax: (408) 725-1580
E-mail: info@portal.com (to receive information automatically) or
support@portal.com (to ask specific questions)
WWW: http://www.portal.com

The WELL

1750 Bridgeway, Suite A200
Sausalito, CA 94965-1900
E-mail: support@well.com
WWW: http://www.well.com
Phone: (415) 332-9200
Fax: (415) 332-9355

National

CRL

P.O. Box 326
Larkspur, CA 94977
E-mail: support@crl.com
FTP: ftp.crl.com/CRL-Info/Basic.Services.Info
Phone: (415) 837-5300
Fax: (415) 392-9000

Netcom Online Services

3031 Tisch Way
San Jose, CA 95128
E-mail: info@netcom.com
WWW: http://www.netcom.com
Phone: (800) 501-8649
Fax: (408) 241-9145

Performance Systems International (PSI)

510 Huntmar Park Drive
Herndon, VA 22070
E-mail: info@psi.com
WWW: http://www.psi.com
Phone: (800) 827-7482
Fax: (800) FAX-PSI1

■ Western Europe

(See also Eastern/Central European listings)

Austria

EUnet Austria

E-Mail: info@Austria.EU.net
Phone: (43) 1 3174969
Fax: (43) 1 3106926

Belgium

Interpac Belgium

Av. Louise 350, boite 11
1050 Bruxelles
E-mail: info@interpac.be
Phone: (32) 2 6466000
Fax: (32) 2 6403638

Denmark

DKnet/EUnet Denmark

Fruebjergvej 3
2100 Copenhagen Oe
E-mail: info@DKnet.dk
Phone: (45) 39 17 99 00
Fax: (45) 39 17 98 97

Finland

EUnet Finland

Punavuorenkatu 1
FI-00120 Helsinki
Phone: (358) 0 400 2060
Fax: (358) 0 622 2626

France

FRANCENET

49 Rue du Faubourg Poissonniere
Paris
WWW: http://WWW.Francenet.fr
E-mail: infos@francenet.fr
Minitel: 36 15 Francenet
FTP: FTP.francenet.fr
Gopher: gopher.francenet.fr
Phone: (33) 1 40 61 01 76
Fax: (33) 1 48 24 46 22

Germany

Interactive Network Informationssysteme GmbH i.Gr.

Spohrstrasse 24
D-60318 Frankfurt am Main
E-mail: johnny@interactive.nacamar.de
Phone: (49) 69 5974099
Fax: (49) 69 555442 or 555683

Interactive Networx GmbH

Hardenbergplatz 2
D-10623 Berlin
E-mail: info@unlisys.net
Phone: (49) 30 25431-0
Fax: (49) 30 25431-299

Greece

EUnet Greece

E-mail: postmaster@Greece.EU.net
Phone: (30) 81 221171
Fax: (30) 81 229342

Holland

EuroNet Internet

Prins Hendrikkade 48
1012 AC Amsterdam
E-mail: info@euro.net or office@euronet.nl
Phone: (31) 20 625 6161
Fax: (31) 20 625 7435

Iceland

EUnet Iceland

E-mail: postmaster@Iceland.EU.net
Phone: (354) 1 694747
Fax: (354) 1 28801

Ireland

IEunet Ltd.

E-mail: info@ieunet.ie or info@Ireland.eu.net
Phone: (353) 1 6790832

Italy

ALPCOM

CSI Piemonte
c.so Unione Sovietica, 216 I-10136
Torino
E-mail: info@alpcom.it or secretary@alpcom.it
Phone: (39) 11 3187407
Fax: (39) 11 4618212

INET S.p.A.

v. A.Bono Cairoli, 34 I-20127
Milan
E-mail: info@inet.it
Phone: (39) 2 26821182
Fax: (39) 2 26821311

Luxembourg

EUnet Luxembourg

E-mail: postmaster@Luxembourg.EU.net
Phone: (352) 470261 361
Fax: (352) 470264

Norway

DAXNET

Enebakkveien 304
Postboks 79 Abilds
N-1105 Oslo
E-mail: daxnet@datametrix.no
WWW: http://www.datametrix.no/
Phone: (47) 22 74 06 20
Fax: (47) 22 74 04 89

Portugal

Telepac Servicos de Telecomunicacoes SA

Rue Dr Antonio Loureiro Borges 1
1495 Lisboa
E-mail: henrique@telepac.pt
Phone: (351) 1 790 7000
Fax: (351) 1 790 7001

Spain

RedIRIS

Fundesco
Alcala 61
28014 Madrid
E-mail: secretaria@rediris.es
Phone: (34) 1 435 1214
Fax: (34) 1 578 1773

Sweden

Bahnhof

Phone: (46) 18-100899
Fax: (46) 18-103737
E-mail: info@bahnhof.se
WWW: http://www.bahnhof.se/

■ Credits

AC/DC contest home page courtesy of ACDContest@aol.com.

ALL-IN-ONE home page created by William Cross. Courtesy of William Cross. Reprinted with permission.

The Amazing Fish Cam! © 1995 Netscape Communications Corporation. Courtesy of Netscape Communications Corporation.

Apple Computer © 1995 Apple Computer, Inc. Courtesy of Apple Computer, Inc.

AT&T Accelerated Learning © 1995 AT&T. All rights reserved. Graphics by Psyberspace. Courtesy of AT&T.

Best of the Net © 1995 Netscape Communications Corporation. Courtesy of Netscape Communications Corporation.

Caligari's Fountain VRML browser image courtesy of Caligari.

Career Mosaic home page created by Bernard Hodes Advertising. Courtesy of Bernard Hodes.

Cool Site of the Day © 1995 InfiNet Company. Courtesy of InfiNet Company.

Echo Websites © 1995 Echo Communications Group. Courtesy of Echo Communications Group.

Find-it! © 1995 Paul Savena. Created by Paul Savena. Reprinted with permission.

Free Acrobat Reader Software © 1995 Adobe Systems, Inc. Courtesy of Adobe Systems.

Ghostscript, Ghostview & GSview home page courtesy of rjl@eng.monash.edu.au.

GNN Map © 1995 Global Network Navigator, Inc. All rights reserved. Courtesy of Global Network Navigator, Inc.

Interactive Age Daily © 1995 CMP Publications. Courtesy of CMP Publications.

Internet Movie Database © 1990-1995 the Internet Movie Database Team. Created by Col Needham. Reprinted with permission.

Internet Underground Music Archive © 1995 Internet Underground Music Archive. All rights reserved. Courtesy of IUMA.

JASC home page courtesy of JASC, Inc.

Jim Clark Website courtesy of Netscape Communications Corporation.

Madlibs Website. Created by the Massachusetts Institute of Technology SIPB. Courtesy of MIT.

Magellan home page © 1995 The McKinley Group, Inc. All rights reserved. Courtesy of the McKinley Group, Inc.

MagicURL Mystery Trip home page created by Ryan Scott. Courtesy of Ryan Scott.

Marc Andreesen home page courtesy of Marc Andreesen.

Mozilla home page courtesy of Tillman Hausherr. Artwork by Vincent Van Mozh.

National Center for Supercomputing Applications © 1993, 1994 University of Illinois Board of Trustees. Courtesy of National Center for Supercomputing Applications. Created by the staff of NCSA.

Netsurfer Digest © 1995 Netsurfer Communications, Inc. Created by Arthur Bebak and Bill Woodcock. Reprinted with permission.

The Palace Web site courtesy of The Palace.

RealAudio © 1995 Progressive Networks. All rights reserved. RealAudio is a trademark of Progressive Networks. Courtesy of Creative Networks.

Rubber Nipple Salesmen home page © 1995 Internet Underground Music Archive. All rights reserved. Courtesy of IUMA.

Tim Berners-Lee home page courtesy of Tim Berners-Lee.

TimesFax © 1995 *The New York Times*. Courtesy of *The New York Times*.

URouLette © 1995 by Matthew T. Abrams and Matthew J. Angell. All rights reserved. Reprinted with permission.

The Virtual Tourist home page courtesy of Kinesava Geographics. Created by Brandon Plewe.

Web Week Wednesday home page created by E. Mullin. Courtesy of the staff of Web Week.

Welcome to Netscape © 1995 Netscape Communications Corporation. Courtesy of Netscape Communications Corporation.

Welcome to the World of Classical Music © 1995 BMG Music. Courtesy of BMG Music.

What's Cool © 1995 Netscape Communications Corporation. Courtesy of Netscape Communications Corporation.

What's New © 1995 Global Network Navigator, Inc. All rights reserved. Created by Ellie Cutler. Courtesy of Global Network Navigator, Inc.

WinZip © 1995 Nico Mak Computing, Inc. Created by Nico Mak. Reprinted with Permission.

Worlds Chat © 1995 Worlds, Inc. Courtesy of Worlds, Inc.

Yahoo! © 1994, 1995 Yahoo. Courtesy of Yahoo!

ZDNet © 1995 Ziff-Davis Interactive. Courtesy of Ziff-Davis Communications.

■ Index

Ziff-Davis Press Survey of Readers

Please help us in our effort to produce the best books on personal computing. For your assistance, we would be pleased to send you a FREE catalog featuring the complete line of Ziff-Davis Press books.

1. How did you first learn about this book?

Recommended by a friend . . . . ☐ -1 (5)

Recommended by store personnel . . . . ☐ -2

Saw in Ziff-Davis Press catalog . . . . ☐ -3

Received advertisement in the mail . . . . ☐ -4

Saw the book on bookshelf at store . . . . ☐ -5

Read book review in: _____ ☐ -6

Saw an advertisement in: _____ ☐ -7

Other (Please specify): _____ ☐ -8

2. Which THREE of the following factors most influenced your decision to purchase this book? (Please check up to THREE.)

Front or back cover information on book . . . ☐ -1 (6)

Logo of magazine affiliated with book . . . . . . ☐ -2

Special approach to the content . . . . ☐ -3

Completeness of content . . . . ☐ -4

Author's reputation. . . . . ☐ -5

Publisher's reputation . . . . ☐ -6

Book cover design or layout . . . . ☐ -7

Index or table of contents of book . . . . ☐ -8

Price of book . . . . ☐ -9

Special effects, graphics, illustrations . . . . ☐ -0

Other (Please specify): _____ ☐ -x

3. How many computer books have you purchased in the last six months? _____ (7-10)

4. On a scale of 1 to 5, where 5 is excellent, 4 is above average, 3 is average, 2 is below average, and 1 is poor, please rate each of the following aspects of this book below. (Please circle your answer.)

Depth/completeness of coverage	5	4	3	2	1	(11)
Organization of material	5	4	3	2	1	(12)
Ease of finding topic	5	4	3	2	1	(13)
Special features/time saving tips	5	4	3	2	1	(14)
Appropriate level of writing	5	4	3	2	1	(15)
Usefulness of table of contents	5	4	3	2	1	(16)
Usefulness of index	5	4	3	2	1	(17)
Usefulness of accompanying disk	5	4	3	2	1	(18)
Usefulness of illustrations/graphics	5	4	3	2	1	(19)
Cover design and attractiveness	5	4	3	2	1	(20)
Overall design and layout of book	5	4	3	2	1	(21)
Overall satisfaction with book	5	4	3	2	1	(22)

5. Which of the following computer publications do you read regularly; that is, 3 out of 4 issues?

Byte . . . . ☐ -1 (23)

Computer Shopper . . . . ☐ -2

Home Office Computing . . . . ☐ -3

Dr. Dobb's Journal . . . . ☐ -4

LAN Magazine . . . . ☐ -5

MacWEEK . . . . ☐ -6

MacUser . . . . ☐ -7

PC Computing . . . . ☐ -8

PC Magazine . . . . ☐ -9

PC WEEK . . . . ☐ -0

Windows Sources . . . . ☐ -x

Other (Please specify): _____ ☐ -y

Please turn page.

6. What is your level of experience with personal computers? With the subject of this book?

	With PCs	With subject of book
Beginner..............	☐ -1 (24)	☐ -1 (25)
Intermediate..........	☐ -2	☐ -2
Advanced.............	☐ -3	☐ -3

7. Which of the following best describes your job title?

Officer (CEO/President/VP/owner)........ ☐ -1 (26)
Director/head......................... ☐ -2
Manager/supervisor.................... ☐ -3
Administration/staff.................. ☐ -4
Teacher/educator/trainer.............. ☐ -5
Lawyer/doctor/medical professional....... ☐ -6
Engineer/technician................... ☐ -7
Consultant........................... ☐ -8
Not employed/student/retired............. ☐ -9
Other (Please specify): _____ ☐ -0

8. What is your age?

Under 20............................ ☐ -1 (27)
21-29............................... ☐ -2
30-39............................... ☐ -3
40-49............................... ☐ -4
50-59............................... ☐ -5
60 or over.......................... ☐ -6

9. Are you:

Male................................ ☐ -1 (28)
Female.............................. ☐ -2

Thank you for your assistance with this important information! Please write your address below to receive our free catalog.

Name: _____

Address: _____

City/State/Zip: _____

Fold here to mail.   3547-19-03

_____
_____
_____